APPLICATION SOFTWARE REENGINEERING

M. Afshar Alam
Department of Computer Science
Hamdard University
New Delhi

Tendai Padenga
Department of Computer Science
Hamdard University
New Delhi

PEARSON
Delhi • Chennai

Assistant Acquisitions Editor: Anant Kumar
Associate Production Editor: Jennifer Sargunar
Composition: White Lotus Infotech Pvt. Ltd, Pondicherry
Printer: India Binding House

ISBN: 978-81-317-3185-7

First Impression, 2010

Published by Pearson India Education Services Pvt.Ltd,CIN:U72200TN2005PTC057128.
Formerly known as TutorVista Global Pvt Ltd, licensees of Pearson Education in South Asia

Head Office: 7th Floor, knowledge Boulevard, A-8(A) Sector-62, Noida (U.P) 201309, India

Registered Office: Module G4, Ground Floor, Elnet Software City, TS -140,Block 2 & 9
Rajiv Gandhi Salai, Taramani, Chennai, Tamil Nadu 600113.,Fax: 080-30461003,
Phone: 080-30461060, www.pearson.co.in email id: companysecretary.india@pearson.com

Printed in India by CMS IT Services Private Limited, New Delhi in the year of 2017.

Contents

Foreword

This book is bound to give very clear-cut, explicit and definite answers to application software reengineering. It is an excellent piece of academic literature intended to help not only honours undergraduate and postgraduate students, but research scholars as well as practitioners in the software industry. It is user friendly and can be used in a non-sequential manner. Provision of simple, comprehensive and understandable illustrations and exercises makes this book an excellent primer to the dynamic field of application software reengineering.

Indeed this book is a culmination of years of experience in teaching and research by the authors who have had a long felt desire to have a simple book that not only addresses and identifies the competence requirements of the next generation of software developers, but also offers a refreshing analysis to application software reengineering trends. It offers a realistic approach to and sufficiently equips its users for the new software environment.

The authors must be commended for coming up with a self-paced guide that helps users answer most questions students, researchers and software engineering practitioners may have.

I feel that this book does offer a mental image of application software reengineering core principles.

Eng. Quinton C. Kanhukamwe
Pro Vice Chancellor
Harare Institute of Technology

Preface

Application software reengineering has become an important part of any software system. Similarly, a course on application software reengineering has become an essential component of any computer science education curriculum. This field is, however, beginning to take shape at a breathtakingly rapid rate as a lot of application software systems are increasingly turning into legacy systems. We present this book as a text for an introductory course in application software reengineering at senior undergraduate and first-year graduate level students. It provides a lucid description of the concepts that underlie application software reengineering. As prerequisites, we assume that the reader is already familiar with basic software engineering principles and programming such as 'C'.

The fundamental application software reengineering concepts and theories covered in this book are often based on those used in existing commercial and open source systems. We introduce these concepts and theories in a general setting that is not tied down to one particular application software. Concepts and theories, herein, are advanced using intuitive descriptions. Important and notable theoretical results are covered, but formal proofs are omitted. The bibliographical notes contain pointers to reputable research papers in which some of the results were first presented and proved as well as references to material for further reading. In place of proofs, figures and examples are used to inherently suggest why we expect the result in question to be true.

How this Book Is Organized

This book is organized for people who have done a course in software engineering with adequate knowledge of the Software Development Life Cycle (SDLC). However, experienced software developers can safely be an exception to this rule. Every effort has been made to make this book user friendly. Each chapter starts with well-defined chapter objectives and ends with an exercise section containing chapter-review questions.

This book need not be read sequentially or from cover to cover. It should rather be used as a reference book when faced with a problem. However, it is advisable for a beginner to start with Chapter 9, Legacy Software. Since the chapter is an introduction to the core principles of application software reengineering, it is important to read it entirely.

Finally, this book ends with a useful list of books and papers to further knowledge.

Mailing List

We provide an ambient environment in which users can communicate among themselves and with us. We have, to that effect, created a mailing list consisting of users of our book with the following address: asr-book@gmail.com. If you wish to be on the list, please send a message to tepadenga@gmail.com indicating your name, affiliation and email address. If you would like to suggest improvements or to contribute exercises, we would be glad to hear from you.

Acknowledgments

We would like to extend our sincere thanks to all the people who participated in the review of this book. We would like to thank the project team at Pearson Education India, in particular Anant Kumar, Jennifer Sargunar and Pradeep Banerjee.

M. Afshar Alam and Tendai Padenga
Hamdard University
New Delhi

About the Authors

Prof. M. Afshar Alam is the Head of the Computer Science department at Hamdard University, New Delhi, India. He is the Dean in The Faculty of Management and Information Technology and also the Dean of Students Welfare. He has written several textbooks and published research papers in various national and international journals of repute. His research interests are quite broad and include but not limited to Intuitionistic Fuzzy Databases and Software Reengineering.

Tendai Padenga is a Zimbabwean national doing his PhD in Computer Science under Prof. M. Afshar Alam. He is a commonwealth fellowship alumni as well as an Indian Council for Cultural Relations scholarship (Government of India) alumni. Earlier, Padenga was awarded a prestigious National Foods Ltd scholarship (Zimbabwe) after attaining outstanding grades at Ordinary level. An active participant in several turnkey IT projects, he was the Group Projects Officer for the Business Process Reengineering exercise of African Banking Corporation Holdings, Zimbabwe, in partnership with the then Indian banking solutions provider I-Flex Solutions. He did his research fellowship at Osmangazi University in the Graduate School of Electrical, Electronic and Computer Engineering in Turkey.

CHAPTER 1

Software Evolution

Objectives

The objective of this chapter is to introduce the student to the concept of software evolution at an introductory level, based on principles of natural evolution. When you have read this chapter, you will be able to:

- Understand the concept of evolution from natural laws and how that relates to software evolution
- Understand the historical background of evolution models and theories
- Distinguish between evolutionistic and evolutionary models
- Understand the general impact of evolutionary biology on software evolution
- Understand the need for laws closely related to and guarding software evolution

1.0 Introduction to Software Evolution

The need for software reengineering has increased greatly as heritage/legacy software systems have become obsolete in terms of their architecture, the platforms on which they run and their suitability and stability to support evolution so as to support ever-changing needs. Software reengineering has indeed become important for:

- recovering and reusing existing software assets;
- putting high software maintenance costs under control;
- establishing a base for future software evolution.

The increasing cost of aging software systems has necessitated software reengineering efforts. A legacy system is subjected to many unavoidable maintenance activities, which causes degradation of the quality of the system. However, when this degradation exceeds a critical threshold, the legacy system needs to be reengineered. There is, however, a constant need for practical, efficient and comprehensive techniques to be used in merging and reengineering legacy systems.

First, let us look at a definition of evolution that covers different scientific and technological disciplines. Lehman and Ramil (2004) provide an appropriate definition. In the definition an attempt has been made to address properties applicable in a general sense though individual disciplines may have additional properties not identified here.

Accordingly, evolution is a process of progressive change and cyclic adaptation over time in terms of the attributes, behavioral properties and relational configuration of some material, abstract, natural or artificial entity or system. Such a definition accommodates:

- "evolutionistic" models that draw attention to stages and direction of developmental progress;
- "evolutionary" models that focus attention on mechanisms, forces or impinging constraints that give rise to evolution.

1.1 Evolution Models and Theories

1.1.1 Historical Background

Theories of biological evolution have been the subject of scientific inquiry and speculation for centuries, with Charles Darwin's Origin of Species (1859) being the most widely known and cited theory. Darwin's theoretical analysis was based in part on his field studies of animal species on the Galapagos Archipelago. His theory sparked a century of scientific debate that included religious and moral undertones. It led to the following concepts:

- developmental biology that examines the role of genetics, reproductive (natural) selection, co-evolution (among co-located species) and adaptation to ecological circumstances shaping the lives of organisms;
- evolutionary biology which accounts for the influence of genetics, reproduction, lineage, speciation, and population growth and diffusion shaping the long-term or transgenerational lives of species of organisms.

The concept of developmental versus evolutionary biology helps draw attention to two alternative ways to view the evolution of a system:

- focusing on a system's life cycle;
- focusing on changes that manifest across generations of related systems.

In addition, the concept of biological systematic further helps draw attention to "progress," direction or (punctuated) equilibrium of evolution by associating the developmental properties (e.g. agency, efficiency, and scope) of living organisms with those found in the fossil and geological objects.

Culture, language and economy, which arise from the social actions and interactions of people, may evolve in ways similar or different from that in the natural science of biology. Culture, for example, may rely on the development, diffusion and assimilation of memes (i.e. concepts, compelling ideas or cultural "genes") that embody recurring social practices, situations, beliefs or myths that can be shared, communicated or otherwise transported as a basis for their evolution. In spite of the differences, "open source" and "free software" remain clear-cut examples of related memes. Thus, rather than conjecturing physical (biological) conditions or circumstances, cultural evolution relies on social actions and narrative records that relate to physical conditions and circumstances that enable the ongoing evolution of diverse cultures and cultural experiences. However, language evolution seems to share and span ideas from culture and biology with respect to efforts that associate language learning, perception and semiotics with neurological mechanisms and human population dynamics. It can be appreciated that elsewhere, topics like competition, resource scarcity, population concentration/density, legitimacy and organizational ecologies appear as factors shaping the evolution of markets, organizations and economies at least at a macro level. Beyond this, the evolution of culture, language and economy continue to be explored experimentally using computational approaches. Overall, it can thus be appreciated that this tiny sample of work draws attention to associations more closely aligned to evolutionary biology, rather than to developmental biology.

It should be noted that the evolution of modern technology has also become the subject of systematic inquiry. In a study of the American automobile industry by Abernathy (1978), it was found that the technical system for developing and manufacturing automobiles associates:

- product design;
- process design within a productive unit;

(i.e. the manufacturing systems within a physical factory or production organization). Each depends on the other, so that changes in one, such as the introduction of new techniques into a productive unit, are propagated into both product design and production process layout/workflow. Similar findings were recorded by King and Kraemer (1984) in their analysis of the evolution of computing systems in organizational settings. In addition, Hughes outlined the same phenomenon in his historical study of the technical system of electrification and draws attention to the role of the infrastructure of electrical production and distribution as spanning not just equipment, mechanisms (e.g. power generators, sub-stations), cabling and power outlets but also the alignment of producers, retailers and consumers of devices/products together with the processes that depend on electrification for their operation. It was Meyer and Utterback (1993) who were among the first to recognize that productive units and technical systems of production and consumption were increasingly organized around product lines that accommodate a diversity of product life cycles centered on the dominant design or product architecture that dominates current retail markets.

From an economic perspective, we have Nelson and Winter (1982) independently terming the overall scheme that associates and aligns products, processes, productive units with producers, retailers and consumers, a technological regime. Lastly, the development, use and maintenance of software are strongly dependent on computer hardware; however, there are now studies that examine how different kinds of computer hardware components exhibit evolutionary patterns across technological generations or regimes. The evolution of technology through technological regimes that depend on:

- product features
- development processes
- infrastructure
- productive units

seem immediately relevant to understanding the evolution of software systems and technologies.

Software programs, systems, applications, processes and productive units continue to develop at an alarming speed. For example, there is a plethora of software innovations in the form of new tools, techniques, concepts or applications, which continue to emerge as more people experience modern computing technology and technical systems. These innovations give rise to unexpected or unanticipated forms of software development and maintenance, as, for example, software systems that are dynamically linked at run-time instead of compile-time. Software innovations are diffused into a population of evermore diverse settings and technical systems via either technology transfer or system migration. Software processes are subject to ongoing experience, learning, improvement and refinement, though there is debate about how to most effectively and efficiently realize and assimilate such process improvements (Conradi and Fuggetta, 2002; Beecham, *et al.*, 2003). Software systems are also subject to cultural forces (Elliott and Scacchi, 2002), narrative and informal documentation (Scacchi, 2002) and economic conditions (Boehm, 1981) within the productive units or work settings that affect how these systems will be developed and maintained. These forces can give rise to similar kinds of systems in similar settings evolving at different rates along different trajectories. This suggests that software systems are developed and evolved within particular organizational and informational ecologies, as well as situated within a technical system of production and larger overall technological regime.

Overall, this brief review of evolutionary theory across a sample of disciplines raises an awareness of the following issues:

- First, in studying software evolution, it is necessary to clarify whether in fact attention is directed at matters more closely aligned to the development of a given system throughout its life or with the evolution of software technologies across generations that are disseminated across multiple populations. It appears that much of what are labeled as studies of "software evolution" are more typically studies of patterns of development of specific systems, rather than patterns of evolution across different systems within one or multiple product lines (or species), at least as compared to work in biological evolution. However, the laws and theory of software evolution articulated by Lehman and associates depend on empirical findings that examine a variety of software systems in different application domains, execution environments, size of system, organization and company marketing the system as their basis for identifying mechanisms and conditions that affect software evolution.
- Second, when considering the subject of software evolution at a macro level, it appears that there is no easily found or widely cited study that examines issues of memes, competition, resource scarcity, population concentration/density, legitimacy and organizational ecology as forces that shape or impinge on software systems or software technology. Therefore, it

can be highlighted that the study of software evolution is still in its infancy. In general, the existing theory of the development or evolution of software does not have a substantial cultural, language or economic basis yet. Lastly, conventional closed source software systems developed within centralized corporate productive units and open source software systems developed within globally decentralized settings without corporate locale represent alternative technological regimes. Each represents a different technical system of production, distribution/retailing, consumption, differentiated product lines, dominant product designs and more. Similarly, software development methods based on object-oriented design and coding, agile development and extreme programming entail some form of alternative technological regime. Concepts from theories of technological evolution and observations on patterns of software development and maintenance can hence be used to help shape an understanding of how software evolves.

1.2 Empirical Studies of Software Evolution

To understand the state of the art in the development of a theory of software evolution and how it might be extended, it is necessary to identify and describe what empirical studies of software evolution have been reported. However, it is encouraging to note that not only proprietary empirical study evolution is taking place but also equally the empirical study evolution of F/OSS evolution has recently become a topic of interest and its study has been recently taken up by several groups around the world.

1.3 Studies of the Laws of Software Evolution

The most prominent studies of software evolution have been directed by M.M. Lehman and colleagues over a 30-year period dating back to the mid 1970s. The studies have given rise to eight laws of software evolution as formulated and refined by Lehman *et al.* (1980–2001). These laws are the result of careful and challenging empirical studies of the evolution of large-scale software systems found in a variety of corporate-based settings. These laws seek to consistently account for observed phenomena regarding the evolution of software releases, systems and E-type applications, as defined by Lehman and colleagues. The laws and theory can be reformulated in a manner suitable for independent test and validation, or refutation, but this requires making assumptions about details that are not explicitly stated in the laws. Thus, there are many challenges in how such empirical testing of these laws should be performed (e.g. how many or what kinds of software systems constitute an adequate or theoretically motivated sample space for comparative study), what the consequences for refutation may be (rejection or reformulation of the laws/theory) and whether or how the laws and theory might be refined and improved if a new or contradictory phenomena arises.

The most recently published study by Lehman and colleagues provides data from evolution of releases primarily from five software systems:

- two operating systems—IBM OS 360, ICL VME Kernel;
- one financial system—Logica FW;

- two versions of a large real-time telecommunications system;
- one defense system—Matra BAE Dynamics.

1.4 Other Empirical Studies of Software Evolution

Here our attention is directed to a sample of studies where non-open source software systems were being investigated. This is mainly intended to see if other studies of software evolution conform, refute or extend and refine the laws and theory of software evolution.

Bendifallah and Scacchi (1987) present qualitative data and analysis of two comparative case studies revealing that similar kinds of software systems in similar kinds of organizational settings have different evolutionary trajectories. They report that the differences can be explained by how system maintainers and end-users deal with local contingencies in their workplace and career opportunities in the course of maintaining their software systems, whereas Tamai and Torimitsu (1992) present data and observations from a survey study of mainframe software system applications across product generations. Among other things, they report that software lifetime in their survey is on average about 10 years; the variance in application lifetime is 6.2 and that small software applications tend to have a shorter life on an average. They also report that applications that constitute what they call administration systems (back office applications) have been proven to live longer than business supporting (mission-critical) systems. On the same note, it has also been shown that application systems that replace previous generation systems tend to grow by a factor greater than 2 against their predecessors. Lastly, they report that some companies follow policies that set the predicted lifetime of an application system at the time of initial release and use this information in scheduling migration to next generation systems.

Cusumano and Yoffie (1999) presented results from case studies at Microsoft and Netscape indicating strong reliance on the incremental release of alpha and beta versions to customers as a business strategy for improving evolution of system features that meet evolving user requirements. They show that user satisfaction can improve and be driven by shortening the time interval between releases. They also find that unstable releases (e.g. alpha and beta versions) will be released to users as a way to enable them to participate in the decentralized testing and remote quality assurance and thus affecting software evolution. Their study does not confirm or refute the laws of software evolution but they introduce a new dynamic into software evolution by making the release activity an independent output variable rather than an input variable.

In a separate study Gall *et al.* (1997) provide data and observations based on software product release histories from a study of a large telecommunications switching system. The growth of this system over 20 releases conforms to the general trends found in the data of Lehman and colleagues. However, they report that though global system evolution follows the trend and thus conforms to the laws, individual subsystems and modules do not. Instead, they sometimes exhibit significant upward or downward fluctuation in their size across almost all releases. Related scenarios also provided data demonstrating that source code decays unless effort and resources are allocated to prevent and maintain the system throughout the later stages of its deployment, and that the decay can be observed to rise and fall in different subsystems and modules across releases. Also a systematic set of data, analyses and comparison with prior studies revealing that problems in software maintenance can be attributed to a lack of knowledge of the maintenance process and of the cause and effect relationships that software maintenance practices and software maintenance outcomes posses. However, their data may be associated with the growth of system complexity and other outcomes over time, which they attribute to the laws observed by Lehman and colleagues.

Perry *et al.* (2001) reported findings from an observational case study of the development of large telecommunications systems that indicate extensive parallel changes being made between software system releases. This notion of parallel changes that may interact and thus confound software maintenance activities is not accounted for in an explicit way by the laws of software evolution. Thus, it does introduce yet another organizational factor that may affect software evolution.

Keywords

legacy software; software maintenance; software evolution; evolutionistic models; evolutionary models; scientific inquiry; theoretical analysis; developmental biology; evolutionary biology; transgenerational; system's life cycle; biological systematics; agency; efficiency; scope; product design; process design; workflow; evolutionary patterns; software innovations; F/OSS evolution; E-type applications

Exercises

1. Define the term evolution.
2. Explain the major difference between evolutionistic and evolutionary models of evolution.
3. Explain the following concepts:
    - developmental biology;
    - evolutionary biology.
4. Why is it important to learn the concepts of developmental and evolutionary biology in viewing the evolution of a system?
5. Discuss the impact of culture, language and economy on evolution.
6. Explain in detail why evolution of modern technology has become the subject of systematic enquiry?
7. Outline any two awareness issues raised by evolutionary theories.

CHAPTER 2

Software Evolution Process

Objectives

The objective of this chapter is to introduce the student to the software evolution process with a close reference to Lehman's laws of software evolution and their implications. When you have read this chapter, you will be able to:

- Understand the activities governing the evolution process
- Understand the factors governing the success of the software evolution process
- Know the existing three program types
- Understand the E-type and S-type program classifications
- Understand the laws of software evolution and their implications
- Understand the evolutionary patterns in open source software

2.0 The Software Evolution Process

Software evolution is the initial development process of a software product, followed by its software maintenance phase. Software evolution of a software system is a continuous change from a lesser, simpler or worse state to a higher or better state. The evolution process includes the fundamental activities of:

- change analysis;
- release planning;

- system implementation;
- releasing a system to customers.

Software evolution processes depend on:

- the type of software being maintained;
- the development processes used;
- the skills and experience of the people involved;
- proposals for change which are the real driver for system evolution.

Change identification and evolution continue throughout the system lifetime. Sometimes urgent changes may have to be implemented without going through all stages of the software engineering process. This could, for example, happen:

- if a serious system fault has to be repaired;
- if changes to the system's environment (e.g., an OS upgrade) have unexpected effects;
- if there are business changes that require a very rapid response (e.g., the immediate release of a competing product).

The changes could sometimes trigger system problems that then have to be tackled very urgently. In such cases, an emergency repair process can be implemented. Emergency repair is prompted by system faults, business changes and environmental changes, all requiring urgent treatment (Fig. 2.1)

Using an emergency repair process can result in the following dangers:

- software becomes inconsistent;
- changes are not reflected in documentation;
- software ageing is accelerated by workaround solutions.

Another problem with emergency repair process is that they have to be completed as quickly as possible. System evolution can be used to implement changes in systems which are not well understood. But it becomes difficult to apply the same processes to legacy systems as they are difficult to change and implement. Hence, many organizations may reengineer systems to improve the system's functionality, performance or implementation.

Figure 2.1 Activities involved in emergency repair process

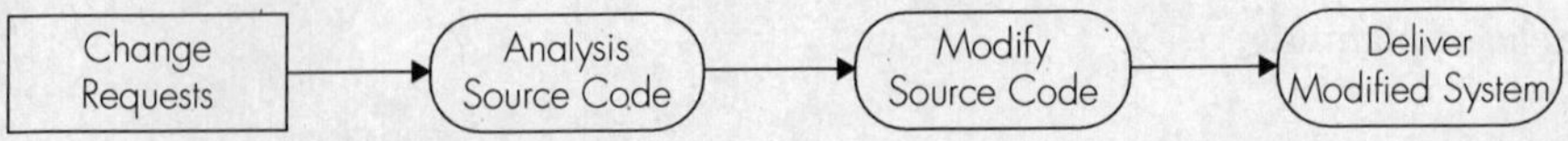

2.1 Program Types

2.1.1 S-type Programs ("Specifiable")

Properties

- In S-type programs (Fig. 2.2), problems can be stated formally and completely.
- This type of software does not evolve.
- A change to the specification defines a new problem hence a new program.

2.1.2 E-type Programs ("Embedded")

Properties

- The E-type system (Fig. 2.3) generally becomes part of the world that it models.
- This software is inherently evolutionary.
- Changes in the software and the world affect each other.

2.1.3 P-type Programs ("Problem-solving")

Properties

- Imprecise statement of a real world problem.
- This software is likely to evolve continuously because the solution is never perfect.
- Can be improved because the real world changes, hence the program (Fig. 2.4) changes.

Figure 2.2 S-type

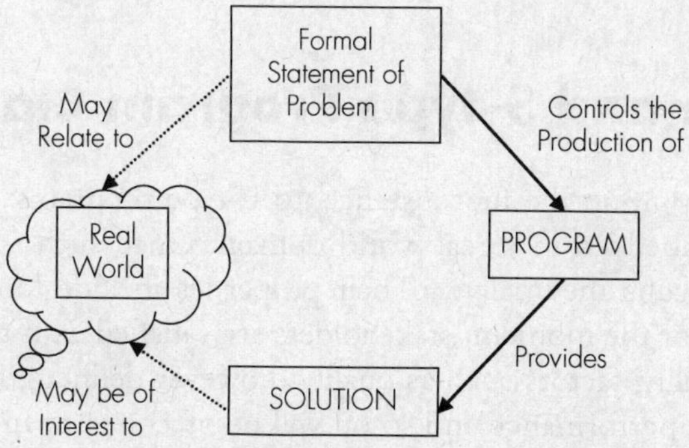

Figure 2.3 E-type

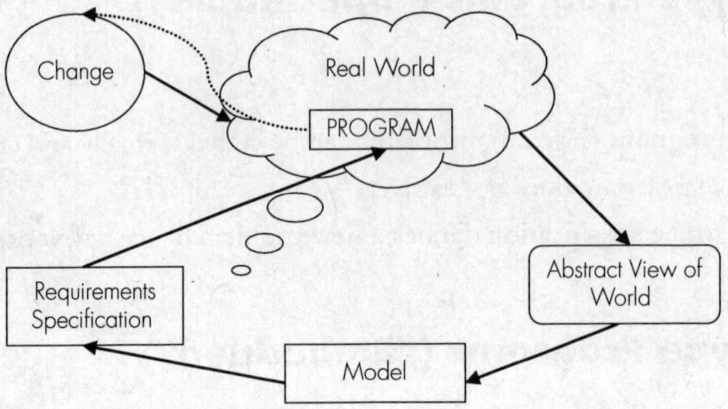

Figure 2.4 P-type

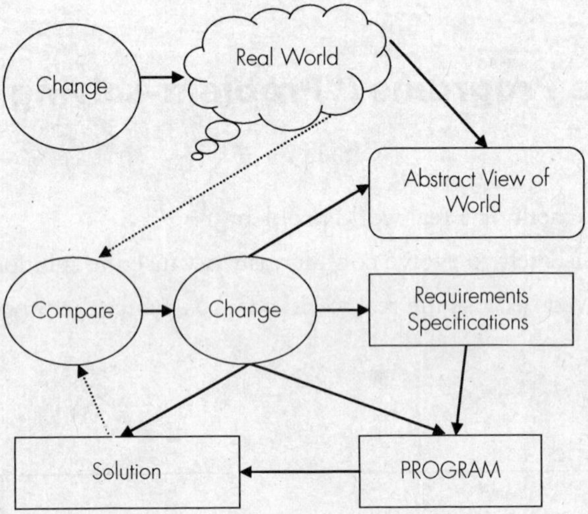

2.2 E-type and S-type Program Classification

Note that the laws apply, in the first instance, to E-type programs. E-type programs – systems actively used and embedded in a real world domain. Once such systems are operational, they are judged by the results they deliver. Their properties include loosely expressed expectations with which, at least for the moment, stakeholders are satisfied with the system as is. However, in addition to functionality, factors such as quality (however defined), behaviour in execution, ease of use, changeability, performance and so on will be of concern. In this they differ from S-type programs where the sole criterion of acceptability is correctness, in the mathematical sense. Only that, which is explicitly included in the specification or follows from what is so included is of concern in assessing (and accepting) the program and the results of its execution. An S-type program is completely defined by and is required to be correct with respect to a fixed and consistent specification. A property not so included may be present or absent, deliberately, by oversight or at the programmer's whim.

The importance of S-type programs lies in their being, by definition, mathematical objects about which one may reason. Thus, they can be verified i.e., proven correct. A correct program possesses all the properties required to satisfy its specification. By their omission from the specification other properties implicitly become "don't care". Once the specification has been fixed and verified, acceptance of the program is independent of any assumption by the implementers; entirely determined by the specification, at least as far as the original contract is concerned. At some later time the program may require fixing or enhancing because of an error in the specification, changes in the purpose for which the program is required, changes in the operational domain or some other reason. An updated specification, including changes to the embedded assumption set can then be prepared and a new program derived. This may be achieved by modification of the old program or by *ab initio* development of a new one.

Since, it is impossible to read the mind of a programmer it is not possible to know what assumption is made during the course of the work. Any such assumption become embedded in and part of the program even though not originally specified. As the operational domain or other circumstances change some assumptions will become invalid and affect program behaviour in unpredictable, possibly unacceptable, fashion. It is, therefore, important to prevent individuals or small groups from unconsciously incorporating assumptions into a program or its documentation. It is equally important to support the process of making and documenting conscious assumptions and to adapt the system as necessary.

The role of S-type programs in the programming process follows. The unconscious, unconsidered, injection of assumptions into S-type and E-type programs may be minimized by providing a precise and complete specification for each assigned task, that is, by assigning only S-type programs to individuals. The lowest level bricks from which larger programs and complex systems are built should be of type S. The main body of assumptions will then be explicit in the specification of these bricks, or implied by omissions from those specifications. Each elemental part of the total system can thus be verified objectively against its specification.

The detection of implied, often unconscious, assumptions is, however, difficult and situations requiring the de facto introduction of new assumptions cannot be avoided. When this occurs, they must, as far as possible, be detected, captured, validated, formally approved, recorded and added to the specification. But some assumptions will slip through the net.

The better the record of assumptions, the more it is updated, the simpler will it be to maintain the programs in a changing world, the less likely it is that the program displays unexpected or strange behaviour in execution, the more confidence one has in the operation of the programs when integrated into a host system and later when operational in the real world. But as the system evolves, the specifications from which the S-type programs are derived will inevitably have to be changed to satisfy the changing domains within which they work and to fulfill the current needs of the application they are serving.

Once integrated into a larger system and when that system is operational, the bricks operate in the real world. In that context they display E-type characteristics. This is, of course, fine provided that records of changes to individual specifications record additions and changes to the assumption set that underlie them. The restriction of the laws to E-type systems does not, therefore, decrease their practical significance. Both S-type and E-type programs have a role to play in system development and evolution.

2.3 The Laws of Software Evolution

The eight laws of software evolution formulated over the 70s and 80s are listed in Table 2.1. The first three laws emerged from a follow up of the 1969 study of the evolution of IBM OS/360 and its successor OS/370. These results were further strengthened during the seventies by other software system evolution studies. Additional support came from an ICL study in the eighties but some criticism directed, primarily, at the inadequacy of the statistical support from Lawrence.

Table 2.1 Current statement of the laws

No.	Brief Name	Law
I 1974	Continuing Change	E-type systems must be continually adapted else they become progressively less satisfactory in use.
II 1974	Increasing Complexity	As an E-type system is evolved its complexity increases unless work is done to maintain or reduce it.
III 1974	Self-Regulation	Global E-type system evolution processes are self-regulating.
IV 1978	Conservation of Organisational Stability	Unless feedback mechanisms are appropriately adjusted, average effective global activity rate in an evolving E-type system tends to remain constant over product lifetime
V 1978	Conservation of Familiarity	In general, the incremental growth and long-term growth rate of E-type systems tend to decline.
VI 1991	Continuing Growth	The functional capability of E-type systems must be continually increased to maintain user satisfaction over the system lifetime.
VII 1996	Declining Quality	Unless rigorously adapted to take into account changes in the operational environment, the quality of E-type systems will appear to be declining.
VIII 1996	Feedback System (Recognised 1971, formulated 1996)	E-type evolution processes are multi-level, multi-loop, multi-agent feedback systems.

The present listing incorporates minor modifications that reflect new insights gained during the FEAST/1 project.

Over the years, the laws have gradually become recognized as providing useful inputs to understanding of the software process and have found their place in a number of university software engineering curricula. Additional support for six of the eight laws has accumulated as the data obtained from its collaborators was modeled and analysed in the FEAST/1 project. The remaining two laws were neither supported nor negated by the evidence acquired from the latest studies because of the absence of relevant data. They appear, however, to reflect a basic truth whose precise nature still needs clarification.

As indicated above, the structure of this section follows the order in which the laws were formulated. It is, however, now recognized that since the laws are not independent they should not be regarded as linearly ordered. Thus, the numbering of Table 2.1 is only historically significant. Its use in structuring this section is a matter of convenience and has no other implication. The question of dependencies and relationships between the laws is currently the subject of further investigation and initial thoughts on that topic are now available. If that development is successful it should put to rest the main criticisms to which the laws have been subjected for many years. These addressed the absence of precise definitions and of statements of assumptions, being based on data from a single, atypical source OS/360 and the system represented an outmoded software technology. The use of the term laws in relation to observations about phenomena directed, managed and reflecting human activity was also questioned.

Human decision was surely the principle determinant of much of the behaviour encapsulated in the laws. In response it was noted that though the demand for more widespread evidence of their validity was undoubtedly justified, the final criticism was not valid. It was precisely human involvement that justified the use of the term. The term law is appropriate and was selected because each encapsulates organizational and sociological factors that are outside the realm of software engineering and the scope of software developers. From the perspective of the latter they must be accepted as such.

2.4 Practical Implications of the Laws

Let us now outline some of the practical implications of the laws and the tools that are suggested by them. Many of the items on the lists that follow will appear intuitively self-evident. What is new is the unifying conceptual framework on which they are based. This framework follows from observed behaviour, interpretation, inference and so on. Together, these provide the basis for a comprehensive theory of software evolution.

A full analysis of the meaning and implications of this classification requires more discussion, than can be provided here, but guidelines that follow from the preceding discussion are listed in this section, others under the headings that follow. It is appreciated that some of these recommendations may be difficult to implement but the potential long-term benefit of their implementation in terms of productivity, process effectiveness, with system predictability, maintainability, changeability makes their pursuit worthwhile. Note that this list (and all others that follow) is to be considered randomly ordered. No implications, in terms of relative importance for example, are to be drawn from the position of any item.

- All properties and attributes required to be possessed by software products created or modified by individual developers should be explicitly identified in the specification. Such key properties serve as task definitions.
- The (long-term) goal should be to express specifications formally within the organization's quality system.
- A goal of every process must be to capture and retain assumptions underlying the specification, both those that form part of its inputs and those arising during the subsequent development process. This should occur during the initial development of specifications, all the implementation steps that follow and any subsequent revisions. Further opportunities arise during verification and/or validation.
- The ideal state has been represented in the previous point. In practice modifications to the specification, assumptions that accompany them and independent assumptions may be recorded in user or other documentation. This is appropriate since users need to be informed of assumptions that affect their usage. To treat that as a replacement for recordings in the system documentation cannot be considered best practice.
- It must be recognized and agreed by all involved that whatever is not included in the specification is left to the judgement of the assignee or whoever he/she wishes to consult. Any such decision must be confirmed as not being inconsistent with the specification and must either:
    a. be documented in an exclusion document;
    b. be formally approved and added to the specification or to other appropriate user documentation.
- Tools to assist in the implementation of these recommendations and to support their systematic application should be developed and introduced into practice.

2.4.1 First Law: Continuing Change: E-type Systems must be Regularly Adapted else they Become Progressively Less Satisfactory in Use

The real world has a potentially unbounded number of attributes. The operational domain and the applications pursued in it are part of the real world, initially undefined and intrinsically unbounded. The E-type software system implemented or supporting the application and, for that matter, the wider total application system are essentially finite. Thus, as a model of an application in the real world, every E-type system is essentially incomplete. A process of bounding, abstraction and transformation is required to specify and implement the system. This finitisation process excludes an unbounded number of attributes of the operational domain and the application from the system specification. Only exclusions specifically identified as such in the specification are determined. All others are left to the implementers' choice, conscious or unconscious and each such exclusion reflects an assumption about required program properties. Some of the assumptions will be explicit, others implicit, some by inclusion, others by exclusion, some recorded, some unrecorded. They will be reflected in the application implementation and/or documentation in a variety of ways, not discussed further here. Note that implicit exclusion from the system is as real in impacting system operation as are inclusions. In summary, every E-type system has embedded in it an unbounded assumption set whose composition will determine the domain of valid application in terms of execution environment, time, function, geography, the detail of many levels of the implementation and so on.

It may be that the initial set of assumptions was complete and valid in the sense that its effect on system behaviour rendered the system satisfactory in operation at the time of its introduction. However, with the passage of time user experience increases, user needs and expectation change, new opportunities arise, system application expands in terms of numbers of users or details of usage and so on. Hence, the greater the number of assumptions the greater the number of problems. This is likely to lead to less than acceptably satisfactory performance in some sense and hence to change requests. On top of that there will be changes in the real world that impact the application or its domain of operation so requiring changes to the system to restore it to being an acceptable model of that domain. Taken together, these facts lead to the first law of software evolution and its practical outcome in the unending maintenance that has been the universal experience of computer users since the start of serious computer applications.

There follows a listing of some of the practical implications of this unending need for change to E-type systems to adapt them to their respective changing operational domains.

- Comprehensive, structured, documentation must be created and maintained to record the growth in content, interdependencies and complexity (see second law) to facilitate control of that growth as changes are applied over the system lifetime, change upon change.
- As the design of change proceeds, all aspects including, for example, the issue being addressed, the reasons why a particular implementation design/algorithm is being used, details of assumptions, explicit and implicit, adopted and so on must be recorded in a way that will facilitate regular subsequent review.
- There must be a conscious effort to control, and reduce complexity and its growth as changes are made locally or in interfaces with the remainder of the system.
- The assumption set must be reviewed as an integral part of release planning and periodically thereafter to detect domain and other changes that conflict with the existing set, or violate constraints. The widespread practice of beta releases should be a help in this regard in relation, for example, to the detection of such changes or violations.
- The safe rate of change per release is constrained by the process dynamics. As the number, magnitude and orthogonality of changes to system architecture in a release increases, complexity and fault rate grow more than linearly. Successor releases focusing on fault fixing, performance enhancement and structural clean up will be necessary to maintain system viability. Models over a sequence of releases of, for example, patterns of incremental growth and of numbers of changes per release can provide an indication of limits to safe change rates. Another useful metric is the number of elements changed (i.e. handled) per release or over a given time period.
- FEAST/1 and earlier incremental growth model, suggest that an excessive number of changes in a release has an adverse impact on release schedule, quality, and freedom of action for following releases. A more precise statement of the consequences remains to be determined.

- It appears, in general, to be a sound strategy to alternate releases between those concentrating primarily on fault fixes, complexity reduction and minor enhancements and those that implement performance improvement, provide functional extension or add new function. Incremental growth and other models provide indicators to help determine if and when this is appropriate.
- Change validation must address the change itself, actual and potential interaction with the remainder of the system and impact on the remainder of the system.
- It is beneficial to determine the number of distinct additions and changes to requirements over constituent parts of the system per release or over some fixed time period to assess domain and system volatility. This can assist evolution release planning in a number of ways, for example, by pointing to system areas that are ripe for restructuring because of high fault rates or high functional volatility or where, to facilitate future change, extra care should be taken in change architecture and implementation.

2.4.2 Second Law: Growing Complexity: As an E-type System is Evolved its Complexity Increases Unless Work is Done to Maintain or Reduce it

One reason for complexity growth as a system evolves, the imposition of change upon change. Though, other reasons do exist. For example, the number of potential connections and interactions between elements (objects, modules, holons, sub-systems, etc.) is proportional to the square of the number n of elements. Thus, as a system evolves, and with it the number of elements, the work required to ensure a correct and adequate interface between the new and the old, the potential for error and omission, the likelihood of incompatibility between assumptions, all tend to increase as n^2. Moreover, with the passage of time, changes and additions that are made are likely to be more remote from the initial design concepts and architecture, so further increasing the interconnectivity. Even, if carefully controlled all these contribute to an increase in system complexity.

The growth in the difficulty of design, change and system validation, and hence in the effort and time required for system evolution, tends to cause a growth in the need for user support and in costs. Such increases will, in general, tend to be accompanied by a decline in product quality and in the rate of evolution, however defined and measured, unless additional work is undertaken to compensate for this. FEAST/1 observations indicate directly that the average software growth rate measured in modules or their equivalent tends to decline as a function of the release sequence number as the system ages. The long-term trend tends to follow an inverse square trajectory with the *mae* (mean absolute error), that is the mean absolute difference, between release sizes as predicted by the model and their actual size of order 6%. Based on this law which reflects the observations, measurement, modeling, analysis and other supporting evidence obtained over the last thirty years, and most recently, in the FEAST/1 project, the following observations and guidelines may be identified:

- The complexity of the system has many aspects. Which include but are not limited to:
  a. Application and functional complexity – including that of the operational domain.
  b. Specification and requirements complexity.

c. Architectural complexity.

d. Design and implementation complexity.

e. Structural complexity at many levels (subsystems, modules, objects, calling sequences, object usage, code, documentation, etc.).

- Complexity control and other anti-regressive activities are an integral part of the development and maintenance responsibility. The immediate benefits of such effort will, generally, be relatively small. The long-term impact is, however, likely to be significant; may indeed, at some stage, make the difference between survival of a system and its replacement or demise. Release planning for one or a series of releases must carefully consider the degree, timing and distribution of anti-regressive activity.
- Effective control of complexity requires that, as part of the maintenance and evolution process, its growth be measured to determine when anti-regressive activity as above should be initiated to reverse adverse trends.
- Determining the level of effort for anti-regressive activity such as complexity control in a release or sequence of releases and what effort is to be applied presents a major paradox. If the level is reduced or even abandoned so as to free resources for progressive activity such as system enhancement and extension, system complexity and future effort/cost are likely to increase, productivity, evolution rates stakeholder dissatisfaction and system quality to decline (law VII). If additional resources are provided, resources for system enhancement and growth are likely to be reduced. Once again the system evolution rate and with it stakeholder satisfaction will decline. In the absence of process improvement that is based on the principles examined in this section, decline of evolution rate appears inevitable. Hence, one must evaluate alternatives and select a strategy most likely to help achieve corporate business or other goals requiring to be optimized.
- The fraction of total activity that should, on average be devoted to anti-regressive work or how this should be divided between releases of any system is likely to vary as a function of factors such as organizational, project, process, application area and so on. The development of models for estimating requires R & D but there is reason to believe that generic parameterized models can eventually be developed. In the meantime it behoves software organizations to investigate this with reference to individual environments.
- Despite the absence of sound models, many strategies for optimizing progressive/anti-regressive work balance can be conceived. One might, for example, alternate between releases focusing primarily on each of the two classes. Alternatively one might seek to set up a sequence along the lines of a new function release (beta?), followed by a fault fixing release followed by an internal release reducing complexity. Selection of a strategy has technical, cost and business implications and requires local exploration and decision but one can conceive developing generic strategies.

2.4.3 Third Law: Self-regulation – Global E-type System Evolution Processes are Self-regulating

This law was first suggested by the growth patterns of OS/360, confirmed by observations on three other systems in the 1970's and most recently reconfirmed for the release-based systems studied in FEAST/1. The detailed growth patterns of the different systems differ but the gross trends are strikingly similar. In particular, inverse square models have yielded unexpectedly good fits to plots of system size S_i, (generally measured in modules or their equivalent) against release sequence number (*rsn*) i in all the release based systems studied under the FEAST projects. The model takes the form:

$$S_{i+1} = S_i + \hat{e}/S_i^2,$$

where $\hat{e}$ can be calculated, for example, as the mean of a sequence of e_i calculated from pairs of neighbouring size measures S_i and S_{i+1}. The predictive accuracy of the models, as measured by the *mae*, are of order 6%. This is a remarkable result since the size of individual releases is mainly determined by management focus on functional needs. With the declining cost of storage, overall system growth is not, in general, consciously managed or constrained. An exception to that observation is illustrated by embedded systems where storage is often limited by physical considerations.

The FEAST projects have identified two exceptions to this surprisingly simple growth model. In the case of VME Kernel, the least square model can be fitted directly to the growth data as for the other systems studied. An improved fit is, however, obtained when the model is fitted by separate segments spanning *rsn* 1 to 14 and *rsn* 15 to 29 respectively. The second exception is OS/360 where a linear model over *rsn* 1 to 19 gives a lower *mae* than an inverse square model. However, its growth rate fluctuated wildly for a further 6 releases before fission into VS1, VS2. Over that region both inverse square and linear growth models are totally inappropriate. Explanations of these exceptions have been proposed but confirmation and with it, determination of their wider implications, are now difficult to come by.

As noted above, with some exceptions, size is not, in general, a managed system parameter. Several growth related factors come to mind. Complexity growth is almost certainly a constraining factor. Increasing capability that may follow growing maturity may help overcome this though current evidence, the widely observed inverse square rate for example, suggests that complexity growth dominates. Further investigation of this issue is clearly of major interest and ripe for further research investigation, and therefore beyond the scope of this book.

A common feature of the growth patterns of all the release based systems observed is a superimposed ripple. These ripples are believed to reflect the action of stabilizing mechanisms that yield the regulation referred to in the law. Feedback mechanisms that achieve such stabilization have been proposed. Their identification in real industrial processes, exploration of the manner in which they achieve control such as process stabilization and the behavioural implication on system evolution, was initiated in FEAST/1 and is being continued in FEAST/2 by means of system dynamic models. Attempts to improve, even optimize, such mechanisms can follow.

The conclusion that feedback is a major source of the behaviour described by the third law is supported by the following reasoning. As for many business processes, one of the goals of the outer loop mechanisms in the software process is stability in technical, financial, organizational and sales terms. To achieve this goal technical, management, organizational, marketing, business, support and user processes and the humans who work in or influence or control them, apply negative (constraining) and positive (reinforcing) information controls guided by indicators of past and present performance, data for future direction and control. Their actions are exemplified by, for example, progress and quality monitoring and control, checks, balances and control on resource usage. All these represent, primarily, feedback based mechanisms as described by the third law. The resultant information loops tend to be nested and intuition suggests that the outer ones will exert a major, possibly dominant, influence on the behaviour of the process as measured from outside the loop structure.

This has been supported by global process behaviour (and, by implication, that of the system) as observed from the outside, the law is entirely compatible with the realities of business. It appears that the mechanisms underlying the third law are strongly feedback related and the law is likely to be closely related to the eighth – Feedback – law. An investigation, in a wider context, of this relationship is about to be initiated in a complex, multi-loop, system such as the software process, it is difficult to identify the sources of the feedback forces that influence individual behavioural characteristics. Thus, for example, stabilization forces and mechanisms in software evolution planning and execution are not explicit, will often be unrecognized, and may not be manageable. Many will arise from outside the process, from organizational, competitive or marketplace pressures, for example. Process changes may have the intended local impact but unexpected global consequences.

Each may work for or against deviations from established levels, patterns and trajectories but lead to counter-intuitive consequences, particularly when decisions are taken in the absence of a global picture. In feedback systems, correct decisions can generally only be taken in the context of an understanding of the system as a whole. In the absence of appropriate global models provision must be made for the unexpected.

As discussed above, important process and product behavioural characteristics are probably determined to a significant degree by feedback mechanisms not themselves consciously controlled by management or otherwise. As a first step, for their identification one should search for properties common to several projects or groups or for correlations between project or group characteristics such as size, age, application area, team size, organizational experience or behavioural patterns. One then may seek quantitative or behavioural invariants associated with each characteristic. To identify the feedback mechanisms and controls that play a role in self-stabilization and to exploit them in future planning, management and process improvement the following steps should be helpful.

- Applying measurement and modeling techniques such as those used in FEAST/1, determine typical patterns, trends, rates and rates of change of a number of projects within the organization. To obtain models with an *mae* of O (5%) data on at least six, possibly eight to ten, releases are likely to be required. Quantitatively, the rules quoted in the FEAST/1 report apply to systems that have evolved over that number of releases. Qualitatively, however, the rules have more general implications.
- Establish baselines, which are typical values, for process rates such as growth, faults, changes over the entire system, units changed, units added, units removed and so on. These may, however, be counted per unit time or per release. Our experience has been that, for reasons well understood, the former yields results that are more regular and interpretable. Initially however, and occasionally thereafter, results over real time and over release sequence number must be compared and appropriate conclusions drawn. Incremental values, that are the difference between values for successive time intervals, should also be determined, as should

numbers of people working with the system in various capacities, person days in categories such as specification, design, implementation, testing, integration, customer support and costs related to these activities. A third group of measures relates to quality factors. These can be expressed, for example, in pre-release and user reported faults, user take-up rates, installation time and effort, support effort, etc.

- New data that becomes available as time passes and as more releases are added, should be used to recalibrate and improve the models or to revalidate them and test their predictive power.
- Analysis of FEAST/1 data, models and data patterns suggests that, in planning a new release or the content of a sequence of releases, the first step must be to determine which of three possible scenarios exists. Let m be the mean of the incremental growth mi of the system in going from release i to release $i+1$ and s the standard deviation of the incremental growth both over a series of some five or so releases or time intervals. The scenarios may, for example, be differentiated by an indicator $m+2s$ that identifies a release plan as safe, risky or unsafe according to the conditions listed below.
- The rules here are expressed in release based units. For observations based on incremental growth per standard real time unit, analogous safe limits are likely to exist. They are likely to be a function of the interval between observations. More work is required to determine whether meaningful relationships can be identified, quantified and modeled for predictive purposes.

    a. As briefly discussed above and in greater detail in the FEAST publications, those studies suggest that a safe level for planned release content mi is that it be less than or equal to m. If the condition is fulfilled growth at the desired rate may proceed safely.

    b. The desired release content is greater than m but less than $m+2s$. This release is risky. It could succeed in terms of achieved functional scope but serious delivery delays, quality or other problems could arise. If pursued, it would be wise to plan for a follow-on clean up release. Even if not planned, a zero growth release may be required. Note that $m+2s$ has long been identified as an alarm limit, for example, in statistical process monitoring/control.

        1. The desired release content is close to or greater than $m+2s$. A release with incremental growth of this magnitude is unsafe. It is likely to cause major problems and instability over one or more subsequent releases. At best, it is likely to require to be followed by a major clean up release which concentrates on fault fixing, documentation updating and antiregressive work such as restructuring, the elimination of dead code and other anti-regressive work.

The application of some form of evolutionary development approach should be considered if the number of items on the "to be done" list for a release in planning would, if implemented in one release, lead to incremental growth in excess of the levels indicated above. Such a strategy would be appropriate whenever the size and/or complexity of the required addition is large. In that event, several alternatives may be considered. They include spreading the work over two or more releases, the delivery to users of the new functionality over two or more releases with mechanisms in place to return to older version if necessary, support group reinforcement, preceding the release with one or more clean up releases or preparing for a fast follow on release to rectify problems that are likely to appear. In either of the last two instances provision must be made for additional user support.

2.4.4 Fourth Law: Conservation of Organizational Stability – Unless Feedback Mechanisms are Appropriately Adjusted, Average Effective Global Activity Rate in an Evolving E-type System Tends to Remain Constant Over Product Lifetime

The observations on which this law is based date back to the late seventies. Further data gathered in FEAST/1 neither supports nor negates it. When first formulated, the feedback nature of the software process had already been identified. Insight into the underlying process mechanisms and related phenomena supported the interpretation encapsulated in the law. Subsequent observations suggested, for example, that the average activity rate measured by the change rate, is stationary but with changes of the mean and variance at one or more points during the observed life time of the released-based systems. The influence of feedback on the process has been apparent since the early 70s but the full extent was not fully appreciated until recently. If further observations yield similar results and when more understanding is achieved, refinement of the law may be indicated. Aspects of the law relating to the role of feedback stabilization and its implications are discussed below. Management implications are not considered further here except in so far that they are reflected in the rules.

2.4.5 Fifth Law: Conservation of Familiarity – In General, the Incremental Growth and Long-term Growth Rate of E-type Systems Tend to Decline

With the exception of OS/360, the decline in incremental growth and growth rate has been observed in all the systems whose evolution has been studied. It might be thought that this could be due to a reduction in the demand for correction and change as the system ages but anecdotal evidence from the market place and from developers indicates otherwise. In general, there is always more work in the "waiting attention" queue than in progress or active planning.

Other potential sources of declining growth rate with age can be identified. Consider, for example, system maintenance over a series of releases. This requires a split of resources between fixing, enhancement and extension. There are many reasons why fixes are likely to increase as a system ages. If investment in system maintenance remains constant, a drop in resources available for system growth and, hence, a declining growth rate is implied as system complexity increases. Equally the budget allocation may be declining because it has, for example, been decided that it is no longer in the organization's interest to expand the system or because it is believed that increasing maintenance productivity, as personal experience and system familiarity increases, permits the reduction of maintenance funding.

As the system ages, as changes and additions to the system become ever more remote from the original concepts and structures, increasing effort and time will be required to implement the changes, to understand them in a changed context, to validate and use the system; in short to ensure that the untouched, the changed and the new portions of the system all operate as required. Thus, changes and additions take longer to design and to implement, errors and the need for subsequent repair are more likely, comprehensive validation is more complex.

Apart from the factors that may be causing the decline identified by the fifth law in the rate of, for example, system growth. There are likely to be others, as well. Though the law refers primarily to long-term behaviour, regular short-term variations in incremental growth have also been observed. FEAST/2 also investigates the relationship between incremental growth which tends to reflect the addition of new functionality and modification of existing software elements to reflect changes in the application, the domain or other parts of the system.

In summary, both developers and users must be familiar with the system if they are to work on or use it effectively. Given the growing complexity of the system, its workings and its functionality, achieving renewed familiarity after numerous changes, additions and removals, restoration of pre-change familiarity after change becomes increasingly difficult. Common sense, therefore, dictates that the rate of change and growth of the system should be slowed down as it ages and this trend has been observed in nearly all the data studied to date. The only exception has been the original OS/360 study where the growth trend appeared to remain constant to *rsn* 19.

The fact that a reduction in growth rate as a system ages is likely to be beneficial has not, to date, been widely appreciated. Its widespread occurrence is, therefore, unlikely to be the result of deliberate management control. It is, rather, feedback from locally focused validation and correction activities that are the likely causes. That is, the decline is believed to be due to the system dynamics and not to human decision. Nevertheless, since such behaviour results from local and sequential control, from correction not specifically aimed at managing growth, the short-term incremental growth rate fluctuates. Such fluctuations reflect, for example, ambitious high content releases dictated by user demand, perceived needs or competitive pressure. These are likely to lead to larger than average growth and growth rates.

Inevitably, clean up and restructuring exercises must follow. The overall effect is stabilization. This and further analysis, in phenomenological terms, of the distributed mechanisms that control evolution rate together with models of related data, suggest the following guidelines for determining release content.

- Collect, plot and model growth and change data as a function of real time or *rsn* to determine system evolution trends. The choice includes objects, lines of code (*locs*), modules (holons), inputs and outputs, subsystems, features, requirements and so on. As a start it is desirable to record several, or even all, of these measures so as to detect similarities and differences between the results obtained from the various measures and to identify those from which the clearest indications of evolutionary trends can be obtained. Once set up, further collection of such data becomes a trivial exercise. Procedures for their capture may already be a part of configuration management or other procedures.
- Develop automatic tools to interpret the data as it builds up over a period of time to derive, for example, the dynamic trend patterns. For example, in FEAST/1 it has been shown how, using a scripting language such as Perl, records, such as change-logs, not conceived for the purpose of metric unplanned, can be used as data sources to estimate such properties element growth and change rate. A degree of discipline, such as the adoption of a fixed standard pattern for change-log data added to change-log preparation, will facilitate data extraction. Once data is available, models that reflect historical growth trends can and should

be derived. Planning and management indicators for future use may then be computed by, for example, fitting an inverse square trend lines or some other appropriate curves.

- Once the model parameters have stabilized (FEAST observations indicated that this requires some six releases of a system) the models should provide first estimates of the trends and patterns of growth and changes per release or time unit as determined by the system dynamics. Somewhat more data points will be required to reach, confidence levels of, say 5%. Measures must be updated and the trend indicator recomputed or redisplayed for each subsequent release and/or at regular time intervals.
- On the basis of the observations reported, in planning further releases the following guide lines should be followed:
  a. seek to maintain incremental growth per release or the growth rate in real time at or about the level m suggested by the trend model(s);
  b. when the expected growth of a release appears to require growth significantly greater than *m*, seek to reduce it, for example, by spreading the additional functionality over two or more releases;
  c. plan and implement a 'preparation release' that precleans the system, if limiting growth to around *m* is difficult or not possible;
  d. alternatively, allow for a longer release period to prepare and handle problems at integration, a higher than normal fault report rate, some user discontentment.
- If the required release increment is near to or above $m+2s$ the steps in 2 - 4 must be even more rigorously pursued. Prepare to cope with and control a period of system instability, provide for a possible need for more than average customer support and accept that, as outlined above, a major recovery release may be required.

2.4.6 Sixth Law: Continuing Growth – The Functional Capability of E-type Systems Must be Continually Increased to Maintain User Satisfaction Over the System Lifetime

This law must be distinguished from the first law which asserts "Continuing Change". The need for change reflects a need to adapt the system to the outside world, the domain being covered and the application and/or activity being supported or pursued. Such exogenous changes are likely to invalidate assumptions made during system definition, development, validation, installation and application or render them unsatisfactory.

The software reflecting such assumptions has to be adapted so as to restore assumptions validity. The sixth law reflects the fact that all software, being finite, limits the functionality and other characteristics of the system (in extent and in detail) to a finite selection from a potentially unbounded set. The domain of operation is also potentially unbounded, but the system can only be designed and validated, explicitly or implicitly, for satisfactory operation in some finite part of it. Sooner or later, excluded features, facilities and domain areas become bottlenecks or not useful. They have to be included if the gap is to be filled. The system needs to evolve to satisfactorily support new situations and circumstances, to the new requirements.

Though, they have different causes and represent, in many ways, different circumstances, the steps to be taken to take cognisance of the sixth law do not, in principle, differ radically from those listed for the first. There are, however, differences due to the fact that the former is, mainly, concerned with functional and behavioural change whereas the latter leads, in general, directly to additions to the existing system and to its growth. In practice, it may be difficult or inappropriate to associate a given change with either law. Nevertheless, since the two are due to different phenomena they are also likely to lead to different but overlapping recommendations. This report, however, does not distinguish between the rules implied by any one.

Some further remarks are, however, appropriate in the context of the sixth law. In general, the cleaner the architecture and structure of the system to evolve the more likely is it that additions may be cleanly added with firewalls to control the exchange of information between old and new parts of the system. There must be some form of penetration from the additions to the existing system. This will, in particular, be so when one considers the continued evolution of systems that were not, in the first instance, designed or structured for dynamic growth by the addition of new components. Sadly, the same remarks, limitations and consequent precautions, apply when one is dealing with systems that are component based or that make widespread use of COTS. They will also evolve, with due time. A sound architectural and structural base and application of the rules of these laws will reduce the effort that will inevitably be required when such systems are extended.

2.4.7 Seventh Law: Declining Quality – The Quality of E-type Systems will Appear to be Declining Unless they are Rigorously Adapted, as Required, to take into Account Changes in the Operational Environment

This law follows the first and sixth laws. As briefly discussed in previous sections, to remain satisfactory in use in a changing operational domain, an E-type system must undergo changes and additions to adapt and extend itself. Functionality as well as behavioural detail must be changed and extended. To achieve this, new blocks of code are attached, new interactions and interfaces are created on top of one another. If such changes are not made, embedded assumptions become falsified, mismatch with the operational domains increases. Additions will tend to be increasingly remote from the established architecture, function and structure. All in all the complexity of the system in terms of the interactions between its parts, and the potential for such interaction, all increase. Performance is likely to decline and the faults potential will increase as embedded assumptions are inadvertently violated and the potential for undesired interactions created. From the point of view of performance, behaviour and evolution, adaptation and growth effort increase. Growing complexity, mismatch with operational domains, declining performance, increasing numbers of faults, increasing difficulty of adaptation and growth, all lead to a decline in stakeholder satisfaction. Each represents a factor in declining system quality.

There are several approaches that can be used to define software quality. The above lists of decline are some of the more obvious ones. However, there are several others. It is not proposed to discuss here possible viewpoints, the impact of circumstances or more formal definitions. To do so involves, on the one hand, organizational and stakeholder concerns and, on the other, issues more adequately discussed in terms of a theory of software evolution. The bottom line is that quality is a function of many factors whose relative significance will vary with circumstances. Users in the field will be concerned with performance, reliability, functionality, adaptability. The concern of a CEO, at the other extreme, will be with the system's contribution to corporate profitability, market share and the corporate image, resources required to support it, the support provided to the organization in pursuing its business and so on.

Once identified as a concern in relation to the business or task being addressed, aspects of quality must be quantified to be adequately controllable. Subject to being observed and measured in a consistent way, associated measures of quality can be defined for a system, project or organization. Their value, preferably normalized, may then be tracked over releases or units of time and analysed to determine whether levels and trends are required or desired. One may, for example, monitor the number of user generated fault reports per release to obtain a display of the fault rate trend with time. A fitted trend line (or other model) can then indicate whether the rate is increasing, declining or remaining steady. One may also observe oscillatory behaviour and test this to determine whether sequences are regular, randomly distributed or correlated to internal or external events. Time series modeling may be applicable to extract and encapsulate serial correlations.

One may also seek relationships with other process and product measures such as the size of or the number of fixes in previous releases, subsystem or module size, testing effort and so on. When enough data is available, and the process is sufficiently mature, models such as Bayesian nets may be useful to predict defect rates. The above examples all relate to fault related aspects of quality. Several other measures may also be defined, collected and analysed in an analogous manner.

In summary we observe that the underlying cause of the seventh law, the decline of software quality with age, appears to relate, primarily, to a growth in complexity associated with ageing. It follows that in addition to undertaking activity from time to time to reduce complexity, practices in architecture, design and implementation that reduce complexity or limit its growth should be pursued.

- Design changes and additions to the system in accordance with established principles such as information hiding, structured programming, elimination of pointers and GOTOs, and so on, to limit unwanted interactions between code sections and control those that are essential.
- Devote some portion of evolution resources to complexity reduction of all sorts, restructuring, the removal of "dead" system elements and so on. Though primarily antiregressive, without immediate revenue benefit, this will help ensure future changeability, potential for future reliable and cost effective evolution. Hence, eventually, the investment turns profitable.
- Train personnel to seek to capture and record assumptions, whether explicit or implicit, at all stages of the process in standard form and in a structure that will facilitate their being reviewed.
- Verify the authenticity of assumptions with users and/or other stakeholders.
- Assess the impact if the assumptions were to be invalid, for example what changes would need to be made to correct the invalid assumption?
- Review relevant portions of the assumption set at all stages of the evolution process to avoid design or implementation action that invalidates even one of them. Methods and tools to capture, store, retrieve and review them and their realization must be developed.

- Monitor appropriate system attributes to predict the need for cleanup, restructuring or replacement of parts or the whole.

2.4.8 Eighth Law: Feedback System – E-type Evolution Processes are Multi-level, Multi-loop, Multi-agent Feedback Systems

This is the key law and underlies the behaviour encapsulated by the other seven. It is hoped to develop a formal theory that covers and describes the observed phenomenology and the relationships between the laws. The behaviour of feedback systems is not and cannot, in general, be described directly in terms of the aggregate behaviour of its forward path activities and mechanisms. Feedback constrains the ways that process constituents interact with one another and will modify their individual, local and collective, global, behaviour. With respect to the eighth law the software process is such a system. This observation must, therefore, be expected to apply. Thus, the contribution of any activity to the global process may be quite different from that suggested by its open loop characteristics. If the feedback nature of the software process is not taken into account when predicting its behaviour, unexpected, even counter-intuitive, results must be expected both locally and globally. For sound software process planning, management and improvement, the feedback nature of the process must be mastered.

Consider, for example, the growth and stabilization processes described by the first and third laws. Positive feedback conveys the desire for functional extension leading to pressure for growth and a need for continuing adaptation to exogenous changes. If the resultant pressure grows beyond a certain threshold it may lead to instability. The observed instability and final break up of that system will be attributed to excessive positive feedback, arising from competitive market and user demand for virtual memory and interactive operation. In any event, management, exercising its responsibility to manage change and the rate of change will, in response to information received about progress, system quality and so on, induce negative feedback, in the form of directives and controls to limit change contain side effects and drive it in the desired direction. Stabilization of results, FEAST/1 and earlier studies have provided behavioural evidence to support this analysis and the eighth law.

The positive and negative feedback loops and control mechanisms of the global E-type process involve activities in the many domains, organizational, marketing, business, usage and so on, within which the process is embedded and evolution is pursued. It eventually develops dynamics that will drive and constrain it. Many of the characteristics of this dynamics are rooted in and will be inherited from its history in wider, global, domains. As a result, there are significant limitations that management can exert on control of the process. The basic message of the eighth law is that in the long-term managers are not absolutely free to adopt any action considered appropriate from some specific business or other point of view. Reasonable decision can, generally, be locally implemented. The long-term, global, consequences that follow may not be what was intended or anticipated.

Fully effective planning and management requires that one takes into account the dynamic characteristics of the process; the limitations and constraints it imposes, as outlined above and in FEAST reports. To achieve this requires models that reflect the dynamic forces and behaviour. The FEAST project and other sources have made progress in such modeling but more, much of it interdisciplinary is required to achieve a systematic, controlled and usable discipline for the design and management of global software processes. FEAST results suggest that feedback loops involving personnel outside the direct technical process may have a major impact on the process dynamics and, therefore, on the behaviour of the evolution process. It follows that the interactions of maintenance, planning, marketing, user support, corporate personnel and others needs at least as much thought and planning as do technical software engineering and other low level issues and activities.

These observations lead to the following recommendations:

- Determine the organizational structures and domains within which the technical software development process operates including information, work flow and management control, both forward and feedback and monitor changes.
- In particular, seek to identify the many informal communication links that are not a part of the formal management structure but play a continuing role in driving and directing the system evolution trajectory and seek to establish their impact.
- Model the global structure using, for example, system dynamics approaches, calibrate and apply sensitivity analysis to determine the influence and relative importance of the paths and controls.
- In developing the models make certain to include all personnel and activities that feedback information or instructions that may be used to direct, control or change the process.
- In planning and managing further work, use the models as simulators to help determine the implications of the influences that are implied by the analysis.
- In assessing process effectiveness, use the models as outlined in *c* above to guide to identify interactions, improve planning and control strategies, evaluate alternatives and focus process changes on those activities likely to prove the most beneficial in terms of the organizational goals.

2.4.9 The FEAST Hypothesis – To Achieve Major Process Improvement of E-type Processes Other than the most Primitive, their Global Dynamics Must be Taken into Account

The FEAST hypothesis extends the eighth law by drawing explicit attention to the fact that one must take the feedback system properties of the complex global software process into account when seeking effective process improvement. The description of the process as complex is an understatement. It is a multi-level, multi-loop, multi-agent system. Chances are the loops might not even be fixed yet; therefore it need not be hierarchically structured. The implied level of complexity is compounded by the fact that the feedback mechanisms involve humans whose actions cannot be predicted with certainty. Thus, analysis of the global process, prediction of its behaviour and determination of the impact of feedback, are clearly not straightforward. One approach to such investigation uses simulation models. The consequences of human decision and action of variable forces and of flow levels may be described by statistical distributions. It is an open question whether such quantitative models must be specific to each system. It is believed that in the long run parameterized generic models can be developed to fit a wide range of circumstances.

Some classes of systems like safety critical, or organizations, e.g. multi-nationals could be expected to benefit from tailored models.

2.4.10 The Uncertainty Principle – The Real World Outcome of any E-type Software Execution is Inherently Uncertain with the Precise Area of Uncertainty also not Knowable

This principle, first formulated in the late 80s as a stand alone observation, is now regarded as a direct consequence of the laws. It asserts that the outcome of the execution of an E-type program is not absolutely predictable. The likelihood of unsatisfactory execution may be small but a guarantee of satisfactory results can never be given no matter how impeccable the previous operation has been. This statement may sound alarmist or trivial (after all there can always be unpredictable hardware failure) but that is not the issue. A proven fact is a fact and by accepting this, identifying the sources of uncertainty and taking appropriate steps even a small likelihood may be further reduced.

Various sources of software uncertainty do exist. The most immediate and one that can be at least partially addressed in process design and management, relates to the assumptions reflected in every E-type program. Some will have been taken consciously and deliberately, for example to limit the geographical range of the operational domain to a specific region or to limit the scope of a traffic control system. Others may be unconscious, for example to ignore the gravitational pull of the moon in setting up control software for a particle accelerator. Others may follow from implementation decisions taken without sufficient foresight such as adopting a two-digit representation for years in dates. These examples illustrate circumstances where errors can eventually arise when changes in the user or the machine world, or in the associated systems, invalidates assumptions and their reflection in code or documentation.

As indicated the real world domain is unbounded. Once any part of that real world is excluded from the system specification or its implementation the numbers of assumptions also become unbounded. Any one of this unbounded set can become invalid, for example, by extension of the operational domain, by changes to the problem being solved or the activity supported by the system or by changes in the system domain under and with which the program operates. Uncertainty is therefore intrinsic since an invalid assumption can lead to behavioural change in the program. Awareness of that uncertainty can, however, reduce the threat of error or failure if it leads to systematic search for and early detection of invalidity through regular checking of the assumption set. The more effectively assumptions are captured, the more carefully they are validated in terms of the current knowledge and in terms of the foreseeable future, the more complete and accessible the records of assumptions, the simpler they are to review and the greater the frequency with which they are reviewed the smaller the threat. Hence, the recommendation in earlier sections to incorporate and enforce the conscious capture, recording and review of assumptions of all types into the software and documentation processes.

So far we have mainly focused on assumptions related to software uncertainty. There are also other sources of uncertainty in system behaviour but the likelihood of their contributing to system failure is small in relation to that stemming from invalid assumptions embedded in the code or documentation. These are, therefore, not further discussed here.

- When developing a computer application and associated systems, estimate and document the likelihood of change in the various areas of the application domains and their spread through the system to simplify subsequent detection of assumptions that may have become invalid as a result of changes.
- Seek to capture by all means, assumptions made in the course of program development or change.
- Store the appropriate information in a structured form, related possibly to the likelihood of change as in *a*, to facilitate detection in periodic review of any assumptions that have become invalid.
- Have all assumptions validated by individuals with the necessary objective and contextual knowledge.
- Review the assumptions database by categories as identified in *c*, and as reflected in the database structure, at intervals guided by the likelihood or expectation of change or as triggered by events.
- Develop and provide methods and tools to ultimately facilitate all of the above points.
- Separate validation and implementation teams to improve questioning and control of assumptions
- Provide for ready access by the evolution teams to all appropriate domain specialists .

Finally and as already noted, the Uncertainty Principle is a consequence of the unboundedness of the operational and application domains of E-type systems and that the totality of known assumptions embedded in it must be finite. However, much understanding is achieved, however faithfully and completely the recommendations listed in the previous sections are followed, the results of execution of an E-type system will always be uncertain. There is no room for escaping. Adherence to the recommendations will, however, ensure that unexpected behaviour and surprise failures can be reduced, if not completely avoided. And when they do occur the source of the problem can be relatively rapidly located and fixed. In view of the increasing penetration of computers into all facets of human activity, organizational and individual, and their societal or economically critical roles, any such reduction in the likelihood of failure is important, must not be ignored.

2.5 Evolutionary Patterns in Open Source Software

F/OSS development has appeared and disseminated throughout the world of software technology in the last ten years. This coincides with the spread, adoption, and routine use of the Internet and the World Wide Web as a global technical system. This infrastructure supports widespread access to previously remote information and software assets, as well as the ability for decentralized communities of like-minded people to find and communicate with one another. This is a world that differs in many ways from the traditional where it is common to assume centralized software development locales, development work, and administrative authority that controls and manages the resources and schedules for software development and maintenance. Thus, to better understand whether or how patterns of software evolution in the technical and social regime of F/OSS conform to or differ from prior studies or models of software evolution, then it is appropriate to start with an identification of the types of entities for F/OSS evolution, then follow with an examination of empirical studies, data and analyses of F/OSS evolution patterns.

2.6 Types of Entities for Studying F/OSS Evolution

The scheme of object types that are suitable to address in studies of software evolution have been identified in the studies by Lehman and colleagues over the years. The primary types of entities are:

- software releases;
- systems;
- applications;
- development processes;
- process models.

Accordingly, each of these can be cast in terms of F/OSS as follows.

2.6.1 F/OSS Releases

In general, large F/OSS systems continue to grow over time and across releases. This suggests intimate consistency with the sixth law of software evolution. Both stable and unstable F/OSS release product versions are being globally distributed in practice. Periodic alpha, beta, candidate, and stable releases are made available to users at their discretion, as are unstable nightly F/OSS build versions released for developers actively contributing software updates to a given release. F/OSS releases for multiple platforms are generally synchronized and distributed at the same time, though may vary when new platforms are added (in parallel). F/OSS releases, thus, evolve within a nontraditional process cycle between full stable releases. F/OSS releases are also named with hierarchical release numbering schemes, sometimes with three or four levels of nested numbering to connote stable versus unstable releases to different audiences. However, the vast majority of F/OSS systems, primarily those for small and medium size F/OSS systems, do not continue to grow or thrive, mostly because the software is not intensively or widely used.

2.6.2 F/OSS Systems

F/OSS systems or programs evolve from first statement of an application concept or a change required, to an existing system released and installed as an operational program text with its documentation. F/OSS systems may

- be small (<5K SLOC2)
- medium (5K–100K SLOC)

- large (100K–1000K SLOC)
- very large systems (>1MSLOC)

Large and very large systems are few in number, but the most widely known. Most large or very large F/OSS systems or programs may exist in related but distinct versions/releases intended for different application platforms (e.g., MS Windows, Solaris, GNU/Linux, Mac OS X). Many F/OSS are structured as distributed systems, systems configured using scripts (e.g., using Perl, Python, Tcl), middleware, or as modules that plug-in to hosts/servers (e.g., Apache, Mozilla, and now Firefox support independently developed plug-in modules). Additionally, some F/OSS are dynamically linked systems configured at run-time, when developed in a programming language like Java or others enabling remote service/method invocation.

2.6.3 F/OSS Applications

A much greater diversity and population of F/OSS applications are being investigated for evolution patterns. Those examined in-depth so far include the Linux Kernel, Debian Linux distributions3, Mono, Apache Web server, Mozilla Web browser, Berkeley DB, GNOME user interface desktop, PostgreSQL DBMS, and about a dozen others. Studies of F/OSS application populations, taxonomy, and population demographics for hundreds to upwards of 40K F/OSS systems have also began to appear.

2.6.4 F/OSS Process

F/OSS are developed, deployed, and maintained according to some software process. It is however unclear whether F/OSS processes, as portrayed in popular literature or are intended only to be viewed as a monolithic process, just the top-level of a decomposable process, or whether specific software engineering activities have distinct processes which may also evolve, either independently or jointly. Furthermore, a small number of recent studies have begun to observe, describe and compare F/OSS development processes with those traditional to software engineering that point to differences in the activities and organization of the F/OSS process. In addition, F/OSS activities surrounding software releases may have their own distinct process that may not reflect the activities involved in the release of closed-source systems examined in the preceding section.

2.6.5 Models of F/OSS Process

Existing models of software development processes do not explicitly account for F/OSS development activities or work practices per se. Thus it is unclear whether models of software evolution processes that characterize closed-source software systems developed within a centralized administrative authority can account the decentralized, community oriented evolution of F/OSS.

Overall, evolving software systems may be packaged and released in either open source or closed source forms. The packaging and release processes and technical system infrastructure may at times differ or be the same, depending on the software system application and development host (e.g., a Web site for open source, a corporate portal for closed source). But the decentralized community-oriented technological regime and infrastructure of F/OSS appears different than the world of the centralized corporate centered regime and infrastructure of the closed source systems that have been examined as the basis of the laws of software evolution. Nonetheless, the laws of software evolution seem to apply, at least at a very high level, in accounting for the evolution of F/OSS.

Keywords

software ageing; S-type programs; E-type programs; P-type programs; dependencies; relationships; organizational factors; sociological factors; conceptual framework; classification; guidelines; process effectiveness; quality system; initial development; subsequent revisions; user documentation; exclusion document; continuing change; implicit exclusion; unbounded assumption; execution environment; system behaviour; system lifetime; release planning; beta releases; process dynamics; system architecture; incremental growth; system volatility; growing complexity; adequate interface; self-regulation

Exercises

1. Define the term software evolution.
2. List four activities carried out during the software evolution process.
3. List four conditions upon which successful software evolution is dependent on.
4. What three potential dangers may arise as a result of using an emergency repair process?
5. Using well-labeled diagrams, draw and list the properties of the three program types.
6. Explain, in detail, the classification relationship between E-type and S-type programs.
7. List Lehman's Laws of Evolution in its proper order.
8. List any three of Lehman's Laws of Evolution highlighting their implications in detail.
9. Discuss Lehman's Laws and their comprehensive inapplicability to open source software.
10. Translate transferable objects of Lehman's Laws to open source software in detail.

CHAPTER 3

Patterns in Open Software Evolution Studies

Objectives

The objective of this chapter is to bring to the student's attention the key differences between the application of software evolution laws to proprietary and open source software. Here we dwell on studies which compare the two blocks. When you have read this chapter you will be able to:

- Appreciate that Lehman's Laws of Evolution are not universally applicable to all kinds of software
- Appreciate the importance of research before adopting a general school of thought
- Understand the importance and role of software models in studying and adopting Lehman's Laws of Evolution
- Understand the software evolution playground, i.e. individual systems, group systems and global population systems and their impact

3.0 Patterns in Open Source Software Evolution Studies

Here we look at examples of studies in which F/OSS systems have been and are still being investigated, with the focus on how their results can be compared with those of Lehman and his colleagues.

Godfrey and Tu (2000) provided data on the size and growth of the Linux Kernel (2M + SLOC) from 1994 to 1999, and found the growth rate to be super-linear (i.e., greater than linear), as portrayed in Figures 3.1 through 3.5. They also found similar patterns in F/OSS for the Vim text

Figure 3.1 Data revealing the size and growth of major sub-systems in the Linux Kernel during 1994–1999

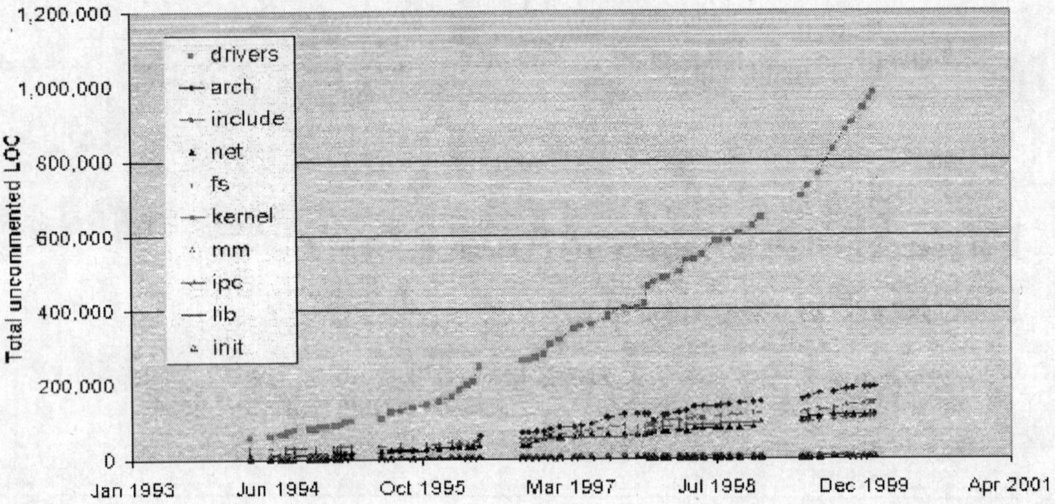

Source: Godfrey and Tu (2000)

Figure 3.2 Data revealing the size and growth of device drivers in the Linux Kernel during 1994–1999

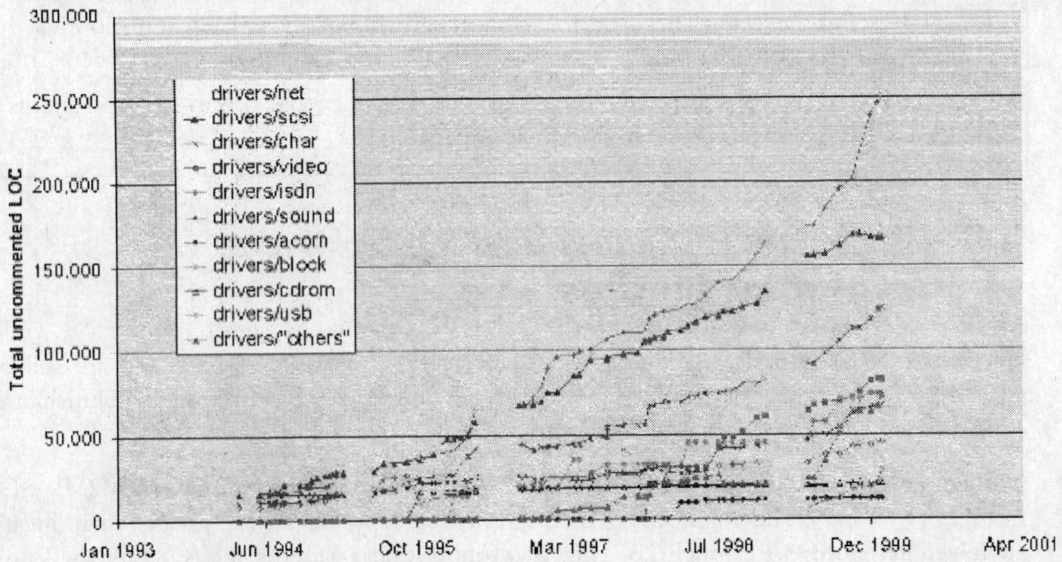

Source: Godfrey and Tu (2000)

Figure 3.3 Data revealing the size and growth of the Linux Kernel for different computer platform architectures during 1994–1999

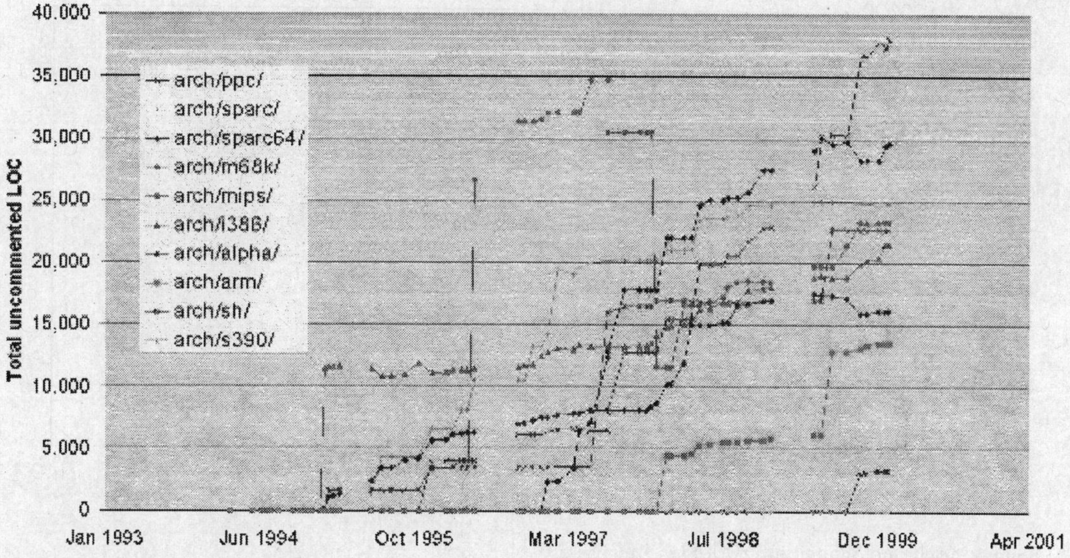

Source: Godfrey and Tu (2000)

Figure 3.4 Measured (discrete points) versus predicted (smooth curves) of common coupling of source code modules in the Linux Kernel across releases

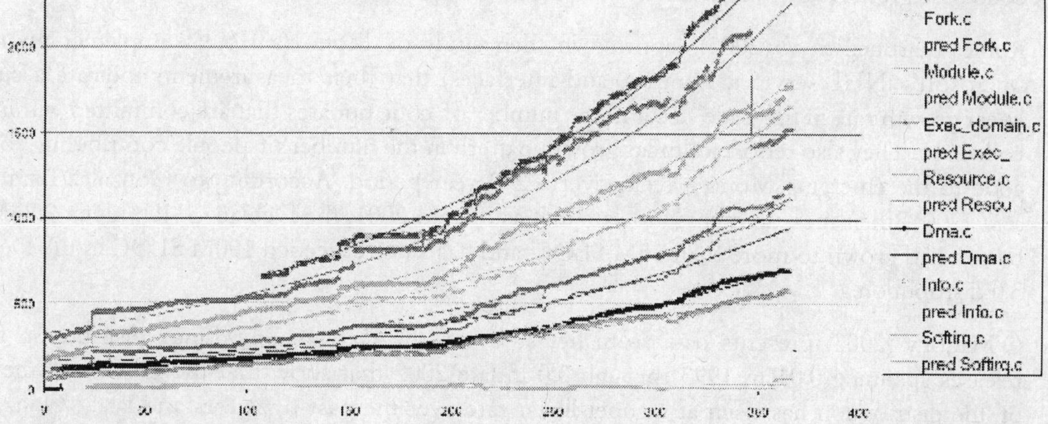

Source: Schach *et al.* (2002)

Figure 3.5 Growth of the lines of source code added as the number of software developers contributing code to the GNOME user interface grows

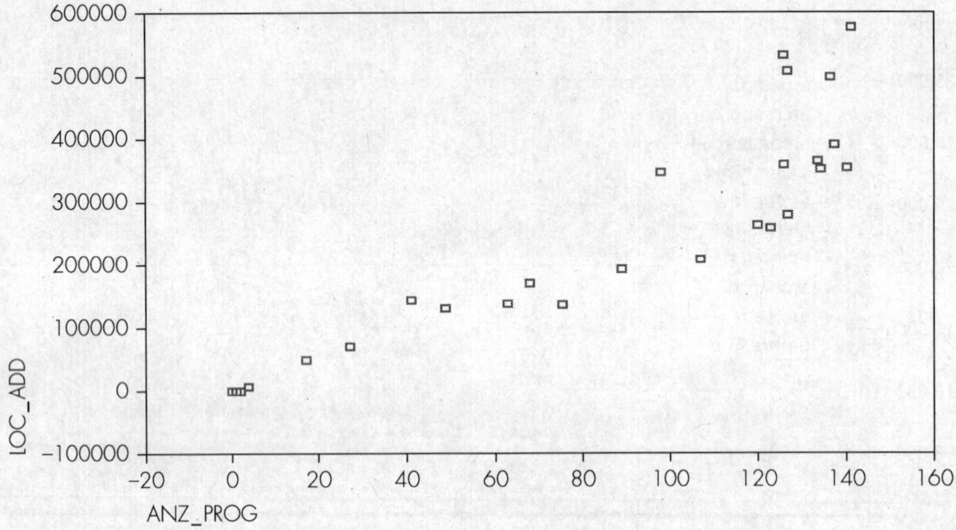

Source: Koch and Schneider (2000)

editor. Schach *et al.* (2002) reported on the result of an in-depth study of the evolution of the Linux Kernel across 96 releases indicating that module coupling (or interconnection) has been growing at an exponential (super-linear) rate. Their data is as displayed in Figure 3.1. They predict that unless effort is made to alter this situation, the Linux Kernel will become unmaintainable over time.

Koch and Schneider (2000) studied the GNOME user interface desktop (2M+ SLOC) and provided data that showed growth in the size of the source code base across releases increased in a super-linear manner as the number of software developers contributing code to the GNOME code base grew. Data from their study is plotted in Figure 3.2.

Robles-Martinez *et al.* (2003) reported in their study of Mono (a F/OSS implementation of Microsoft's .NET services, libraries, and interfaces) that their measurements indicate a super-linear growth rate in the code size and the number of code updates that are committed within the code base. They also report a similar growth pattern in the number of people contributing source code to the emerging Mono system over a 2–3 year period. According to Gonzalez-Barahona *et al.* (2001) their measurements indicate that as of mid-2001, the Debian GNU/Linux 2.2 distribution had grown to more than 55M SLOC, and has since exceeded 100M SLOC in the Debian 3.0 distribution.

O'Mahony (2003) presents data from her study of the Debian Gnu/Linux distribution from releases spanning 0.01 in 1993 through 3.0 in late 2002 that show that the growth of the size of the distribution has risen at a super-linear rate over the past five years and lastly, Gonzalez-Barahona *et al.* (2004) also provided data on the growth of the Apache project community and number of modules, revealing, once again, a superlinear growth pattern over the five year period (1999–2004) covered in their data.

The intriguing question is why there is such a high growth rate for some F/OSS systems like the Linux Kernel, Vim, GNOME, Mono, the Debian GNU/Linux distribution, and the Apache project, but not for other F/OSS. Godfrey and Tu (2000) reported in the case of the Linux Kernel that:

- much of the source code relates to device drivers, as seen in Figure 3.2;
- much of the code is orthogonal and intended for different platforms, as suggested in Figure 3.3; and
- the contributions to the code base are open to anyone who makes the requisite effort;
- Linux Kernel source code configurations (or "builds") are specific to a hardware platform or architecture (see Figure 3.4), and use as little of 15% of the total Linux Kernel source code base.

It is possible but still uncertain whether these conditions also apply to GNOME, Vim, Mono and the Apache project, since they may have source code configurations that are specific to different operating systems (Linux, BSD, Windows, or Mac OS/X). However, it is still not clear why they would or would not apply to Fetchmail, X-Windows, Gcc and Pine. Perhaps it might be because the latter systems are generally older and may have originally been developed in an earlier (pre-Web) technological regime.

3.1 Software Models

Models are also of a wide variety. Usually, when one thinks of a model, one thinks of a graphic representation along the lines of a construction plan with entities and connecting arrows. Earlier, models were made up of tree diagrams and flow diagrams. Later, models consisted of entity/relationship diagrams, sequence diagrams and state transition diagrams. The Unified Modeling Language (UML) attempts to unify all the previous diagram types plus some new ones into a common, all encompassing set of diagrams intended to describe a software system.

Diagrams or pictures are not the only way to describe a system. One can argue that the program code is also a description of the system, albeit a very low level one, but it contains all the details required to really understand the system. Abstraction means suppressing details, which also means losing them. Thus, a model can only be a partial description whereas the code is the complete description. The sum of all the program sources – the workflow languages, the interface description languages, the database schemas, the header files and the classes make up a comprehensive and complete description of the system developed.

On the other hand, there are specification languages like Z, VDM and OCL which are high level descriptions of the system to be developed. These languages are closer to the way a user would view the system provided he is familiar with set theory. With them one can describe a complete solution independent of the technical implementation. Whether the user can understand them is another question.

Finally, there is the natural language itself, which is also an abstract description of a proposed or existing system. More often, requirement specifications are formulated in some restricted form of a natural language. The history of mankind has proven that a natural language is the preferred means of describing situations whether or not they physically exist or only exist in the minds of men. Situations and minds differ and so do natural languages. Of course, there are situations in which diagrams are more expressive than words – in which case, diagrams can be used to supplement words. Good descriptions of real or imagined phenomena are more often combinations of text and diagrams, which is how most software systems are described.

3.1.1 Top-down and Bottom-up Software Evolution

The problem with software evolution is how to keep the description of the system synchronized with the system itself i.e., how to synchronize the code with the model, when the system is changing rapidly and significantly. The implied goal of model driven software evolution is that the model is changed and that the changes are automatically propagated to the real code as depicted in Figure 3.6.

This assumes some kind of automatic transformation between the higher level description of the system and the lower one. If a function is added to the model, that same function pops up somewhere in the code or perhaps in many places in the code. The prerequisite to really applying such an automatic transformation is that the modeling language is closely related to the programming language i.e., the higher level description of the software is not far removed from the lower one. The further the modeling language is from the code being modeled, the more difficult and error prone is the transformation.

Figure 3.6 Top-down model driven approach

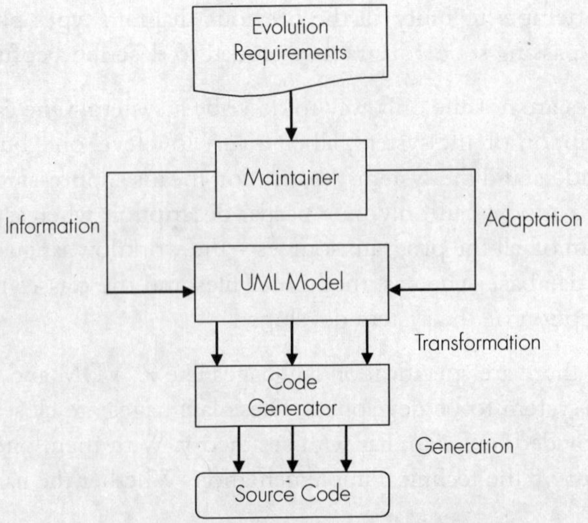

The model driven approach builds on the classical top-down approach to software development, which is in itself a fallacy. The advocates of this approach have a naïve belief in the ability of commercial developers to understand what they are doing. In reality they do not have the slightest idea. They play around with a problem until they have found an acceptable solution. Apparently, in actual practice, development steps are not refinements of the original specification, but instead redefine the specification itself. There is a much more intertwined relationship between specification and implementation than the standard rhetoric.

As an example, Balzer had the opportunity to observe commercial developers at work for almost 40 years. He found it difficult to accept the hypothesis that developers working with UML tools understand the problems they work on any better than they did 20 years ago working with CASE tools based on structured analysis and design. The problem then was the human operator, which is still the problem. Developers, especially the run of the mill programmers working in the industry, are not able to conceptualize the solution to a complex problem no matter what language they use to express themselves in or what tool they use to implement the language. As Michael Jackson put it blatantly: "System requirements can never be stated fully in advance, not even in principle, because the user does not know them in advance – not even in principle".

The bottom-up approach is more contrary. The changes are made to the low level description of the system i.e., to the code itself, and are then propagated by means of reverse engineering techniques to the upper level description. Thus, if an interface is added to the code, that interface description is updated in the model automatically. This approach ensures that the model is always a true description of the system itself. However, here too, for this to work, the modeling language must be closely related to the programming language. All the constructs in the programming language must have some equivalent in the modeling language otherwise they will be distorted, which is often the case in translating natural languages. Figure 3.7 depicts the bottom-up approach.

Figure 3.7 Bottom-up model driven approach

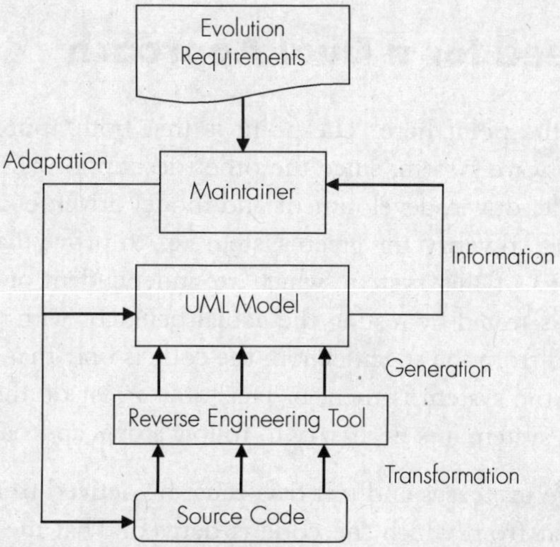

The biggest drawback of both, the top-down and the bottom-up approaches to model driven software evolution is that in both cases, there really is only one description of the system. The other description is only a translation of the original one in a different language. In the case of the top-down approach, the original description is the model. The code is merely a copy of the model in another form. In the case of the bottom-up approach, the code is the original description and the model is derived from it. As such, the model is only another, somewhat higher level description of the code, both of which are descriptions of the real systems.

The frequently posed question is what is easier to change – the graphical, higher level description, or the textual, lower level description. Theoreticians would argue that it is easier and better to change the diagrams or the higher level notations. Practicing programmers would argue that it is easier and better to change the code or the low level notations. Both have good reasons for their choice.

After 15 years of research on automatic programming, Rich and Waters came to the conclusion that "to write a complete specification in a general purpose specification language is seldom easier and often incredibly harder than writing a program. Furthermore, there has been little success in developing automatic systems that compile efficient programs from specifications".

Theoreticians often claim that diagrams are easier to comprehend and offer a better overview. Practitioners, on the other hand, often argue that the code is the most exact description of what is going on and that it offers a more detailed view. Besides, practitioners argue that they really do not know what will happen when they invoke a change, so they must first try out many variations until they find the right one. This goes much faster in the code itself.

The top-down approach assumes that the system maintainers know what they are doing (which is not often the case), that they are able to project the affects of their model changes on the underlying code. Maintenance programmers are by nature hackers so when they have a change to make they experiment with different variants of that change until they find one that fits.

Consequently, software evolution at the lowest level is a trial and error process, which is often repeated many times before the right solution is found. For this reason, it is open to debate which approach is really better. It may depend on the system type and the knowledge of the maintainer.

3.1.2 The Need for a Dual Approach

However, this is not the point here. The point is that both approaches are based on a single description of the software system, since the other description is only a translation. Is that fact what makes both model driven development and model driven evolution unacceptable for verification and validation? To verify any given system i.e., to prove that a system is true, one needs at least two descriptions of that system, which are independent of one another. Testing implies comparing. A system is tested by testing the actual behavior with the specified behavior. If the code is actually derived from the specification, the code is only that same specification in another notation. The test of the system is then, in fact, only a test of the transformation process. To assure the quality of a system it is necessary to follow a dual approach as depicted in Figure 3.8.

In testing a system, the test cases and test data must be derived from another description of the system, other than that from which the code is derived. That means that there should be two

Figure 3.8 Dual approach

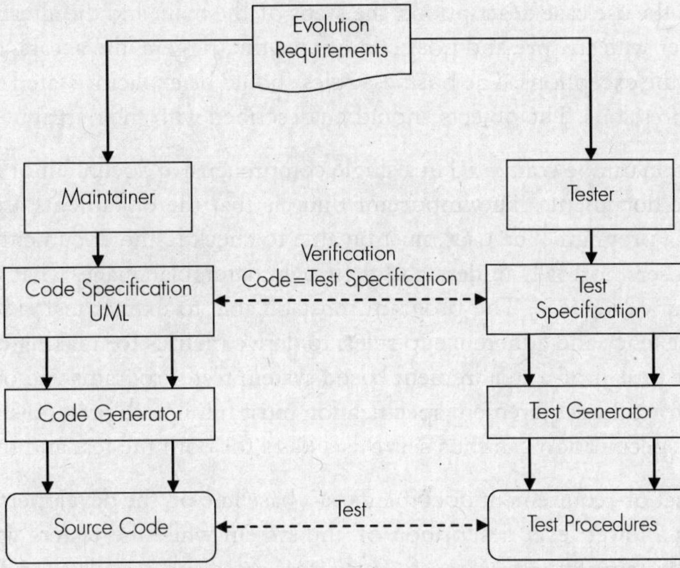

independent descriptions of the final solution, preferably in two different languages. The one should be in the language of the developers, the other in the language of the users and that is their natural language.

3.1.3 Using the Requirements as a Model

The developers may choose between using a programming language or a modeling language or they may use both. In either case, users will have their own languages which will be some form of a natural language. For processing as well as for documenting the requirements, it will be necessary to put the natural language into some kind of regular form. This could be a combination of texts, tables and diagrams. The requirements themselves should be listed out as a series of numbered texts. This list of requirements should be enhanced by a set of tables including:

- a table of user interfaces
- a table of system interfaces
- a table of business objects
- a table of business rules
- a table of business processes
- a table of system actors
- a table of system resources and
- a table of use cases.

The use cases should be described with their attributes in separate tables enhanced by a use case diagram. In all the tables the texts should be written out as full sentences or as proper names. This same rule applies to the requirements. Every requirement should be a paragraph with two or more full sentences. In the use case descriptions, the steps of the main and the alternate paths should be listed out together with the pre and post conditions, the triggers, the actors, the rules, the inputs and outputs and the exceptions. The business rules should be explicitly stated as logical conditions or arithmetic expressions. The objects should be described with their attributes.

All this information can be contained in a single comprehensive document or it can be distributed in many separate documents. The important thing is that the documents are both readable for the user and for a program. The user must be able to check if the document really reflects what he wants. Since users normally understand their own natural language, what they want has to be described in natural language. The program must be able to extract test cases from the text to check it for consistency and adherence to rules, to derive metrics for making cost estimations and for providing the design of a requirement based system test. Programs can only work on regular grammar. Therefore, the requirement specification must fulfill both prerequisites. If it can do this, the requirement specification can thus serve as a basis for both the test and the development.

Using the same set of requirement documents as a base line or, the developers will produce either a higher level or a lower level description of the system while the testers will produce another description of the same system in the form of test cases and test data. In this way, two separate interpretations of the requirements will be made, one from the viewpoint of developers and another from the viewpoint of testers. At the end, these two independent interpretations will be compared to determine the correctness of the system.

3.2 Requirement-driven Software Evolution

Having thus understood the above, where does it leave us, as far as evolution is concerned? It certainly leaves us with the necessity of maintaining and evolving two separate descriptions of the software being evolved – one in a normalized natural language and one in a graphic or programming language. It is, therefore, absurd to believe that a graphic or modeling language description will ever be able to replace the natural language one. For that, we would need to replace our users by software technicians. This applies to all the other fields as well. Few house builders are able to understand the construction plans created by the architect, but they still can visualize what they want and express it with pictures and natural language.

Therefore, in software evolution, there is no real need of a modeling language like UML. If the maintenance personnel would like to have an overview of their code in graphical form, they can use a reverse engineering tool to have it on demand. Though we know for sure that the users, managers and testers will never ask for it but they will stick to their natural language description. The maintainers are usually best served by a software repository and a flexible query facility which provides them with information on demand.

After all is said and done, model-driven software evolution will boil down to a requirement-driven software evolution. It will be absolutely essential to evolve the requirement documents and not the UML. UML is not a requirement language and was never intended to be. It is a language for software technicians and not for users. It may help to improve the communication between developers, but aside from the use cases, it does not help in promoting communication with end users. For that there is no substitute for well structured natural language. The requirement-driven model is depicted in Figure 3.9.

In the requirement model, three descriptions of the system exist, namely:

- the requirements document;
- the source code; and
- the test procedures.

For every change or enhancement, both the source code and the test procedures must be adapted. It is important that this be done by two different people with two different perspectives:

- the programmer; and
- the tester.

On the side of the code, the programmer will have to map the requirement changes on to the source code. On the side of the test, old test cases will have to be altered and new test cases will have to be generated. Both the programmer and the tester will require information on the impact

Figure 3.9 Requirement-driven approach

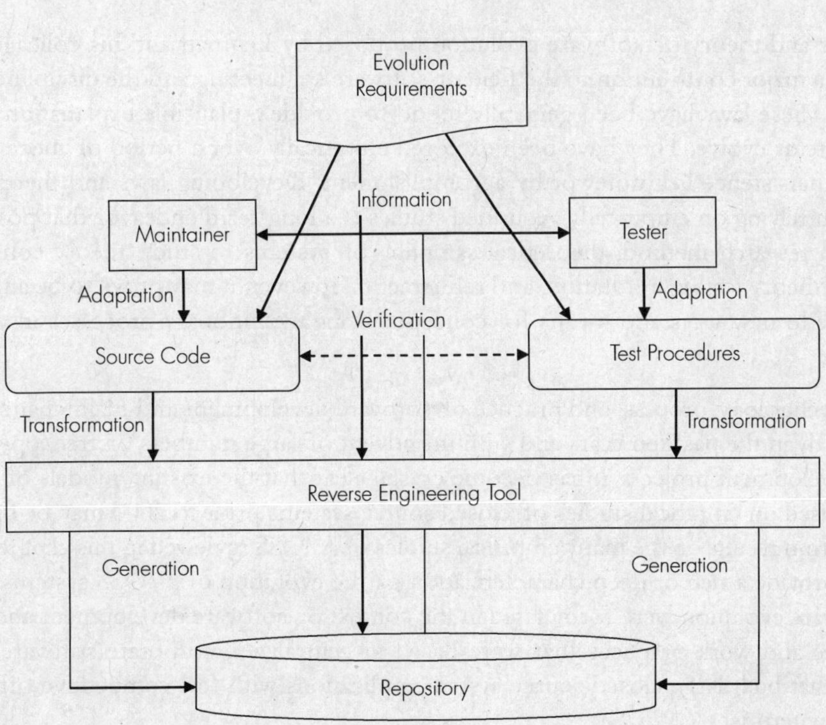

of their changes. For this purpose, there should be an invisible model of the software system contained in a software repository. This repository should be populated via source code analysis as well as by requirement analysis and test case analysis. In this way, any requirement change can be linked directly to the code units affected.

In software maintenance and evolution, the testers are the representatives of the users. Thus, there are two groups working along side each other – the maintenance team and the test team. Both can get any information they want about the system on demand through a query facility. Their questions should be answered directly without forcing them to ponder through a series of UML diagrams. They will then be able to see what the impact domain of the new or changed requirement is, but nothing will be updated automatically since this would violate the principle of comparing two independent solutions.

The maintainer will have to alter or enhance the code manually, based on his interpretation of the change request. The tester will alter existing test cases or create new ones, based on his own particular interpretation of the requirement. In this way, the duality is preserved. The costs may be higher, but that is the price of quality. To have only a single description of a system which satisfies both the testers and the developers is not only a misguided illusion, but also a gross violation of the verification principle. The goal should be to maintain two independent descriptions in two different languages. The price is that of preserving separate user/tester and developer views of an evolving system.

3.3 Conclusions

The laws and theory of software evolution proposed by Lehman and his colleagues are recognized as a major contribution to the field of software engineering and the discipline of computer science. These laws have been generally found to provide a plausible explanation for how software systems evolve. They have been explored empirically over a period of more than 30 years, so their persistence is a noteworthy accomplishment. Developing laws and theory of software evolution relying on empirically grounded studies is a long-term endeavor that poses many challenges in research method, theoretical sampling of systems to study, theory construction, and ongoing theory testing, refutation, and refinement. However, it may prove to be an endeavor that gives rise to new ways and means for conceptualizing evolutionary processes in other domains of study.

As the technology, process, and practice of software development and maintenance has evolved, particularly in the past ten years and with the advent of large numbers of free/open source software development projects, it has become crystal clear that the existing models of software evolution based on empirical studies of closed source systems prior to 2000 may be breaking down, at least from results of the many empirical studies of F/OSS reviewed in this chapter. The models do not provide a rich or deep characterization of the evolution of F/OSS systems. Prior models of software evolution were formulated in the context of software development and maintenance processes and work practices that were based in centralized, corporate software development centers that built large closed source system applications with few competitive offerings for use by large enterprises.

Large F/OSS systems, on the other hand, are developed and maintained in globally decentralized settings that collectively denote a loosely-coupled community of developers/users who generally lack the administrative authority, resource constraints, and schedules found in centrally controlled software centers. These F/OSS systems are typically competing alternatives to closed source commercial software product offerings. Subsequently, it may be better to consider whether the primary evolutionary dynamic associated with F/OSS is the reinvention, renovation, or revitalization of established software systems or applications that have proved to be useful, but now merit redevelopment, refinement, and new extensions or extension. Similarly, as large F/OSS are sometimes observed to exhibit sustained super-linear or exponential growth, whether such rates of growth go on unabated, or will the concurrent growth of system complexity eventual change the shape of the growth curve to something more like an "S" curve, with exponential growth in the early stages, followed by inverse-square growth in the later stages remains an area to be studied.

There is a growing base of data, evidence, and findings from multiple studies of F/OSS systems that indicate that F/OSS systems co-evolve with their user-developer communities, so that the growth and evolution of each depends on the other. Co-evolution results of this kind are not yet reported for closed source systems, and it is unclear whether such results will be found. In short, prior models of software evolution were developed within and apply to systems maintained and used in a corporate world and technological regime that differs from the socio-technical communities, global information infrastructure, and technological regime which embeds open source software.

We, therefore, need a more articulate explication and refinement of the models of software evolution if they are to account for the evolution of F/OSS systems. One way this might be done is to embrace and extend the reliance of the ontology of feedback control systems theory. This would entail identifying the types, operations, behaviors, and interconnection of mechanisms that embody and realize a complex, multi-level, multi-loop, and multi-agent feedback system. Building computational models and simulations of such a system (or family of systems) could be a significant contribution.

3.4 The Future of Software Evolution

The future of research in software evolution must include the technological regime of F/OSS as a major element. This will be an increasingly practical choice for the empirical study of:

- individual systems;
- groups of systems of a common type;
- larger regional or global populations of systems.

This is due in part to the public availability of the source code and related assets on the Web for individual versions/releases of hundreds of application systems, as well as data about their development processes, community participants, tools in use, and settings of development work. Not that collecting or accessing this data is without its demands for time, skill, effort and, therefore, cost, but that useful and interesting data can be accessed and shared without the barriers to entry and corporate disclosure constraints of intellectual property claims or trade secrets.

It, however, seems unlikely that the software engineering community will get open access to the source code, bug report databases, release histories, or other "property or secrets" of closed source systems that are in widespread use (e.g., Microsoft Windows operating systems, Internet Explorer, Word, Outlook, Office, Oracle DBMS, or SAP R/3) in ways that can be shared and studied without corporate trade secrets, non-disclosure agreements and publication constraints. In contrast, it is possible today to empirically study the ongoing evolution of the GNU/Linux operating systems (Kernel or alternative distributions), the Mozilla Web browser, Open Office, SAP DB, Apache project, or GNU enterprise, which together with their respective technically and socially networked communities, have publicly accessible Web portals and software assets that can be shared, studied, and redistributed to support research into models, laws, and theory of software evolution. The future of research in software evolution should be free, open and constructive, since it is likely that it will take a community of investigators to help make substantial progress in developing, refining, sharing, and publishing models, laws, and theories of software evolution.

Keywords

automatic programming; bottom-up approach; device drivers; GNOME; linux kernel; natural languages; platform architectures; super-linear growth; top-down approach; user interface; vim

Exercises

1. Explain why the size of source code across releases developed in Open Source Software increases in a super-linear manner.
2. Apart from diagrams and/or pictures, how can a system be described?
3. With the aid of well-labeled diagrams explain the major differences between top-down and bottom-up software evolution concepts.
4. Discuss the role of the maintainer in the top-down approach.
5. Explain what takes place at the transformation stage in the bottom-up approach.
6. Outline the need for a dual approach in software evolution.
7. State the reason for using requirements as a model and its implications.
8. What is the requirement-driven approach? Explain with diagrams.

CHAPTER 4

Taxonomy of Software Evolution

Objectives

The objective of this chapter is to introduce the student to the concept of "naming and organizing things" i.e., Taxonomy. Our aim is to focus on the technical aspects of evolution – when, where, what and how of software changes. When you have read this chapter you will be able to:

- Understand the overall concept of "Taxonomy" with respect to software evolution
- Understand and appreciate the four dimensions of software evolution and
- Understand software evolution models

4.0 Taxonomy of Software Evolution

4.0.1 Introduction

Evolution is critical in the life cycle of all software systems particularly those serving highly volatile business domains such as banking, e-commerce and telecommunications. An increasing number of evolution mechanisms and tools are becoming available and many systems are being built with some change support in place. Because of this, there is a need for a common vocabulary and a conceptual framework to categorize and compare the evolution support offered by the various tools and techniques.

More than two decades ago, Lientz and Swanson proposed a mutually exclusive and exhaustive software maintenance typology that distinguishes between perfective, adaptive and corrective maintenance activities. This typology was further refined into an evidence-based classification of 12 different types of software evolution and software maintenance: evaluative, consultive, training, updative, reformative, adaptive, performance, preventive, groomative, enhancive, corrective and reductive. This work is very important and relevant, in that it categorizes software maintenance and evolution activities on the basis of their purpose (the why aspect of software changes).

In this section, we will take a complementary view of the domain, by focusing on the technical aspects i.e., the when, what, where and how of software changes. These questions are used as a basis to propose a taxonomy of the characteristics of software change mechanisms and the factors that influence these mechanisms. By the phrase "change taxonomy" we mean "a system for naming and organizing things . . . into groups that share more or less the same qualities". "Change mechanisms" are the software tools used to achieve software evolution and the algorithms underlying these tools (although it is intended that this taxonomy should be extended to consider the formalisms used and the methods employed to carry out software evolution).

The purpose of this taxonomy is:

- To position concrete software evolution tools and techniques within this domain;
- To provide a framework for comparing and combining individual tools and techniques;
- To evaluate the potential use of a software evolution tool or technique for a particular maintenance or to change context;
- To provide an overview of the research domain of software evolution.

Each of these purposes is essential, given the proliferation of tools and techniques within the research field of software evolution.

Figure 4.1 Dimensions of software evolution

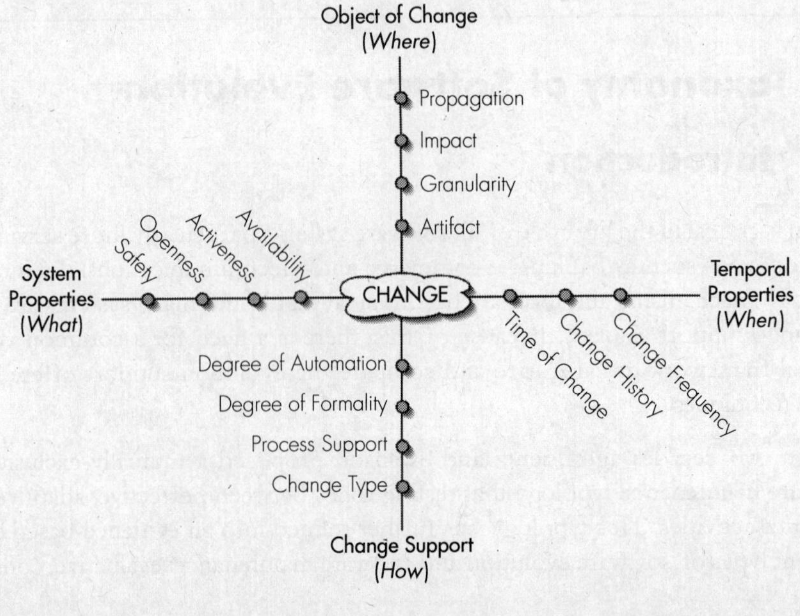

4.1 Dimensions of Software Evolution (Taxonomy)

4.1.1 Temporal Properties (When)

The when question addresses temporal properties such as when a change should be made, and which mechanisms are needed to support it.

4.1.1.1 Time of Change

Depending on the programming language, or the development environment being used, it is possible to distinguish between different phases of the software life-cycle, such as compile-time, load-time, run-time, and so on. These phases have been used indirectly as a basis for categorizing software evolution tools. Using these phases, at least three categories become apparent, based on when the change specified is incorporated into the software system.

- **Compile-time**. The software change concerns the actual source code of the system in question. Consequently, the software needs to be recompiled for the changes to become available.
- **Load-time**. The software change occurs during the time when software elements are being loaded into the executable system.
- **Run-time**. The software change occurs during the execution of the software.

The traditional approach to software maintenance, in which the programmer edits or extends the source code of a software system, and re-compiles (possible incrementally) the changes into a new executable system, is compile-time evolution. Here, typically, a running software system has to be shut down and restarted for the change to become effective. Instead of compile-time evolution, one often uses the term static evolution.

On the other hand, run-time evolution deals with cases when the changes are made at run-time. Here, systems evolve dynamically for instance by hot-swapping existing components or by integrating newly developed components without the need for stopping the system. Run-time evolution has to be either planned ahead explicitly in the system or the underlying platform has to provide means to effectuate software changes dynamically. Run-time evolution is often referred to as dynamic evolution.

Load-time evolution exists between these two extremes. It refers to changes that are incorporated as software elements are loaded into an executable system. In general, load-time evolution does not require access to the source code, but instead applies changes directly to the binaries of a system. Load-time evolution is especially well-suited for adapting statically compiled components dynamically on demand, so that they fit into a particular deployment context. The most prominent example of a load-time evolution mechanism is Java's ClassLoader architecture. It is based on classfile modifications on the byte-code level. Depending on whether load-time coincides with run-time (like in Java) or it coincides with a system's startup-time, load-time evolution is either static or dynamic.

It can be concluded that the time of change influences the kind of change mechanism to be implemented. For example, systems that allow dynamic evolution must ensure, at run-time, that the system's integrity is preserved and that there is an appropriate level of control over the change. Otherwise, when the change is implemented, the running system will crash or behave erroneously.

4.1.1.2 Change History

The change history of a software system refers to the history of all (sequential or parallel) changes that have been made to the software. Tools that make this change history explicitly available are called version control tools, and are used for a variety of purposes. One can distinguish between mechanisms that support versioning and those that do not provide means to distinguish new from old versions. In completely unversioned systems, changes are applied destructively so that new versions of a component override old ones. In this scenario, old versions can easily get lost in the process of evolution. In systems that support versioning statically, new and old versions can physically coexist at compile-time or load-time, but they are identified at run-time and therefore cannot be used simultaneously in the same context. In contrast to this, fully versioned systems do not only distinguish versions statically, they also distinguish versions at run-time, allowing two different versions of one component being deployed simultaneously. This is particularly relevant to the dynamic evolution of systems. Here, safe updates of existing components often require that new clients of the component use the new version whereas existing clients of the component continue to use the old version. In such a context, two versions of a component coexist until the old version reaches a quiescent state which allows the safe removal of the old version.

Such versioning mechanisms have been extensively used for schema evolution in object-oriented databases in order to support forward and backward compatibility of applications with schemas and existing objects. We classify here the different kinds of versioning, and the mechanisms needed to support them. It is possible that software changes may be carried out sequentially or in parallel (see Fig. 4.2). With sequential software evolution, multiple persons cannot make changes to the same data at the same time. To enforce this constraint, we need some form of concurrency control, for example, a locking or transaction mechanism to avoid simultaneous access to the same data. With parallel evolution, multiple persons can make changes to the same data at the same time. Parallel evolution is needed when different software developers simultaneously make changes to the same software component.

Figure 4.2 Sequential versus parallel evolution

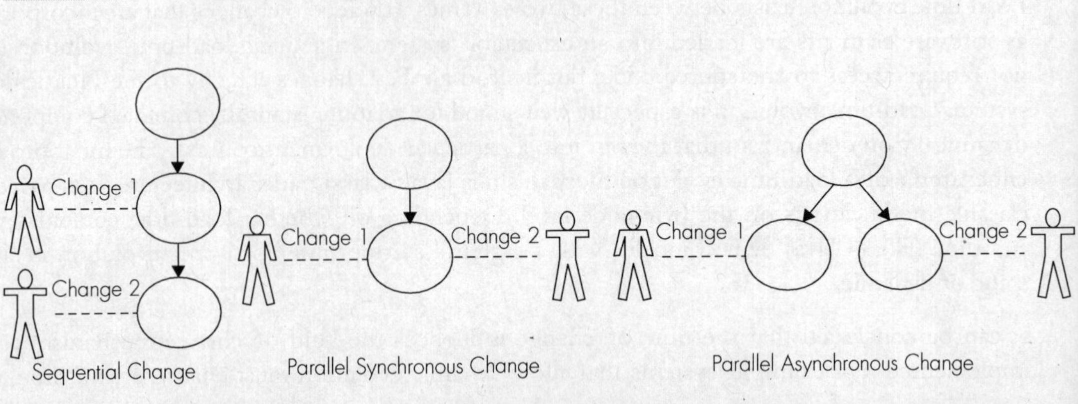

Figure 4.3 Convergent versus divergent parallel changes

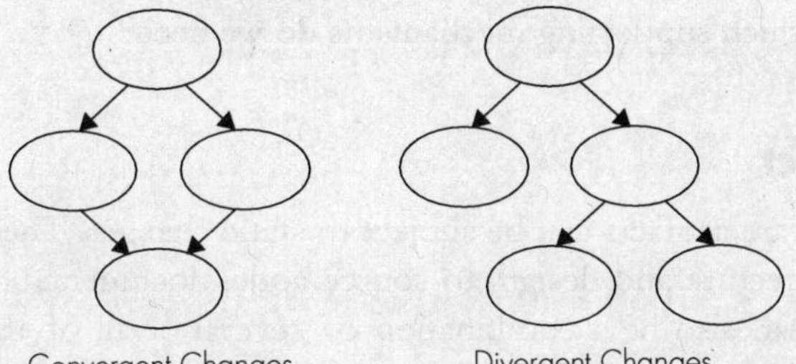

Within parallel evolution, one can further distinguish between synchronous changes and asynchronous changes (see Fig. 4.2). In the case of synchronous changes, the same data is shared by all people. This is usually the case when computer-supported collaborative work is carried out. It requires mechanisms such as a shared work surface, a permanent network connection to the server where the data resides.

In the asynchronous case, all the people who change the data work on a different copy. Because the data is not shared, we can have convergent changes or divergent changes (see Fig. 4.3). With convergent changes, parallel versions can be merged or integrated together into a new combined version. For divergent changes, different versions of the system co-exist indefinitely as part of the maintenance process. This is, for example, the case in framework-based software development, in which different invasive customizations of an application framework, i.e. destructive changes directly applied to the framework by different customers, may evolve independently of one another.

Please note that an asynchronous convergent change process subsumes a completely synchronous process, if one looks only at the final product and not at the creation history, in which different versions of some data may exist temporarily in the asynchronous case.

4.1.1.3 Change Frequency

Another important temporal property that influences the change support mechanism is the frequency of change. Changes to a system are flexible and they may be performed continuously, periodically, or at arbitrary intervals. For example, in traditional management-information systems (MIS), users frequently request changes but these changes are incorporated into the system only periodically, during scheduled downtimes. Other systems, for example interpreted systems, allied with less-formal change processes, may allow developers to incorporate changes continuously, as they are required.

The frequency of change is very important, because it has a direct influence on the change mechanisms used. For example, if a system is being changed continuously, the need for fine-grained version control over the system is increased. Otherwise, it would become very difficult to roll-back the system to specific earlier versions, when required.

4.1.2 Object of Change (Where)

The second group in our taxonomy addresses the where question. Where in the software can we make changes, and which supporting mechanisms do we need?

4.1.2.1 Artifact

Many kinds of software artifacts can be subject to static changes. These can range from requirements through architecture and design, to source code, documentation and test cases. There is a possibility that it can also be a combination of several or all of the above. Obviously, these different kinds of software artifacts influence the kind of change support mechanisms that will be required. Dynamic evolution mechanisms evolve run-time artifacts such as modules, objects, functions.

4.1.2.2 Granularity

Another influencing factor on the mechanisms of software change is the granularity of the change. Granularity refers to the scale of the artifacts to be changed and can range from very coarse, through medium, to a very fine degree of granularity. For example, in object-oriented systems, coarse granularity might refer to changes at a system, subsystem or package level, medium granularity might refer to changes at class or object level and fine granularity might refer to changes at variable, method, or statement level. Traditionally, researchers have distinguished only between coarse grained and fine grained artifacts with the boundary specified at file level. Anything smaller than a file was considered a fine-grained artifact.

4.1.2.3 Impact

Related to the granularity is the impact of a change. This impact of change can range from very local to system-wide changes. For instance, renaming a parameter of a procedure would only be a local change (restricted to the procedure definition), while renaming a global variable would have, in the worst case, an impact on the whole source code. Sometimes, even seemingly local changes in the software may have a global impact because the change is propagated through the rest of the code. The impact of a change can span different layers of abstraction, if we are dealing with artifacts of different kinds. A source code change may require changes to the documentation, the design, the software architecture, and the requirements specification.

4.1.2.4 Change Propagation

To address all the above problems, we need to resort to mechanisms or tools that help with change impact analysis, change propagation, traceability analysis and effort estimation. Change propagation refers to the phenomenon in which a change to one part of the software creates a need for changes in other parts of the software system. A change to the implementation may have an overall effect in the source code, but may also impact the design, the documentation and the requirements specification. In the same way, single changes to one system part may lead to a propagation of changes throughout the software system. Change impact analysis aims to assess or measure the extent of such a change propagation. Traceability analysis can help with change impact analysis, since it establishes explicit relationships between two or more products of the software development process. Like impact, the traceability relationship can remain within the same level of abstraction (vertical traceability) or across different levels of abstraction (horizontal traceability). In quite a large number of cases, changes that have a high impact seem to require a more significant effort to make the changes. This effort can be measured by effort estimation techniques. In some situations this effort can be reduced by the use of automated tools. Renaming entities on the source code level is typically a global change with a high change impact, but the corresponding change effort is low because it can proceed in an automated way.

4.1.3 System Properties (What)

A logical grouping of factors that influence the kinds of changes allowed as well as the mechanisms needed to support these changes has to do with the properties of the software system that is being changed, as well as the underlying platform, and the middleware in use.

4.1.3.1 Availability

Most software systems evolve continuously during their lifetime. Availability indicates whether the software system has to be permanently available or not. For most software systems, it is acceptable that the system is stopped occasionally to make changes (e.g., to enhance the functionality) by modifying or extending the source code. Alternatively, some software systems like telephone switches, have to be permanently available. Therefore, it is mandatory not to stop them during run-time to incorporate changes. Such systems require more dynamic evolution mechanisms such as dynamic loading of component updates and extensions into the running system (run-time evolution).

4.1.3.2 Activeness

The software system can be reactive (changes are driven externally) or proactive (the system autonomously makes changes to itself). Typically, for a system to be proactive, it must contain some monitors that record external and internal state. It must also contain some logic that allows self-change based on the information received from those monitors. A system is reactive if changes must be driven by an external agent, typically using some sort of user interface. Given this scenario, the system can respond to external events initiated by the user.

For a system to be proactive, the time of change must be run-time (dynamic software evolution). If this is not the case, the system will not be able to detect its own monitors and trigger the specified changes on itself.

4.1.3.3 Openness

Software systems are open if they are specifically built to allow for extensions. Open systems usually come with a framework that is supposed to facilitate the inclusion of extensions. While they support unanticipated future extensions (statically or dynamically), it is difficult to come up with a framework that allows for flexible extensions without being too restrictive concerning all possible evolution scenarios.

It is important to understand that a system cannot be open to every possible change. However, closed systems do not provide a framework for possible extensions. Such systems can be referred to as self-contained, that is they have their complete functionality fixed at build time. This does not imply that closed systems are not extensible. It simply means that they are not specifically designed for it. So it is possible to evolve closed systems, but usually with more effort. It should be borne in mind that operating systems are probably the most prominent open systems. For these systems, the ability to create and run user programs that extend the functionality of the underlying operating system is essential. A second example of open systems could be that of extensible programming languages. Extensibility in languages is either supported with explicit reflective capabilities (Smalltalk, Lisp) or with static meta-programming (OpenJava).

Similarly, some database systems like KIDS , Navajo and SADES support the incorporation of new functionality or the customization of existing functionality by using component-based and aspect-oriented techniques. A partially open system can, thus, be defined as a system that allows for plug-ins at run-time. While the plug-in modules may be unknown in advance, the ability to add them to the system at run-time is explicitly provided. A plug-in based system cannot be defined as fully open since it exposes limited capacity for "extensions". An open system would also allow you to do subtractions and modifications in a clearly defined framework.

4.1.3.4 Safety

In the context of continuous evolution, safety becomes an essential system property. We distinguish between static and dynamic safety. The system features static safety if we are able to ensure, at compile time, that the evolved system will not behave erroneously at run-time. The system provides dynamic safety if there are built-in provisions for preventing or restricting undesired behavior at run-time. Note that there are a number of different notions of safety. One of them is security, which means, to protect the software from viruses (in the case of dynamic evolution) or to prevent unauthorized access to certain parts of the software or to certain resources. A good example of such a mechanism is Java's concept of security managers, mainly exploited in web browsers to restrict the access of dynamically loaded applets to the local machine.

Another is behavioral safety, which means that no crashes, or unpredictable or meaningless behavior will arise at run-time due to undetected errors. Yet another notion is backward compatibility which guarantees that former versions of a software component can safely be replaced by newer versions without the need for global coherence checks during or after load-time. Directly related to this is the well-known fragile base class problem in class-based object-oriented programming, in which independently developed subclasses of a given base class can be broken whenever the base class evolves.

- The structural variant of this problem is dealt with in IBM's SOM approach, by allowing (in some cases) a base class interface to be modified without needing to recompile clients and derived classes dependent on that class. This therefore leads to what is clearly a static form of safety.

- The semantic variant of the problem is more complex and requires a dynamic approach, because the implementation of the base class can be changed as well. This gives rise to the question of how a superclass can be safely replaced by a new version while remaining behaviorally compatible with all of its subclasses.

Obviously, the kind and degree of safety that is required has a direct influence on the change support mechanisms that need to be provided. For example, a certain degree of static safety can be achieved by a programming language's type system at compile-time, while dynamic type tests can be used for those cases that are not covered by the static type system. Moreover, systems that support dynamic loading need additional coherence checks at load-time to ensure that new components "fit" in the rest of the system.

Such checks are even necessary for systems that guarantee certain aspects of safety statically because of components' separate compilation. As a final example, systems in which two versions of a single component can coexist together during a transition phase need not only dynamic checks to ensure consistency, but also need some form of monitoring which is capable of mediating between the two versions actively. Object database systems, for example, provide mechanisms for adapting instances across historical schema changes.

4.1.4 Change Support (How)

During a software change, various support mechanisms can be provided. These mechanisms help us to analyze, manage, control, implement or measure software changes. The proposed mechanisms can be very diverse: automated solutions, informal techniques, formal representations, process support, and many more. This section describes some orthogonal dimensions that influence these mechanisms or that can be used to classify these mechanisms.

4.1.4.1 Degree of Automation

Here we propose to distinguish between automated, partially automated, and manual change support. In the domain of software re-engineering, numerous attempts have been made to automate, or partially automate, software maintenance tasks. Typically, these are semantics-preserving transformations of the software system. In reality, however, these automated evolutions incorporate some form of manual verification and thus can be considered only partially automated. Within the specific domain of refactoring (i.e., restructuring of an object-oriented source code), tool support also ranges from entirely manual to fully automated. Tools such as the refactoring browser support a partially automatic approach while other researchers have demonstrated the feasibility of fully automated tools.

4.1.4.2 Degree of Formality

A change support mechanism can either be implemented in an ad hoc way, or based on some underlying mathematical formalism. For example, the formalism of graph rewriting has been used to deal with change propagation and refactoring.

4.1.4.3 Process Support

Process support is the extent to which activities in the change process are supported by automated tools. As an example of process support, one can consider a refactoring tool as a way to automate the activity of refactoring, which is a crucial part of the extreme programming process. By resorting to such a tool, as opposed to performing the refactorings manually, potential errors can be reduced significantly. The process to support dimensions is orthogonal to both previous dimensions. First, the degree of automation of a change process can range from fully manual to automatic. Second, we can have a formal change process that relies on an underlying mathematical formalism by resorting to formal methods. Their mathematical basis makes it possible to define and prove notions such as consistency, completeness and correctness.

4.1.4.4 Change Type

The characteristics of the change can influence the manner in which that change is performed. Because an extensive typology of software changes was already presented in, we will restrict ourselves here to the distinction between structural and semantic changes only. This distinction is an important influencing factor on the change support mechanisms that can be defined and used.

Structural changes are changes that lead to the altering of the structure of the software. In many cases, these changes will alter the software behavior as well. A distinction can be made between addition (adding new elements to the software), subtraction (removing elements from the software), and modification (modifying an existing element in the software e.g., renaming). Intuitively, it seems likely that addition is better suited to late run-time preparation than subtraction and alteration. Subtraction and alteration suggest that changes will occur within the existing system, whereas addition suggests that extra functionality can be hooked on to the existing system.

Next, to structural changes. A distinction should be made between semantics-modifying and semantics-preserving changes. In object-oriented systems, for example, relevant semantic aspects are the type hierarchy, scoping, visibility, accessibility, and overriding relationships, to name a few. In this context, semantics-preserving changes correspond to the well-known concept of software refactoring. In the wider context of re-engineering, semantics-preserving changes are accommodated by restructuring activities, such as the replacement of a *for loop* by a *while loop*, or the removal of *goto* statements in spaghetti code.

Note that a change may only be semantics-preserving with respect to a particular aspect of the software semantics, while it is semantics-modifying when taking other aspects of the semantics into account. For example, a typical refactoring operation will preserve the overall input-output semantics of the software, but may modify the efficiency or memory use, which is another aspect of the software semantics that may be equally important.

This type of change can be described as clearly orthogonal to the previous dimensions. First, some semantics-preserving changes can be fully automated, while semantics-modifying changes typically require a lot of manual intervention. Second, semantics-preserving changes can be supported

Table 4.1 Dimensions that characterize or influence the mechanism of change

Group	Dimension	Section	Characterizing Factor	Influencing Factor
Temporal properties (*when*)	Time of change	4.1.1.1	•	•
	Change history	4.1.1.2	•	
	Change frequency	4.1.1.3		•
Object of change (*where*)	Artifact	4.1.2.1		•
	Granularity	4.1.2.2		•
	Impact	4.1.2.3		•
	Change propagation	4.1.2.4		•
System properties (*what*)	Availability	4.1.3.1		•
	Activeness	4.1.3.2	•	
	Openness	4.1.3.3		•
	Safety	4.1.3.4		•
Change support (*how*)	Degree of automation	4.1.4.1	•	
	Degree of formality	4.1.4.2		•
	Process support	4.1.4.3	•	•
	Change type	4.1.4.4	•	•

by a formal foundation or they need not be. Third, semantics-preserving changes can be a crucial part in the change process, as in the case of extreme programming.

4.2 Dimensions as Characterizing Factors

In determining the dimensions that characterize the change mechanism, we adhered to two simple heuristics. The first was to review existing literature to determine if the dimension had been frequently used to position software evolution tools. So, for example, in the literature, software tools have often been introduced as run-time or load-time (with compile-time being implicitly accepted otherwise). The second heuristic was to put the dimension in a simple sentence of the form: "The change mechanism is dimension". If such a sentence makes sense, the dimension must reflect the essence of the change mechanism and is thus classified as a characterizing mechanism. For example, because we can say that "The change mechanism is compile-time/load time/run-time", the time dimension is a characterizing factor. In a similar way the dimensions of "change history", "activeness", "degree of automation", "process support" and "type of change" are classified as characterizing factors.

Perhaps, the most surprising of these is the "activeness" dimension, as it refers to the system under change. However, it should be noted that when a system is active in changing itself it is also part of the change mechanism. Thus, a sentence of the form: "The change mechanism is proactive" can be sensibly formed.

4.3 Dimensions as Influencing Factors

In determining if the dimension was an influencing factor we followed a third heuristic. For each dimension, the group tried to find an example of a way in which it could influence the change mechanism. For example, system "availability" could inadvently affect the change mechanism process. If a system is required to be highly available, it suggests a run-time change mechanism. However, low availability would facilitate run-time or compile-time changes. It is no coincidence that Table 4.1 classifies all the dimensions of group "object of change" as influencing factors, as these dimensions are in general independent of concrete change mechanisms and rather describe particular properties that can be supported or unsupported by a concrete change mechanism.

Note that the fact that it being a characterizing factor and that also being an influencing factor cannot be mutually exclusive. For example, "time of change", apart from being a characterizing mechanism, also influences the change mechanism by prompting additional change activities like state management.

4.4 Models for Software Evolution

4.4.1 Introduction

The phenomenon of software evolution has been described with several models of different nature being proposed to understand and explain the empirical observations. Some of these models purport to be universally applicable to all software development processes. However, the models in this book were built mainly observing software developed using a traditional centrally-managed waterfall development process, or one of its variants.

This area has been approached from two different perspectives. One considers the processes, methods and techniques to implement and evolve software – the how. The other applies systematic observation of empirical data to achieve an understanding of the causes and general characteristics of the phenomenon – the what/why. Both perspectives are related: the study of the what/why is important in order to achieve an appropriate plan, manage and control the various software engineering activities and to guide the development of new processes, methods and tools, that is, to guide the how.

The link between the how and the what/why perspectives is governed by several guidelines that are derived from Lehman's laws of software evolution. The output of the what/why study is exemplified by empirical generalizations such as Rajlich and Bennett's model of the lifecycle and Lehman's laws of software evolution. Therefore, we expand and refine the empirical hypothesis presented in the staged model of software evolution so that it can be applied to FLOSS projects. For this, we compare and contrast the existing empirical knowledge (as derived from studies of proprietary systems evolved under traditional processes with the emergent FLOSS paradigm). This revision will help FLOSS developers and practitioners to characterize any FLOSS system in terms of which phase it is currently undergoing, or which phase it will more likely move to.

4.4.2 The Staged Model

The staged model for software evolution represents the software lifecycle as a sequence of steps. Based on the traditional commercial projects, the core idea of the model is that software systems evolve through distinct stages.

The initial development, or alpha stage, includes all the phases (design, first coding, testing) achieved before the first running version of the system. In this stage, usually no releases are made public to the users.

- Evolutionary pressures enhance the system with new features and capabilities in the phase of the evolution changes: binary releases and individual patches are made available to the users, and feedback is gathered to further enhance the system.
- As long as the profitability of either new enhancements or changes to the existing code base is overcome by the costs of such modifications, the servicing phase is reached. The system is considered mature, changes are added to the code base, but no further enhancements (apart from patches) are provided to the end users.
- When the service is discontinued and no more code patches are released, the stage of phase-out is meant to declare the system's end. This can be associated with the presence of a new enhanced system substituting the old one.
- The old system serves as a basis for the new one and then it is closed down.

It is possible to analyze each of the phases of the cited model, and observe when and how differences and commonalities arise.

4.4.2.1 Initial Development

Traditional commercial systems are typically built by a fixed number of designers, developers and testers. Also, software is usually published (as executables) only after the first release is deemed "correctly running". The recipients of this release are the end users. It is a rare event that source code access is granted too: we are aware of just one specific case in which a commercial software house, using an agile development process, gives the possibility for users to download the application from the public versioning system repository. FLOSS systems, on the other hand, typically start with a small number of early developers, and eventually new developers join after a certain initiation period. FLOSS systems, instead, may be released (in binaries as well as in source code) well before they are complete or working. Recipients are not only end-users, but also any other developer; read-only access to the versioning system is given to anybody, which leads to the already mentioned continuous release even before the first official release. In what follows, results from empirical case studies are reported to justify the mentioned differences.

Case studies

Successful FLOSS projects have been studied and characterized in the past, but empirical evidence on their behavior in the initial development, and the transition to a larger "evolution" phase has not been proven yet. The initial development phase in FLOSS projects has been characterized as a cathedral-driven software process, as contributions from external developers are not yet encouraged.

The process is hence controlled, the infrastructure for the project is not always in place, and the feedback from end-users is limited. Major differences appear when a FLOSS project either never leaves this initial stage, as documented for a large majority of the projects hosted on SourceForge; or when it leverages a "bazaar", i.e., a large and ever growing number of developers.

A closed process, performed by a small group of FLOSS developers, has some commonalities with traditional software development: one observed system (Arla, a Network File System) was shown to have remained, through its lifecycle, an effort of a small team, or a "cathedral". Also the output was shown to be following the same constant trend. These results were not attributed to an unsuccessful FLOSS project, but interpreted as a potentially missed opportunity in establishing a thriving community around a project.

Specific actions from the core developers (or lone project author) have also been identified when a FLOSS project was to leave this initial stage. It has been shown that new developers in both the analysed systems prefer to work on newly added modules, rather than older ones: therefore, it was argued that core developers should create new avenues of development to let new developers join in. Further analyzing this system, a decreasing trend of new module creation was detected, which prevented new developers from joining in. In another case study (Wine, a free implementation of Windows on Unix), a growing trend of developers and output produced was observed. Also, the amount of new modules inserted by the core developers follows a similar growing trend. This helped with the recruitment of new developers and to leave the initial stage for a "bazaar" stage.

This first difference between traditional and FLOSS systems is annotated in the revised model displayed in Figure 4.4: the box containing the "initial development phase" is highlighted, as it could be the only phase available in the evolution of a FLOSS system. Also, in the same phase, a different handling of the versioning system is achieved.

4.4.2.2 Evolution Changes

Several releases are observed both in traditional commercial and FLOSS systems. The staged model, as proposed, also incorporated the possibility of evolution through several branches of

Figure 4.4 Staged model adapted to FLOSS systems

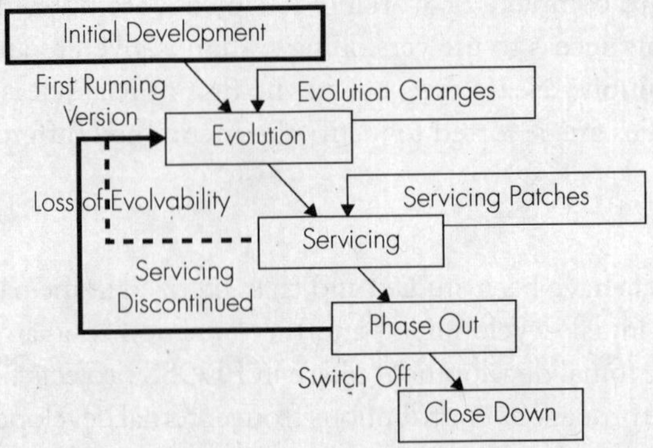

releases. In traditional commercial systems, most of the changes are distributed and applied as patches on the existing code base. New versions of the software systems are distributed regularly, albeit a higher frequency is perceived as an instability factor. A feedback is provided by users in the form of requests for change or bug signaling, and collected as a set of new requirements for new releases, or in intermediate code patches.

In FLOSS systems, new releases of systems and patches are available more often, and this is usually perceived by FLOSS developers as a vitality factor. Although traditionally many FLOSS projects published a new release "once it is ready", in recent times several FLOSS projects have moved to a time-based release planning, offering a new stable version for end-users on a periodic basis (for Ubuntu and GNOME, for instance, every six months). A feedback is provided by users in the same forms as in commercial systems, but also under the form of code patches that users write themselves, and which possibly will be incorporated into new releases of the system.

The loop of evolution changes presented in Figure 4.4 may be accomplished through many years. Both traditional commercial and FLOSS systems have shown the characteristics of long-lived software. For instance, operating systems like OS360, the various flavors of UNIX, or the Microsoft Windows, as well as the FLOSS Linux kernel, FreeBSD or OpenBSD, have been successfully evolving for decades. It is noticeable that while the evolution loop can be found both in commercial and FLOSS environments, research has shown that growth dynamics in both cases differ significantly, at least in the case of large projects. Some FLOSS projects have a superlinear growth rate (for example, Linux), while a majority of the large projects studied grow linearly. Both behaviors (superlinearity and linearity) seem to be in contradiction to Lehman's laws of software evolution which imply that size over time shows a decelerated pattern.

4.4.2.3 Servicing

This phase was first described for traditional commercial systems, when new functionalities were not added to the code base, whilst fixes to existing features were still performed. The transition from evolution to servicing is typically based on the economic profitability of the software system. When revenues from a software product are not balanced by the costs of its maintenance, the system is no longer evolved, and it may become a legacy system. For FLOSS systems, on the other hand, the evolutionary behavior shows often stabilization points, where the size of the overall system does not change, albeit several releases are made available, and a long time interval is achieved. Although a servicing stage could be detected, a new evolution period is later found. Researchers have also assessed that some 20% of the overall number of projects within SourceForge are "tragedies of growth" i.e., they evolved for a period, but then fewer and fewer additions were made.

The presence of servicing stages has been detected in the past through an overall small increase of the code base (say, less than 10% over several releases and temporal time). It was observed, in some of the systems, a very fast increase in size, and a corresponding fast evolution, followed by a stabilization phase which led to the complete abandonment of the project. For some other analyzed systems (e.g., the Gaim system), albeit the same initial fast growth rate, and a transition from evolution to servicing, were observed, a new period of evolution was also found. In yet other systems (the Grace system), it was possible to observe an overall growing pace even when the system was abandoned by the initial lone developer, and was handed over to a new team of developers, followed by a later stabilisation period. The dashed arc between the evolution and servicing stages of Figure 4.4 displays this possibility.

4.4.2.4 Phase Out

In traditional commercial systems, the phase out of a software system happens when the software house declares that neither new functionalities, nor the fixing of existing ones will be performed. The system becomes then a legacy application. The same behaviour is detectable in FLOSS systems, when development teams declare their intention not to maintain the system any more. The main difference between the traditional commercial approach and the FLOSS cases is the availability of the source code. In some specific cases new developers may take over the existing system, and with the availability of the source code, bring it to a new stage of evolution.

Many FLOSS projects have been reported to renew their core groups. For instance, three different categories of FLOSS projects were identified: code gods, generations and mixed behavior. Code gods projects are maintained by the same group of developers during the whole lifetime of the project. Generations projects exhibit a renewal in the core group of developers; the group of people that were the main developers at an early moment in the lifetime are not the main developers in posterior moments. Therefore, a generational relay has taken place in the project. Mixed projects exhibit neither a pure code god or generations profile, but an intermediate state among these two extremes.

Keywords

perfective maintenance; adaptive maintenance; corrective maintenance; evaluative; consultive; training; updative; reformative; adaptive; performance; preventive; groomative; enhancive; corrective; reductive; taxonomy; temporal properties; compile-time; load-time; run-time; static evolution; hot-swapping; version control; sequential evolution; parallel evolution; synchronous change; asynchronous change; convergent change; divergent change; application framework; roll-back; object of change; granularity; vertical traceability; horizontal traceability; run-time evolution; extreme programming

Exercises

1. Define the term taxonomy.
2. List the 12 different types of software evolution and software maintenance according to Lientz and Swanson's evidence-based classification.
3. What is the purpose of software evolution taxonomy?
4. Draw a well-labeled diagram of the dimensions of software evolution.
5. Discuss any two dimensions of software evolution in detail.
6. Tabulate the dimensions that characterize or influence the mechanism of change in software evolution.
7. Discuss the FLOSS staged evolution model.

CHAPTER 5

Software Evolution in Software Design and Software Evaluation Techniques

Objectives

The objective of this chapter is to introduce and equip the student in how to identify the context of the evolution problem in an effort to help him select the software evolution mechanisms practical to a particular scenario. To do this, we consider the most well-known design and evaluation techniques and describe them. When you have read this chapter you will be able to:

- Understand well-known design and evaluation techniques relating to software evolution
- Understand the challenges in software evolution
- Classify the software evolution challenges
- Enumerate the software evolution challenges

5.0 Software Evolution in Software Design and Software Evaluation Techniques

In this chapter, we describe what we mean by the gap between software design/evaluation techniques and design patterns/styles. We consider the most well-known design and evaluation techniques and describe how identifying the context of the evolution problem helps in the choice of the software evolution mechanisms.

5.0.1 The Unified Process

The Unified Process is a use-case driven, iterative and architecture centric software design process. The life of a system is composed of cycles and each cycle concludes with a product. Each cycle is, therefore, divided into four distinct phases. The first phase is the inception phase and in this phase the requirements are analyzed and a general vision about the product is developed. This phase is followed by the elaboration phase in which the architectural baseline of the product is developed. During the third phase the product is built and this phase is labeled as construction.

The last step, called transition, involves the manufacturing of the product. To support the evolution of the Unified Process, there must be link between the transition phase of the previous cycle and the inception and elaboration phases of the current cycle. With this link, the designer, while gaining a perspective about the old system, can also develop ideas about integrating new requirements to the system. That is, with this link the designer can identify the evolution problem he is faced with, select the suitable evolution technique and then apply this technique to the design. For example, if the new requirements extend the current system, the designer can choose to delegate the current system with new requirements. Thus, the new system can be designed using means of delegation mechanisms such as call forward protocols.

5.0.2 Software Architecture and Synthesis Process

The Software Architecture and Synthesis process (Synbad) is an analysis and a synthesis process, which is widely used in problem solving in many different engineering disciplines. The process includes explicit steps that involve searching solutions for technical problems in solution domains. These domains contain solutions to previously solved, well established, similar problems. The selection of which solution to use from the solution domain is done by evaluating each solution according to a quality criteria. The method consists of two parts, which are solution definition and solution control. The solution definition part involves the identification and the definition of solutions. In this part the client requirements are first translated into technical problems; these are the problems that are actually going to be solved. These technical problems are then prioritized and a technical problem is selected according to this priority order. The solution process involves identifying the solution domain for the problem and searching possible solution abstractions in this domain. The selected solution abstractions are, then, extracted from the solution domain and specified to solve the problem in consideration. In the last step of the solution definition part, the specified solutions are composed to form the architectural description of the software. The solution abstractions may cause new problems to be found; thus there is a relation, labeled "discover", between the solution abstraction and the technical problem.

The solution control part of Synbad represents the evaluation of the solutions. The evaluation conditions (e.g., constraints on applying the solution) are provided by the sub-problem and by the solution domain. The solutions extracted from solution domains are expressed as formal models for evaluation. Then optimizations are applied to the formal model in order to meet the constraints and the quality criteria. The output of these optimizations is then used to refine the solution. Synbad treats each problem separately and the solutions of each problem are composed to form the solution of the overall problem the software is going to solve.

Thus, this process inherently supports the addition of new requirements to evolve the software. When new requirements arrive, their technical problems are analyzed and the solution abstractions for these technical problems are extracted from the solution domain. Each extracted solution abstraction causes a new technical problem to be identified, which can be stated as "given a solution, what are the techniques to compose this solution to the system". For this problem, the solution abstraction and the system define the quality criteria and constraints. Here, the quality criteria are the non-functional requirements of the system. The constraints, on the other hand, are the factors that affect the selection of the composition mechanisms. For example, if the extracted solution is already implemented and its source code cannot be changed, the composition mechanism should be a run-time solution.

5.0.3 Scenario-based Evaluation Techniques

There are many scenario-based techniques that evaluate software architectures with respect to certain quality attributes. Scenario-based Architecture Analysis Method (SAAM), is a method for understanding the properties of a system's architecture other than its functional requirements. The inputs to SAAM are the requirements, the problem description and the architecture description of a system. The first step of SAAM is scenario creation and software architecture description.

During this, all stakeholders of the system must be present; scenarios are considered to be complete when a new scenario does not affect the architecture. In the last step, scenarios are evaluated by determining the components and the component connections that need to be modified in order to fulfill the scenario. Then the cost of the modifications for each scenario is estimated in order to give an overall cost estimate. In recent years, SAAM has been specialized to focus on a quality attribute such as modifiability and extended to find the trade-off between several quality attributes.

These methods can easily be used or adapted to find the impact of evolution requests. Though, after finding the impact, software engineers are faced with the problem of finding the mechanisms that are applicable to the evolution problem in consideration. When with scenarios were certain components are found to be hard to evolve, how can the software engineer make them easier to evolve? For this, the evolution problem should be analyzed in detail; the constraints of the software system and the evolution mechanisms should be identified and the most applicable mechanisms should be used to replace/change the components. That is, the context of the software evolution should be identified in order to select the applicable mechanisms. Currently, none of the evaluation techniques has steps that include such an analysis. Here, we identify the contexts of the evolution problems and mechanisms. Thus, after finding the impact, the software engineer can find the applicable evolution mechanisms by selecting the context of the problem he is dealing with.

5.0.4 Design Pattern and Styles

In the software engineering domain there are many mechanisms that can cope with the various evolution problems. Some design patterns, make it easier to add new behavior to the system. In their study of comparing design patterns to find simpler solution for maintenance, Prechelt *et al.* (2001) conclude that due to new requirements design patterns should be used, unless there is an important reason to choose the simpler solution, because of the flexibility they provide. Mens and Eden list some of these evolution mechanisms and determine how helpful they are for some evolution situations. Their analysis shows that these mechanisms are very costly to use for certain evolution problems while for others they are not. This clearly shows that there are contexts for these techniques. Thus, identifying these contexts and then selecting the mechanism to use may greatly ease the procedure for the evolution of the software. The major problem here is that these contexts are not clearly analyzed. We know that design patterns and styles can ease evolution operations but what the applicable mechanisms are for a given evolution problem is not known.

5.1 Challenges in Software Evolution

5.1.1 Introduction

Today's information technology society increasingly relies on software at all levels. This dependence on software takes place in all sectors of society, including government, industry, transportation, commerce, manufacturing and the private sector. The productivity of software organisations and software quality generally continue to fall short of expectations, and software systems continue to suffer from symptoms of aging as they are adapted to changing requirements. One major reason for this problem is that software maintenance and adaptation is still undervalued in traditional software development processes.

The only way to either overcome or avoid the negative effects of software aging is to place change in the center of the software development process. Without explicit and immediate support for change and evolution, software systems become unnecessarily complex and unreliable. The negative influence of this situation is rapidly increasing due to technological and business innovations, changes in legislation and continuing internationalisation.

One must therefore advance beyond a restricted focus on software development, and provide better and more support for software adaptation and evolution. Such support must be addressed at multiple levels of research and development. It requires:

- Basic research on formalisms and theories to analyse, understand, manage and control software change;
- The development of models, languages, tools, methods, techniques and heuristics to provide explicit support for software change;
- More real-world validation and case studies on large, long-lived, and highly complex industrial software systems.

5.2 Classification of Challenges

To increase the readability, the challenges are classified according to a number of more or less orthogonal dimensions. Below is a comprehensive overview of all these challenges using this classification.

Time horizon: Is a short, medium or long-term effort required in order to achieve results?

Research target: Is the challenge related to the management, control, support, understanding or analysis of software evolution?

Stakeholders: Who is interested in, involved in, or affected by the challenge? Given the diversity of challenges, many different people can be involved: managers, developers, designers, end-users, teachers, students, researchers.

Type of artifact under study: Which type of artifact(s) does the challenge address? Artifacts should be interpreted in the broad sense here since they can refer to formalisms, tools, techniques, models, metamodels, languages, programs, processes, systems, and many more.

Type of support needed: Which type of support is needed in order to address the challenge? Although this question is completely different from the previous one, the list of possible answers is the same. One can provide formal support, tool support, language support, process support and so on in order to address software evolution.

5.3 Enumeration of Challenges

5.3.1 Preserving and Improving Software Quality

The phenomenon of software aging, coined by Dave Parnas (1994), and the laws of software evolution postulated by Manny Lehman agree that, without active countermeasures, the quality of a software system gradually degrades as the system evolves. In practice, the reason for this gradual decrease in quality (such as reliability, availability and performance of software systems) is, for a large part, caused by external factors such as economic pressure. The negative effects of software aging can and will have a significant economic and social impact in all sectors of industry. Therefore, it is crucial to develop tools and techniques to reverse or avoid the intrinsic problems of software aging. Hence, the challenge is to provide tools and techniques that preserve or even improve the quality characteristics of a software system, whatever its size and complexity.

5.3.2 A Common Software Evolution Platform

A major difficulty when trying to address the previous challenge has to do with scalability. The need is to develop solutions that are applicable to long-lived, industrial-size software systems. Many of the tools that must be built to manage the complexity intrinsic to software evolution are too complex to be built by single research groups or individuals. Therefore, a closely related challenge, raised by Michele Lanza (2001), is to develop and support a common application framework for doing joint software evolution research. This challenge raises issues such as tool integration and interoperability, common exchange formats and standards, and so on. As an example of such a shared framework that served as a common software evolution research vehicle within the RELEASE network is the Moose reverse engineering environment. A concrete goal could be to try to extend this framework with tools to analyse, manage and control software evolution activities.

Another candidate that may serve as a common platform is Eclipse. It has the advantage of visibility and industrial acceptance and also permits the reuse of certain components (e.g., Java parsing). An important disadvantage is its lack of control over releases. One researcher once mentioned that he had to keep several versions of the platform because not all plug-ins work on all versions. There is also the issue of exploratory prototyping, which is better supported by environments such as Smalltalk. Both options should probably co-exist, although this of course implies the duplication of effort.

5.3.3 Supporting Model Evolution

Although the support for software evolution in development tools can still be advanced in many ways, there are already a number of success stories. One of them is program refactoring, introduced by Opdyke (1992) as a way of improving the structure of object-oriented programs without affecting their desired external behaviour. Since the publication of Martin Fowler's (1999) book on refactoring, this program transformation technique has gained widespread attention. Today, refactoring support has been integrated in many popular software development environments.

Unfortunately, it is observed that almost all existing tool support for software evolution is primarily targeted to programs (i.e., source code). Design and modelling phases (supported by UML CASE tools) typically provide much less support for software evolution. Taking the example of refactoring, we did not find any modelling tool providing adequate means for refactoring design models. Research in model refactoring is just starting to emerge. This can be generalised into the following challenge: software evolution techniques should be raised to a higher level of abstraction in order to accommodate not only the evolution of programs, but also the evolution of higher-level artifacts such as analysis and design models, software architectures, requirement specifications, and so on. Since the advent of model-driven software engineering, this challenge becomes increasingly more relevant, and techniques and tools for dealing with model evolution are urgently needed.

5.3.4 Supporting Co-evolution

A challenge that is related to the previous one is the necessity to achieve co-evolution between different types of software artifacts or different representations of them. A modification in one representation should always be reflected by corresponding changes in other related ones to ensure the consistency of all involved software artifacts. To give a few examples, support for co-evolution is needed between:

- Programs (source code) and design models or software architectures;
- Structural and behavioural design models. This is, for example, the case with UML, in which different models are used to express structure (class diagrams) and behaviour (sequence diagrams and state-transition diagrams);
- Software (at whatever level of abstraction) and the languages in which it is developed. Whenever a new version of the programming, modeling or specification language is provided, it is quite possible that programs that worked perfectly in a previous version of the language fail to function in the new version;

- Software and its business, organisational, operational and development environment. Changes in each of these environments will impact the software and conversely. This feedback loop is well-known in software evolution research;
- Software and its developer or end-user documentation.

To provide better support for co-evolution, it is worthwhile to take a look at other domains of science that can perhaps provide better insights into the matter. Linguistic theory and the history of natural language evolution may increase the understanding of how software languages evolve. In order to better understand software co-evolution, it could be interesting to look at co-evolution in biology. In fact, the term co-evolution originated in biology, and is borrowed by computer scientists to describe a similar situation in software development.

5.3.5 Formal Support for Evolution

According to Wordsworth, "a formal method of software development is a process for developing software that exploits the power of mathematical notation and mathematical proofs." For several decades, formal methods have been advocated as a means of improving software development, with an emphasis on software specification, verification and validation. Nevertheless, as Robert Glass observes "Formal methods have not, during that extended period of time (well over 30 years by now), had any significant impact on the practice of software engineering." He points out a major cause of this problem: "What in fact most practitioners tell me about specifications is that the needs of the customers evolve over time, as the customer comes to learn more about solution possibilities, and that what is really needed is not a rigorous/rigid specification, but one that encompasses the problem evolution that inevitably occurs."

Unfortunately, existing formal methods provide very poor support (or even none at all) for evolving specifications. Let us take the example of formal verification, which aims to prove mathematically that the implementation of a software system satisfies its specification. Specialists that were consulted in relation to this question agreed that even today there are no truly incremental verification approaches available. With current verification tools, even if small localized changes are made to the specification of a program, the entire program needs to be verified again. This makes the cost of verification proportional to the size of the system. What is desired is that it be proportional to the size of the units of change. This leads to the next challenge in software evolution: In order to become accepted as practical tools for software developers, formal methods need to embrace change and evolution as an essential fact of life.

Besides the need for existing formal methods to provide more explicit support for software evolution, there is also a clear need for new formalisms to support activities specific to software evolution.

5.3.6 Evolution as a Language Construct

As a very interesting research direction, programming (or even modelling) languages should provide more direct and explicit support for software evolution. The idea would be to treat the notion of change as a first-class entity in the language. This is likely to cause a programming paradigm shift similar to the one that was encountered with the introduction of object oriented programming. Indeed, to continue the analogy, one of the reasons why object-oriented programming became so popular is because it integrated the notion of reuse in programming languages as a first-class entity. The mechanisms of inheritance, late binding and polymorphism allow a subclass to reuse and refine parts of its parent classes.

It can be pointed out that explicit support for software evolution is considerably easier to integrate into dynamically typed languages that offer full reflective capabilities. Classboxes are also a new module system that control the scope of changes in an application. Changes can be introduced in a system without impacting existing clients; changes are only visible to new clients desiring to see the changes.

5.3.7 Support for Multilanguage Systems

Mohammad El-Ramly *et al.* (2002) pointed out that another crucial, and largely neglected, aspect of software evolution research is the need to deal with multiple languages. Indeed, in large industrial software systems often multiple programming languages are used. More than three languages are the rule rather than the exception. Therefore, software evolution techniques must provide more and better support for multi-language systems. One way to tackle this problem is to provide techniques that are as language-parametric (or language-generic, or language-independent) as possible. Note that this challenge is becoming increasingly more relevant as the number of languages needed or used in software systems is increasing. Programming languages, modelling languages, specification languages, XML-based languages for data interchange, domain-specific languages, business modeling languages, and many more are becoming more widely used.

5.3.8 Integrating Change in the Software Lifecycle

It is important to investigate how the notion of software change can be integrated into the conventional software development process models. A typical way to include support for change in a traditional software process model is resort to an iterative and incremental software development process. So-called agile software processes (including the well-known extreme programming method) acknowledge change as an essential fact. Other processes, such as the staged life-cycle model, have been proposed as an alternative to provide explicit support for software change and software evolution.

5.3.9 Increasing Managerial Awareness

Besides better understanding of, and better support for, evolutionary process models, there is also a need to increase the awareness of executives and project managers of the importance and inevitability of software evolution. Training is needed to convince them of the importance of these issues, and to teach them to plan, organise, implement and control software projects in order to better cope with software changes. We suggest that the importance of software evolution be explained through the SimCity metaphor. This computer game simulates a city and is a typical example of a highly complex dynamic system in which continuous corrective actions of the "manager" are needed in order to avoid deteriorating the "quality" of the city and, ultimately, its destruction or desertion.

5.3.10 Need for Better Versioning Systems

Although the support for software evolution in software development tools can still be improved in many ways, there are already a number of success stories. One of them is version management. Version control is a crucial aspect in software evolution, especially in a collaborative and distributed setting, in which different software developers can (and will) modify the program, unaware of the other changes that are being made in parallel.

A wealth of version control tools is available – commercial as well as freeware. The most popular one is probably CVS (www.cvs.org). Nevertheless, for the purpose of analysing the evolution of software systems, these version repositories clearly fall short because they do not store enough information about the evolution. Therefore, the challenge is to develop new ways of recording the evolution of software that overcome the shortcomings of the current state-of-the-art tools. When addressing this challenge, it is necessary to communicate and coordinate with the research community on Software Configuration Management (SCM), that is trying to address these very related issues.

5.3.11 Integrating Data from Various Sources

One promising approach to reason about the evolution history of software systems is the integration of data from a wide variety of sources: bug reports, change requests, source code, configuration information, versioning repositories, execution traces, error logs, documentation, and so on. Besides all of the above information, it is equally important to take into account information about the software process during the analysis of change histories: the software team (size, stability, experience), individual developers (age, experience), the project structure (hierarchical, surgical, flat), the process model (waterfall, spiral, agile), the type of project (open source), and so on. Indeed, Conway's law postulates that the architecture of a software system mirrors the structure of the team that developed it (and, more generally, the structure of a system tends to mirror the structure of the group producing it). The main challenge here is to find out how these different kinds of data can be integrated, and how the support for this integration can be provided. Having a flexible and open-meta model as one of the Moose reengineering environment supporting entity annotations and version selection should be regarded as a first step in that direction.

5.3.12 Analysing Huge Amounts of Data

Given the sheer amount of data that needs to be processed during the above analysis, new techniques and tools are needed to facilitate the manipulation of large quantities of data in a timely manner. In order to achieve this, one can probably borrow from related areas of computer science that deal with similar problems. For example, one may consider using data mining techniques as used by the database community, or techniques related to DNA sequence analysis as used in bioinformatics.

These techniques could be implemented as an extension of current tools such as CodeCrawler that already supports the management of large data sets via polymetric views (views enriched with semantical information). Another attempt that has been made to address this challenge is a technique that suggests to the developer the changes to be performed based on the co-occurrence of past changes.

5.3.13 Empirical Research

In the context of software evolution there is a need for more empirical research. Among others, comparative studies are urgently needed to measure the impact of:

- **Process models.** In an industrial setting, which software process is most appropriate for which type of evolution activity?
- **Tools.** To which extent does the use of a tool facilitate the execution of a particular evolution activity compared to the manual execution of the same activity? How does one compare the performance of different tools to carry out the same evolution activity?
- **Languages.** What is the impact of the programming language on the ease with which certain evolution activities can be performed? For example, dynamically typed languages with reflective capabilities seem to be more suited than other languages to support the task of run-time evolution
- **People.** To which extent does the experience, background and training of a software developer contribute to his ability to carry out certain software evolution activities?

5.3.14 Need for Improved Predictive Models

Predictive models are crucial for managers in order to assess the software evolution process. These models are needed to predict a variety of things: where the software evolves, how it will evolve, the effort and time that is required to make a change. Unfortunately, the existing predictive models, typically based on software metrics, are far from adequate.

To counter this problem, it was suggested that one looks at metrology research, the science of measurement, which explicitly takes into account the notion of uncertainty that is also inherent in software evolution. Girba's "Yesterday's Weather" measurement is another step in the same direction. This measurement characterizes the climate of changes in a system and helps assessing the trust that may be placed in the continuity of changes (based on the assumption that assets that have changed in the recent past are more likely to change in the near future).

5.3.15 Evolution Benchmark

In order to adequately test, validate, and compare the formalisms, techniques, methods, and tools to be developed for the other challenges, it is useful to come up with, and reach a consensus on, a common set of evolution benchmarks and case studies which, together, are representative for the kinds of problems needing to be studied. Given the amount of long-lived, industrial-size, open-source projects available today, it should be feasible to come up with such a benchmark.

5.3.16 Teaching Software Evolution

One of the best ways to place change and evolution in the center of the development process is to educate the future generations of software engineers. However, classroom programming exercises are usually well specified, have a single release, and are small in size. Capstone projects are more amenable to convey the need for dealing with software evolution, but on the one hand they are often supervised in a rather lose mode, and on the other hand it is preferable to prepare students in earlier courses with the concepts and tools they need to handle changes in their project. Therefore, a big challenge for everyone involved in teaching concerns how to integrate the ideas, formalism, techniques and tools for software evolution into our computer science curriculum in a meaningful way. As a community, we need to decide upon what we want to teach, how we want to teach it, and provide the necessary course material for it.

5.3.17 A Theory of Software Evolution

It seems that often researchers either do empirical investigations into the evolution of a given system over its life-time, or propose tools and techniques to facilitate evolution. But it is definitely not always clear that what one gets from all the collected data nor even if the tools actually used were informed by typical evolution patterns. One needs to study and compare evolution activities before and after the installation of some tool supporting such activities. To undertake such studies, it is necessary to develop new theories and mathematical models to increase the understanding of software evolution, and to invest in research that tries to bridge the gap between the what (understanding) of software evolution and the how (control and support) of the software evolution process.

Nevertheless, this theory still remains to be formalized and enriched. For example, Lehman suggested that many software failures are due to changes that impact on the initial (often implicit) assumptions, and therefore a theory of software evolution must take assumptions into account.

5.3.18 Postdeployment Run-time Evolution

The maintenance and evolution of continuously running systems have become a major topic in many areas, including embedded systems, mobile devices, and service infrastructures. There is an urgent need for the proper support of run-time adaptations of systems while they are running, without the need to pause them, or even to shut them down. For that, further steps are needed to make the deployment, application, and exploration of dynamic adaptations more comprehensible. Dynamic Service Adaptation (DSA) is a promising approach trying to address these issues by providing appropriate means to introspect and navigate basic computational structures and to adjust them accordingly. While evolution support at run-time via dynamic adaptation addresses many of the requirements stated above, it does not address program or system comprehension. On the contrary, systems that are changed dynamically are harder to understand using contemporary approaches. Proper tool support is needed for the exploration and manipulation of both basic and enhanced run-time structures as well as change events and their history.

Keywords

unified process; baseline; solution definition; solution control; solution abstraction; quality criteria; technical problem; problem description; architecture description; quality characteristics; scalability; tool integration; interoperability; common exchange formats; common exchange standards; exploratory prototyping; program transformation; model refactoring; co-evolution; reuse; inheritance; late binding; polymorphism; Classboxes; multiple languages; SimCity; database community; CodeCrawler; evolution benchmarks; industrial-size; run-time adaptations; system comprehension

Exercises

1. List and describe any three design and evaluation techniques mentioned in this chapter.
2. Describe the Software Architecture Synthesis Process.
3. What does the acronym "S.A.A.M" stand for?
4. List the challenges of classification.
5. Explain how co-evolution can be supported.
6. Discuss how better software versioning can assist in its evolution.
7. Narrate the role of universities in Software Evolution.

CHAPTER 6

The Software Maintenance Process

Objectives

The objective of this chapter is to introduce the student to the concept of the software maintenance process and its related activities. When you have read this chapter you will be able to:

- Understand software maintenance and its related activities
- Understand software redocumentation and renovation concepts
- Understand the technologies and architectures upon which redocumentation and renovation rests on
- Appreciate the role of the software maintenance process in the lifecycle of a software product and
- Understand, by intuition, the position of the software maintenance process in the discipline of software development and its lifecycle

6.0 The Software Maintenance Process

To implement a software maintenance process requires that two key activities be fully mastered regarding software engineering:

1. Software configurations management;
2. Change management.

The above two well-known activities shall not be described in detail here. However, it is important to stress another activity which is relatively little used: *measurement.* Indeed it is not possible to control a process without metrics. Apart from elementary indicators such as days*man-day, or number of Lines of Code (LoC) modified per person, it is important to measure:

- the technical quality of each component;
- the economical value of each component;
- the evolution of metrics over a given period of time.

This should be weighted with the context of the application, and it should be possible to aggregate these measures vertically per groups of programs and per application, and horizontally according to features such as portability, reliability and ease of maintenance. Once the domains of non-quality are identified, a decision model should be available in order to choose the corrective actions.

6.1 Software Redocumentation

Documentation has always been the weak link in the set of deliverables related to software projects. This is confirmed by a study by IEEE which shows that 95% of software documentation is obsolete and or not complete. The study shows that in 89% of the cases, developers are obliged to use the source code as the main source for documentation. It follows that the greater part of the maintenance time is spent looking for information, reading it and trying to understand it rather than modifying the code.

A really useful documentation is more than just comment lines explaining a line of code or a group of instructions. It includes all the information required for the maintenance of the application, notably:

- how the application is organized (who is the owner, what is the functional or structural decomposition);
- exactly, which components are involved (JCL, programs, files and data bases, transactions and so on);
- what are the relations within a component and between components;
- the Data Dictionary.

It should be appreciated here that a wealth of information is not the only criteria of a good and useful documentation. This documentation should also be up to date, available to all, and easy to use, which implies:

- processes for automatic update and shared access;
- adaptativeness to the user's cognitive model;
- easy navigation within a component and between components;
- a familiar usage metaphor;
- a dynamic capacity for impact analysis intra- and inter-components

Since application knowledge resides in the source codes and with the experts, a good redocumentation system should include an automated engine for analyzing the sources, and an infrastructure to capture the experts' knowledge.

Today, it is possible with technology to find and automatically exploit all the knowledge contained in the source codes. In addition to this knowledge recovery advantage, one should add that the source codes are the most valuable source since they contain the most up-to-date information. As an example, the automated re-documentation of an application in the insurance industry comprising about 5 million LoC, generates around 500 000 HTML pages of exhaustive documentation. This plainly shows that:

- without an automated process such a large volume of documents cannot be generated nor kept updated within a reasonable budget and period of time;
- without the use and availability of hypertext navigation such an amount of information cannot be exploited.

It is not possible to complctely automate the capture of the experts' knowledge, called semantic assignment. However, it is facilitated, on the one hand, by a man-machine interface consisting of a documentation tool with data-entry fields, and on the other hand, by the technology of object-data bases which allows an automatic storage and the management of this knowledge. Indeed, a comment is only one of the attributes of an object in data-processing.

The redocumentation process generally consists of three main phases which include seven activities. The phases can, thus, be highlighted as:

Preparation phase: Analyse the state of the software and its documentation;

Planning phase: Decide which parts of the system should be redocumented first and which the general approach will be;

Redocumentation phase: Recreate the various documents that constitute the core of the redocumentation process.

There are two activities in the preparation phase:

System inventory: The goal of the first activity is to get an idea of the size of the problem and provide the basic information needed in the following activities. It answers questions like:

- what exactly make up the system?
- what exactly do we know about that system?
- where exactly can we find this information?

The inventory is performed along three main axes:

i. software components and functionalities,
ii. documentation
iii. people.

Figure 6.1 Activities of the redocumentation process

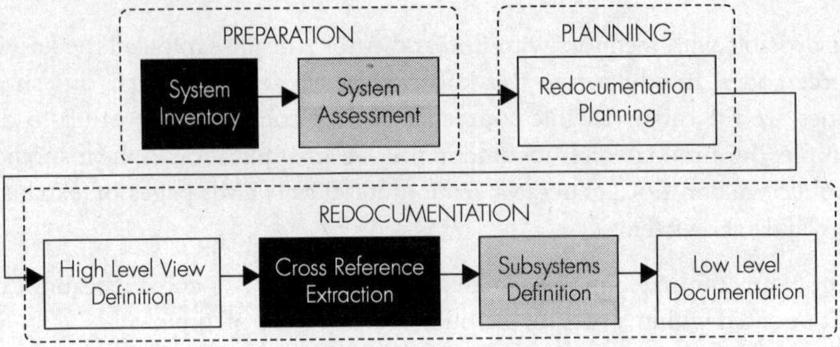

System assessment: The second step consists in assessing the level of confidence one can have in the code, the documentation and the other sources of information. This is useful to plan the redocumentation in itself and the maintenance in general.

There is only one activity in the planning phase:

Redocumentation planning: This activity is the prelude to the redocumentation work. It consists in defining how the redocumentation will be performed and what the priorities are. The planning will be based on results of the preceding phase. Other important points to consider are the maintenance load expectancy and the strategic evaluation of the importance of each part of the system.

There are four activities in the redocumentation phase:

High level view definition: In this activity, one must document a first high level view of the system: functionalities, interaction with other systems or specific hardware. Each functionality listed in the system inventory should be shortly described.

Cross references extraction: This activity will result in the identification of cross references:

- "routine to routine" (call graph),
- "routine to data" (CRUD table),
- "data to data" (data model), and
- "functionality to routine".

It will be important to do such things as impact analysis, feature location and so on.

Subsystems definition: This activity will result in a top down view of the system, its subsystems and their components. If the architectural decomposition is known and agreed upon by all, each subsystem listed in the system inventory must be documented, describing its objective, and what components and functionalities it contains.

Low level documentation: In this final activity, each independent item identified during the planning will be commented on. This activity is, to a large extent, a manual one. The software engineers must consider each item independently, analyse it and document it.

6.2 Software Renovation

The first goal of renovation is to improve the maintainability of code in order to reduce maintenance costs. Beyond this point, renovation definitely has an impact on the strategy for the evolution of applications. When an application becomes too complex to maintain, the management faces two options:

- re-write the application;
- replace that application with another or with a software package.

In some cases these options cannot be avoided, but are high-risk, because they are of the big bang type, and are costly. The third way, renovation, which is now possible thanks to current technologies, leads to a quick reduction of maintenance costs, to an extension of the lifetime of the application, and therefore to the decrease of the global cost. Furthermore, renovation is a low-risk solution because it allows for reverse actions, can be divided in activities of reasonable size, and can be automated in great part.

Renovation covers redocumentation, restructuration, restoration and reengineering techniques. Redocumentation was discussed hereabove. Restructuration includes a number of techniques which are very automated such as:

- the removal of dead codes and of unused variables;
- the reduction of the number of GOTO;

Figure 6.2 Economics of software reengineering (Sneed, 1991)

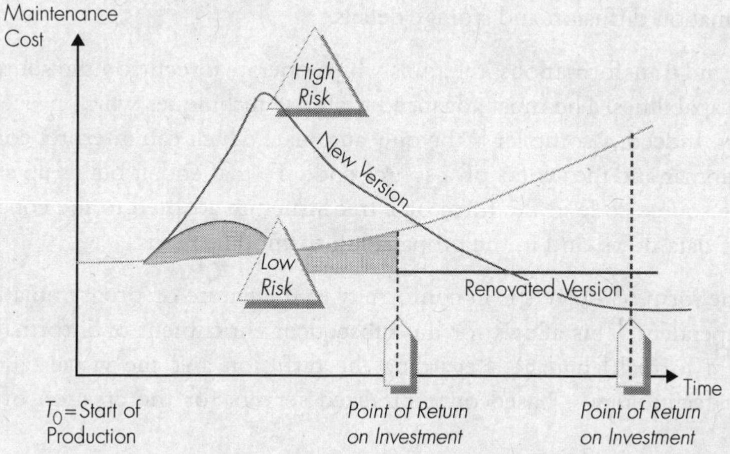

- the removal of backward GOTO;
- the restructuration of data;
- the deletion of unnecessary files;
- the reduction of Dominance Trees (for example, reduction of nested IF);
- the alignment of the precision of numerical data;
- the standardization of names and of code.

In a later stage, it is possible to tackle operations such as:

- restoring the meaning of functions;
- re-engineering.

These operations require more human interventions, but are made easier with the tools described above, and by other automated techniques such as slicing which allows the grouping of the Lines of Code according to the type of processes (display, access to data) and to assign them to functions (concept of Function Mining).

A Renovation Project has to start with an initial diagnosis. It rests on measuring the quality of the source code and of the economical value of the components. It allows choosing: the sub-set of components with the highest economical value in the application, the most adequate renovation techniques for this subset. The technical and economical metrics of components and of applications which have been previously mentioned play a key role in the Renovation process. Not only do metrics allow targeting the renovation actions, but they allow monitoring how quality evolves over a period of time, and therefore to correct any deviation through specific actions.

6.3 Technologies and Architectures

Redocumentation and renovation rest on various technologies:

- analysis of source code;
- manipulation of source code;
- information diffusion and storage details.

For analysis and transformations, the tools which operate directly on the source code have generally limited capabilities. The most advanced tools use techniques which proceed from work done on compilers. Indeed, a compiler is the only automate which can interpret correctly and exhaustively the grammar and the syntax of a source code. To that end, it builds up an abstract representation of the source code in the form of a tree structure adapted to the construction of control flows and of data flows, and to the propagation of modifications.

Storing in the form of objects is in conformity to the nature of programmatic objects which are very interdependent. This allows for the subsequent enrichment of information and to interrogate it with a formal language. Regarding the diffusion and the visualization of information, the Internet technology – based on centralized servers for the creation of HTML and XML pages – and workstation-servers provided with navigators are very adapted to the documentation of applications. They offers major advantages:

- the concept of a central server allows to control the integrity of documentation, its synchronization with that of software configurations, and the accesses;
- the navigators alleviate the installation and the maintenance of the proprietary code on each workstation;
- intuitive navigation thanks to hypertext and hypergraph interactions, while XML makes it possible to exploit the full content of the collected information;
- the Web metaphor, thus, reduces the training time to a few hours.

An architecture based on client/server models allows the creation of documentation servers which have no impact on the mainframes nor on the workstations. Moreover, the servers can be spread over several computers in order to reach the desired scalability. One would wonder why the solutions presented here are not widely used. There may be several reasons to that:

- very few companies master the compiler technology;
- furthermore it is also necessary to master the mass production process required for the treatment of application systems of several millions LoC;
- few people have the know-how to productize such technologies;
- until the relatively recent past, the required processing capacities and memory sizes were an obstacle to solutions which were economically acceptable;
- the Internet technology which forms the basis for the diffusion of information is also a relatively recent tool for maintenance teams;
- the traditional suppliers of redocumentation software tools are handicapped by the old concepts: workstations oriented (instead of servers), proprietary presentation interfaces, low performance of the data base implementation when millions of lines of codes are to be.

Figure 6.3 Documentation server

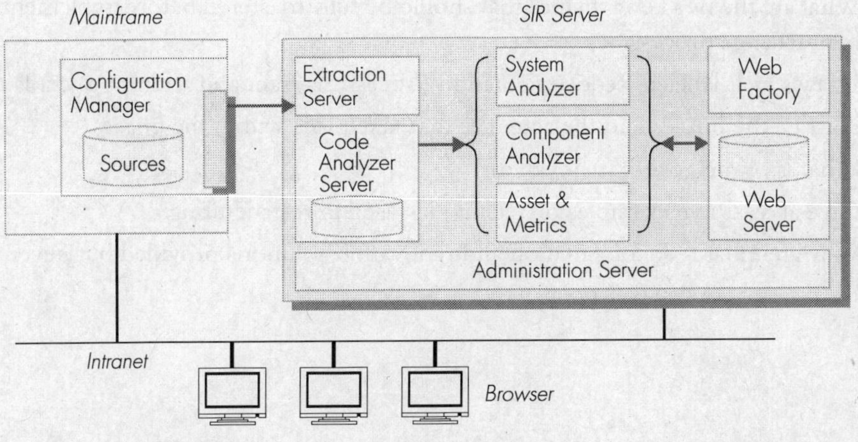

Surprisingly, it is the software houses which came last into the software maintenance market who have been able to capitalize on all these new technologies and which offer well architectured, evolutive, and economical solutions.

6.4 Measurable Benefits

The solutions which have been recommended in this section have been implemented in real cases that have provided valuable information:

- compared to a traditional documentation approach, using an automatic hypertext redocumentation and navigation tool can reduce research time from 5 hours to 1 hour 30 minutes;
- the improvement of the maintenance and of the documentation processes, and the restructuration of the application codes can be allowed to process 9% more of requests in 18% less of man-days.

From the qualitative point of view, one should stress the need to provide maintenance teams with efficient tools having a high technological content in order to boost their motivations. As for management, using these tools allows them to regain control of the maintenance process and put them in a position to engage into a real quality policy.

Keywords

measurement; elementary indicators; technical quality; economical value; portability; reliability; decision model; software redocumentation; functional decomposition; structural decomposition; automatic update; shared access; cognitive model; adaptativeness; dynamic capacity; knowledge recovery; hypertext navigation; semantic assignment; maintenance load; strategic evaluation; dead code; function mining; programmatic objects; quality policy

Exercises

1. What are the two key activities that should be fully mastered before implementing a software maintenance process?
2. Draw a well-labeled Redocumentation Process diagram and attempt to explain it.
3. Narrate the phases and the activities that take place within the phases.
4. What is prime goal of renovation?
5. Give at least five examples of techniques used in restructuring.
6. Why are most redocumentation and renovation solutions provided but never widely used?

CHAPTER 7

Program Comprehension

Objectives

The objective of this chapter is to introduce the student to the basic concepts of program comprehension and its relationships with software maintenance at an introductory level. When you have read this chapter you will be able to:

- Understand what program comprehension is
- Understand the basic concepts underlying program comprehension
- Understand the relationships between program comprehension and the software maintenance process
- Understand the impact of program comprehension on the software maintenance process
- Understand the need and universal environment for software reengineering from a program comprehension point of view

7.0 Introduction

Program comprehension is widely recognized as the main activity within many software maintenance and software development tasks. Particularly within software maintenance activities, program comprehension is the vital first task of any maintenance, whether it is adaptive, perfective, corrective or preventative. Despite being such a key activity, program comprehension has not received much research activity until recently with work from a number of key authors. This initial flurry of activity has since receded and again research into program comprehension has made little major progress.

This chapter will introduce the components of program comprehension and highlight any commonality between them. Throughout the chapter the term maintainer will be used wherever possible to describe the person performing the comprehension task. The reason for this choice over the more popular term programmer is due to the almost monopoly position which software maintenance has on program comprehension activity. Thus, the term maintainer removes the generality and places program comprehension within its typical context. Another terminology issue is the use of the terms cognitive model and mental model.

Within this chapter, the term mental model will refer to the maintainer's internal (mental) representation of the software or the results of the comprehension process. The term cognitive model will refer to the complete set of processes, knowledge, heuristics and mental model used during program comprehension. Thus it is the cognitive model which is the subject of the various theories and the focus of this chapter. However, program comprehension can be further characterized by both the theories that provide rich explanations about how programmers understand software as well as the tools that are used to assist in comprehension tasks.

We will now give an overview of the key theories developed in program comprehension. This will begin by highlighting and defining any commonality, standard terms or standard concepts. This will be followed by a more detailed summary of each of the theories proposed by the various authors. But before we do that, here are some important terminologies to remember.

7.1 Concepts and Terminology

A mental model describes a developer's mental representation of the program to be understood whereas a cognitive model describes the cognitive processes and the temporary information structures in the programmer's head that are used to form the mental model. Cognitive support refers to support provided for cognitive tasks such as thinking or reasoning (Walenstein, 2003).

Programming plans are simply generic fragments of source code that represent typical scenarios in programming. For example, a sorting program will contain a loop to compare two numbers in each iteration (Soloway and Ehrlic, 1984). Programming plans are also often referred to as clichés and schemas. Delocalized plans occur when a programming plan is implemented in disparate areas of the program (Soloway and Ehrlic, 1984).

Beacons are recognizable, familiar features in the code that act as cues to the presence of certain structures (Brooks, 1983). For example, a procedure name can indicate the implementation of a specific feature. Rules of programming discourse capture the conventions of programming, such as coding standards and algorithm implementations (Soloway and Ehrlic, 1984). The rules of discourse invoke certain expectations in the mind of the programmer.

7.2 Theories of Program Comprehension

7.2.1 Cognitive Models

Mayrhauser (1995) identifies a commonality between the various program comprehension theories. This commonality exists in the software engineers' cognitive model, and to some extent in the way the model is created and maintained. All the comprehension theories agree that the program comprehension process uses existing knowledge coupled with a comprehension strategy in order to acquire new knowledge.

This new knowledge should, through a process of additions and revisions eventually achieve the required level of understanding of the code. The various comprehension strategies used in obtaining this new knowledge have a commonality in that they all formulate hypotheses which can then be refined, revised or rejected. Formulating and verifying these hypotheses makes use of both the existing knowledge and the newly acquired knowledge.

The three main components in the cognitive model are the knowledge base, the mental model and the assimilation process. The knowledge base, which has already been described briefly, contains the maintainers' understanding of the domain and any related field. The mental model, which is different from the cognitive model, is the maintainers' internal representation of the program. Within this chapter the term mental model will be used to describe this internal representation, whereas the term cognitive model will be used to describe the overall cognitive system or process used in program comprehension. Finally, the assimilation process is the glue which binds the knowledge base to the mental model, manipulating both to create and revise hypotheses which can then be used to update the knowledge base or the mental model. The actual processes involved in this assimilation are the subject of the various theories of program comprehension. The three main components of the cognitive model will be described in greater detail here.

7.2.2 Knowledge Base

The knowledge base consists of both existing knowledge and newly acquired knowledge. This knowledge will also consist of two general types – general knowledge and task-specific knowledge. During the comprehension process, the maintainer will obtain more task-specific knowledge, but may also require additional general knowledge which will typically be obtained on an "as-needed" basis. The general knowledge represents information not specifically related to the software itself. Such knowledge could include experience with programming languages, the understanding of the implementation platform, or even knowledge of the operational domain of the software – for example business rules, control systems or database systems. Task specific knowledge is directly related with the comprehension task and will include knowledge such as design information, the programming styles used and the overall goals of the program.

Existing knowledge and general knowledge are strongly related, with the majority of existing knowledge being non-task related. However, if the maintainer has prior knowledge of the program, the existing knowledge will contain any fragments of task-specific information related to the program, including any mental model of the software. In contrast, new knowledge is oriented more towards task specific knowledge, which is gleaned during the comprehension process. This new knowledge could include information on control flow, data flow, software structure, implementation details or styles. New knowledge can be obtained at any abstraction level and can range from low level implementation details to higher level structural information.

7.2.2.1 Knowledge-base model

Letovsky views programmers as opportunistic processors capable of exploiting both bottom-up and top-down cues (Letovsky, 1986a). There are three components to his model:

- The knowledge base encodes the programmer's expertise and background knowledge. The programmer's internal knowledge may consist of application and programming domain knowledge, program goals, a library of programming plans and rules of discourse;
- The mental model encodes the programmer's current understanding of the program. Initially it consists of a specification of the program goals and later evolves into a mental model which describes the implementation in terms of the data structures and algorithms used;
- The assimilation process describes how the mental model evolves using the programmer's knowledge base together with the program source code and documentation.

The assimilation process may be a bottom-up or top-down process depending on the programmer's initial knowledge base. Letovsky describes two recurring patterns: asking questions and conjecturing answers (Letovsky, 1986a). He referred to such activities as inquiries. An inquiry may consist of a programmer asking a question (for example, what is the purpose of the variable *x*?), conjecturing an answer (*x* stores the maximum of a set of numbers), and then searching through the code and documentation to verify the answer (the conjecture is verified if *x* is in an assignment statement in which two values are compared to see which is greater). According to Letovsky there are three major types of hypotheses:

- why conjectures (questioning the role of a function or piece of code);
- how conjectures (what is the method for accomplishing a goal);
- what conjectures (what is a variable or one of the program functions).

7.2.3 Mental Model

The mental model is the maintainers' internal representation of the program and can be composed of a number of inter-dependent semantic constructs. The various theories of program comprehension proposed offer a wide variety of forms for these semantic constructs. These constructs include text structures, chunks, plans, hypotheses, beacons, and rules of discourse. The mental model is continuously updated and amended by the assimilation process. Mayrhauser (1995) identifies the dynamic process used in creating these semantic constructs as a combination of behaviours such as strategies, actions, episodes, and processes.

Text structure constructs are formed from the program source code and its structure. The structure of the program text can be derived in two forms. In well presented or styled code, an initial structure can be derived from the text layout, using indentation, comment blocks or blank areas to identify textual chunks.

This initial structure can then be refined further to give it a more syntactic meaning such as function blocks, iteration blocks and conditional constructs. The organisation of text structures within the mental model can include nesting and dependencies. For example, an iteration block may be nested or contained within a function block, and two function blocks may be related by a function call.

Chunks are simply semantic or syntactic abstractions of text structures within the source code. Shneiderman (1980) describes a process in which maintainers abstract portions of the source code (text structures) into chunks. Collections of these chunks can then be abstracted further into higher level chunks.

Chunks can be constructed from either semantic or syntactic knowledge and need not be fully understood or identified immediately, and can be returned to at later time for revision. It seems a reasonable assumption to say that typically a chunk formed on the basis of syntactic knowledge, a syntactic chunk, will be revised later to form a semantic chunk. For example, a syntactic chunk derived from a function block or a nesting level will be revised later with semantic meaning or purpose, such as a sort algorithm.

Plans, best described by Mayrhauser (1995) are "knowledge elements for developing and validating expectations, interpretations, and inferences". Plans, otherwise known as clichés or schemas, are derived from research by Soloway and Ehrlich (1984) which attempted to apply theories from text comprehension to program comprehension. The notion of plans proposed by Soloway and Ehrlich corresponds directly to the notion of schemas in text comprehension in which schemas are "generic knowledge structures that guide the comprehender's interpretations, inferences, expectations, and attention when passages are comprehended" (Graesser, 1981). Similarly, plans in the context of program comprehension also capture the maintainers' attention during the comprehension process.

Mayrhauser describes plans as belonging to two categories – slot types and slot fillers. Slot types can be thought of as generalised templates which the maintainer can apply to a number of specific problems to create slot fillers. Slot fillers are specific to a particular problem. Slot types can thus be thought of as an abstraction of a possibly infinite collection of slot fillers. An example of a slot type could be a function such as a sort routine, whereas a slot filler could be a particular implementation of a sort routine, for example a quick sort. Slot fillers are related to slot types by either *a kind-of* or an *is-a* relationship.

Plans can be further categorised into programming plans and domain plans (Mayrhauser, 1995). A simple analogy can be drawn between these types of plan and the knowledge contained within the knowledge base.

Programming plans, analogous to task specific knowledge, are plans specific to the task at hand. They can exist at a variety of abstraction levels, ranging from the low-level program code to the abstract function of the program as a whole. Domain plans, analogous to general knowledge, are plans which incorporate all other knowledge of the problem area excluding that contained within the program plans (i.e., the details pertaining to the software). Domain plans give a general concept of the task and how it can be completed. These generally exist at a higher level of abstraction than the actual software system.

Hypotheses are introduced by Brooks (1983) in a paper which suggests how programmers use an iterative, hierarchical method of forming, refining and possibly rejecting hypotheses at varying levels of abstraction during the comprehension process. Brooks states that the program comprehension process is complete when the maintainers' mental model contains a complete hierarchy of correct hypotheses.

This hypothesis hierarchy is described as a bridge between the various domain levels of the problem, the complete model thus bridging from the high level "This program is a ..." hypothesis to the low level hypotheses regarding implementation details. The program comprehension process using hypotheses will be described in greater detail below.

Letovsky (1986a) investigates the use of hypotheses further in an experiment involving the study of maintainers undergoing a given comprehension task. Letovsky refers to hypotheses as conjectures and describes the mental processes of the maintainers as they create, question and revise these conjectures.

Conjectures are associated with a degree of certainty which affects the way in which they are revised or discarded at a later stage. The level of certainty can range from a guess to complete certainty. From the study, Letovsky identifies three main types of conjecture:

- Why conjectures are hypotheses which question design choices, implementation decisions or function purpose. For example "Why use a bubble sort?";
- How conjectures are hypotheses which attempt to discover the method with which to accomplish a particular task. For example "How is the array indexed?";
- What conjectures hypothesise classification, for example a variable, function or variable type.

7.2.4 Assimilation and Knowledge Acquisition

The assimilation process is the method which the maintainer uses in undergoing the comprehension task. This process makes use of the mental model and the knowledge base in conjunction with the source code and any related documentation, to build upon or revise the mental model and thus the maintainer's understanding of the program. The exact assimilation process used by the maintainer is the subject of research which will be discussed in greater detail below. A number of methods or processes can be identified which contribute to the assimilation process and belong to a number of the comprehension theories. Mayrhauser (1995) classifies these as being dynamic elements of the mental model, however they appear more fitting as a process by which the mental model is created. Before describing these processes, two features which aid in facilitating them, beacons and rules of discourse, will be described.

Beacons, first identified by Brooks (1983) then explored further by Wiedenbeck (2001), are recognisable or familiar features within the source code or other forms of (possibly higher level) knowledge. Beacons thus act as cues to the presence of certain structures or features and can be used in either the verification or the creation of hypotheses. Brooks' well cited example of a beacon is the swapping of two variables which could be a beacon for a sorting routine. Even at a higher level, beacons such as the name of a particular procedure or source module are equally valid and useful information. Beacons are used in gaining a higher level of understanding than that in which the beacon occurs i.e., abstracting from a code chunk to a process or function.

Rules of discourse, as identified by Soloway and Ehrlich (1984), are rules or conventions within programming such as code presentation or naming standards. For example, one rule of discourse is that a variable name should usually agree with its function. Rules of discourse set up expectations in the mind of the maintainer. These expectations can be very powerful, allowing the pre-fetching of knowledge from long-term storage, though they can also be problematic if discourse rules are violated. Soloway and Ehrlich (1984) describe an experiment which shows that comprehension performance is greater for programs which obey the rules of discourse (plan-like programs). Conversely the study also showed that when the rules of discourse are violated, the comprehension performance is hampered, both for expert and novice maintainers. This implies that unconventional algorithms, unusual data structures or the unexpected use of a known algorithm as well as unconventional programming styles will render programs more difficult to comprehend.

Strategies define the sequence of actions performed by a maintainer while following a plan to achieve a particular goal. Littman *et al.* (1986) identify two such strategies, the systematic strategy and the as-needed strategy. These two strategies are defined within the context of comprehending an entire program, hence the systematic approach attempts to comprehend the program as a whole before any attempt at maintenance is made. The as-needed approach attempts to localise the comprehension process to only the areas of the program which must be understood to perform the maintenance task. These are reviewed further down.

Two comprehension mechanisms which are aided by strategies are chunking and cross-referencing. The chunking process creates new, higher level chunks from lower level structures or chunks. As structures at the lower level are recognized they are abstracted into a chunk and labeled. These labels can then be used again in forming new, higher level chunks. An example of the chunking process could be the formation of the "bubble sort" chunk from iteration, comparison and variable swapping chunks. Cross-referencing forms relations between different abstraction levels by mapping program parts to functional descriptions. Cross-referencing is essential to the building of a mental representation spanning a number of abstraction levels.

7.2.5 Top-down Comprehension

Brooks theorizes that programmers understand a completed program in a top-down manner where the comprehension process is one of reconstructing knowledge about the domain of the program and mapping this knowledge to the source code (Brooks, 1983). The process starts with a hypothesis about the general nature of the program. This initial hypothesis is then refined in a hierarchical fashion by forming subsidiary hypotheses. Subsidiary hypotheses are refined and evaluated in a depth-first manner. The verification (or rejection) of hypotheses depends heavily on the absence or presence of beacons (Brooks, 1983).

Soloway and Ehrlich (1984) observed that the top-down understanding is used when the code or type of code is familiar. They observed that expert programmers use beacons, programming plans and rules of programming discourse to decompose goals and plans into lower-level plans. They noted that delocalized plans add to the complication of program comprehension.

7.2.6 Bottom-up Comprehension

The bottom-up theories of program comprehension assume that programmers first read code statements and then mentally chunk or group these statements into higher level abstractions. These abstractions (chunks) are aggregated further until a high-level understanding of the program is attained (Shneiderman, 1979). Shneiderman and Mayer's cognitive framework differentiates between the syntactic and semantic knowledge of programs. Syntactic knowledge can be described as a language dependent and concerning the statements and basic units within a program. On the other hand, semantic knowledge is an independent language and it is built within the progressive layers until a mental model is eventually formed describing the application domain.

Pennington managed to describe a bottom-up model (Pennington, 1987). She observed that programmers initially develop a control-flow abstraction of the program at hand which, in turn, captures the sequence of operations in the program. This model is referred to as the program model and is developed through the chunking of microstructures in the text (statements, control constructs and relationships) into macrostructures (text structure abstractions) and by cross-referencing these structures. Only when the program model has been fully assimilated will the situation model be developed. The situation model encompasses knowledge about data-flow abstractions and functional abstractions (the program goal hierarchy). The programmer's understanding is further enhanced through the cross referencing of artifacts in the program model and situation model.

7.3 Opportunistic and Systematic Strategies

Littman *et al.* observed programmers enhancing a personnel database program (Littman, 1986). They observed that programmers either systematically read the code in detail, tracing through the control-flow and data-flow abstractions in the program to gain a global understanding of the program, or that they take an as-needed approach, focusing only on the code relating to a particular task at hand. Subjects using a systematic strategy acquired both static knowledge (information about the structure of the program) and causal knowledge (interactions between the components in the program when it is executed). This enabled them to form a mental model of the program. However, those using the as-needed approach only acquired static knowledge resulting in a weaker mental model of how the program worked. More errors tend to occur since the programmers fail to recognize the causal interactions between the components in the program.

7.4 Impact of Program Characteristics

Programs that are carefully designed and well documented will be easier to understand, change or reuse in the future. Pennington's experiments showed that the choice of language has an effect on the comprehension processes (Pennington, 1987). COBOL programmers consistently fared better at answering questions related to data-flow than FORTRAN programmers, and FORTRAN programmers consistently fared better than COBOL programmers for control-flow questions.

Programming paradigms impact comprehension strategies in a way. Object-oriented (OO) programs are often seen as a more natural fit to problems in the real world because of *is a* and *is-part-of* relationships in a class hierarchy and structure, but others still argue that objects do not always map easily to real world problems (Détienne, 2001). In OO programs, additional abstractions that capture domain concepts are achieved through encapsulation and polymorphism (Détienne, 2001). Message-passing is used to communicate between class methods and hence programming plans are dispersed (i.e., scattered) throughout classes in an OO program. Corritore *et al.* (1999) compared how experts comprehend object-oriented and procedural programs. They noted that experts make more use of domain concepts in the initial understanding of object-oriented programs.

7.5 Influence of Individual Programmer Differences

There are many individual characteristics that will impact how a programmer tackles a comprehension task. These differences have an impact on the requirements for a supporting tool. There is a huge disparity in programmer ability and creativity which cannot be measured simply by their experience (Curtis, 1981). Vessey presents an exploratory study to investigate expert and novice debugging processes (Vessey, 1985). She classified programmers as expert or novice based on their ability to chunk effectively. She notes that experts used breadth-first approaches and at the same time were able to adopt a system view of the problem area, whereas novices used breadth-first and depth-first approaches but were unable to think in system terms.

Détienne (2001) also notes that experts make more use of external devices as memory aids. Experts tend to reason about programs according to both functional and object-oriented relationships and consider the algorithm, whereas novices tend to focus on objects. Burkhardt *et al.* (1998) performed experiments to study how object oriented programs are comprehended. They observed that novices are less likely than experts to use inheritance and compositional relationships to guide their comprehension. Finally, Davies (1993) notes that experts tend to externalize low level details, but novices externalize higher levels of representation related to the problem.

7.6 Effects of Task Variability in Program Comprehension

According to Clayton there is no real agreement on what it is about a program that needs to be understood (Clayton, 1998). This is not surprising as program comprehension is not an end goal, but rather a necessary step in achieving some other objective. Tasks that involve comprehension steps include maintenance such as fixing an error, reusing code, refactoring, impact analysis of proposed changes and changing the functionality of the program. Other tasks include software inspection, evaluating quality metrics (such as reusability, performance, security), and testing.

Obviously the type and scope of the ultimate programming task has to have an impact on the comprehension process followed. If a task is simple, the change probably only affects a small portion of the code. For more complex changes, the programmer has to consider global interactions, which reqires the programmer to have a thorough understanding of the causal relationships in the entire program.

Pennington's research indicates that a task requiring recall and comprehension resulted in a programmer forming a program model (control-flow abstraction) of the software whereas a task to modify the program resulted in a programmer forming a situation model containing data-flow and functional information (Pennington, 1987).

For a programmer, a reuse task requires that he/she first understand the source problem, retrieve an appropriate target solution, and then adapt the solution to the problem. The mapping from the problem to the solution is often done using analogical reasoning (Détienne, 2001) and may involve iterative searching through many possible solutions. Davies noted that the task, whether it is a development or comprehension task, influences which information is externalized by experts (Davies, 1993).

7.7 Discussion: Implications for Tool Research

Many of the researchers that developed the traditional cognitive theories for program comprehension discuss the implications of the developed theories on tool design and in some cases also discuss how education and program design could be improved to address program understanding challenges. However, in many cases, the connection to tools and how they could be improved or evaluated according to the theories could be stronger. Moreover, some of these results were also criticized because the researchers studied novice programmers doing fabricated tasks (Curtis, 1986). Vans and von Mayrhauser are an example of notable exceptions. Despite these criticisms, program comprehension research does contain many gems of advice on how tools can be improved. The advantage for tool designers is that they can use these theories to help them understand, not only what features are needed, but also why some features may neither be appropriate nor sufficient in assisting comprehension tasks. Moreover, the research which explores the differences in programmers, programs and tasks can be used to guide tool designers to meet specific needs.

7.7.1 Key Theories in Program Comprehension

This section attempts to give a summary of the most notable program comprehension theories proposed by various authors. These theories vary significantly, yet they all relate to the above outline of the cognitive model to some degree. That is, they all subscribe to the idea of a knowledge base, mental model and some form of assimilation process. The exact representation and formation of these components does, however, vary throughout the theories.

7.7.2 Brooks Cognition Model

Brooks (1983) proposed a theory for program comprehension based on a number of domains existing through the comprehension model. The theory argues that program comprehension is complete when a complete set of mappings can be made from the top level domain (problem domain) to the bottom level domain (programming domain). The developer of the software initially produces these mappings, whereas the maintainer must recover them.

Brooks identifies two types of information which must be obtained in order to reconstruct these mappings. Intra-domain knowledge will contain information about the objects within each domain. This will include their properties and relationships, operations which can be performed on them and the sequence in which these operations are applied. Inter-domain knowledge will contain information about relationships between objects and operators occupying neighbouring domains. Brooks highlights that these relationships are generally not one to one, and new operations in one domain may be built up from both objects and operators in a previous domain. An example could be a sort routine in an algorithm domain which would map on to a series of statements (operators), variables and functions (objects) in the programming domain.

Brooks' mental model is constructed in a top-down manner through a hierarchy of hypotheses, as opposed to the more usual idea of a bottom-up process beginning at the source code (Shneiderman, 1979; Basili *et al.*, 1982). Robson *et al.* (1988) misinterpret this model and see it as a bottom-up approach which works from the source code using beacons to form initial hypotheses. Brooks' theory asserts that the primary hypothesis will be formed as soon as the maintainer obtains information about the task that the program performs.

This information can be as little as the program name, or a short description of its function. The level of detail of the primary hypothesis is obviously dependent on the task and the maintainer, though it will generally specify the global structure of the program with respect to inputs, outputs, and major data and processing constructs. No matter how weak the initial hypotheses are, they may be of considerable aid in further the comprehension of the program.

Hypothesis generation in Brooks' model relates strongly to the program writing tasks involved in creating a piece of software. Earlier work by Brooks (1977) proposed a model for this writing process – one property of which was the use of learned patterns or structures in moving top-down from the problem domain to the program domain. Brooks thus sees the program writing process as retrieving known structural units with varying granularity to fit a particular aspect of the problem, then assembling and possibly modifying them into programs. He sees the hypothesis generation process used in his comprehension theory as retrieving the same units and using these as the formation of further hypotheses.

Obviously, these structures will undergo far less assembly and modification, typically sufficient to result in a hypothesis which can be verified against the code. This process is heavily dependent on the maintainer's knowledge of the problem domain. A weak knowledge of a particular feature implemented in the code, for example an unusual sorting routine, will result in problems in verifying hypotheses.

Brooks proposes that hypotheses be formed in a top-down, breadth-first manner and the descent of this hierarchy is terminated when the lowest level hypotheses can be verified against the code.

This verification occurs when the operations or data structures specified in the hypotheses can be associated with features or details visible in the code or documentation. Brooks then identifies the notion of beacons which are used in this verification. He also states that beacons can themselves lead to the generation of subsidiary hypotheses or a more rapid verification of later hypotheses. When the comprehension process is complete, a hierarchy of hypotheses will exist with the primary hypothesis at the top and subsidiary hypotheses below. Each subsidiary hypothesis will be bound to a segment of the program code, with no un-bound sections of code remaining.

7.7.3 Shneiderman and Mayer Cognition Model

Shneiderman and Mayer (1979) proposed that program comprehension is based on two forms of programming knowledge – syntactic and semantic. They further categorise this into three main types of knowledge, syntactic knowledge – general semantic knowledge, and task related semantic knowledge.

The maintainers' syntactic knowledge contains details of the domain in which the comprehension is to take place. This knowledge will include syntactic details of the programming language used such as keywords, language syntax and available library routines in addition to other relevant areas of the problem domain such as hardware specific details. Syntactic knowledge grows with experience but will typically also fade with lack of use.

The general semantic knowledge of the programmer consists of more general concepts of programming which are not necessarily domain specific. The semantic knowledge may consist of both high level concepts such as tree traversal algorithms, or low-level concepts such as the semantic meaning of programming constructs, for example the FOR...NEXT loop. The maintainer will also possess task-related semantic knowledge which relates directly to the problem domain. This knowledge could be quite specific such as the semantic meaning of various program portions, or more general such as the knowledge of the environment within which the program resides, for example the knowledge of accountancy or medicine. The authors argue that the comprehension process involves the application of syntactic knowledge to create a semantic model of the program.

The maintainer's semantic model of the program may consist of either high-level representations or low level representations, or both. The former favours a top-down approach to comprehension where the maintainer has a general view of the program structure or purpose and must then discover the low-level details of how it operates (similar to Brooks' theory). The low-level representation favours a bottom-up approach in which the maintainer attempts to discover the structure or intent of higher level program entities from the low-level implementation details. Shneiderman and Mayer see the program comprehension task as predominantly unidirectional, starting with the program code and continuing in a bottom-up manner until the problem statement is recovered.

Shneiderman (1980) in later works describes an information chunking process employed by maintainers during program comprehension. Programmers abstract portions of the source code into chunks, collections of chunks being abstracted further into higher level chunks. Chunks can be constructed from either semantic or syntactic knowledge and need not be fully understood or identified immediately, being returned to at later time. It seems a reasonable assumption that typically a chunk formed on the basis of syntactic knowledge, a syntactic chunk, will be revised later to form a semantic chunk. For example, a syntactic chunk derived from a function block or a nesting level will be revised later with semantic meaning or purpose, such as a sort algorithm.

7.7.4 Letovsky Cognition Model

Letovsky (1986a) performed an empirical study of programmers attempting to perform a maintenance operation on unfamiliar code. The maintenance task required the maintainers to first obtain an understanding of the code structure and operation then plan the appropriate modifications. The study concentrated on the program comprehension task and attempted to trace the subjects through processes by encouraging them to "think aloud".

The analysis of the study results concentrated on two recurring behaviours in which the subjects asked questions then conjectured answers. Letovsky proceeded to create a taxonomy of both questions and conjectures then to define his interpretation of the maintainers' cognitive model.

The cognitive model suggested by Letovsky was subdivided into three components, namely a knowledge base, a mental model and an assimilation process. The knowledge base encapsulates the experience and expertise of the programmer, including a syntactic knowledge and, more generally, a problem domain knowledge. The mental model represents the maintainers' internal representation or conception of the program and is further subdivided by Letovsky into the specification, implementation and annotation layers. These layers contain the high-level abstract view of the code, the low-level implementation details, and any known mappings between the two, respectively. Finally, the assimilation process pulls on the knowledge base and any available external help such as the source code or documentation in order to generate and update the mental model. Letovsky suggests that this assimilation process can occur either as bottom-up or top-down where the bottom level is the source code and the top level is the most abstract view of the program. It is also suggested that the maintainer may switch between these techniques in an opportunistic manner, selecting whichever is appropriate at the time to gain the highest return in knowledge gain.

7.7.5 Littman *et al.* Cognition Model

Littman *et al.* (1986) state that program comprehension is based on two distinct strategies – the systematic strategy and the as-needed strategy. This conclusion stems from the results of monitoring the behaviour of a number of expert programmers given a maintenance task to perform upon a small program. From this study they also conclude that the comprehension strategy used strongly influences their resulting knowledge of the program. In addition, they discovered that the extent of a maintainers' knowledge of the program directly determines their ability to perform successful modifications. A programmer's choice of systematic or as-needed strategy is dependent on the extent to which he wants to understand the program.

The systematic strategy is used when the programmer wants to obtain a full understanding of the program operation before commencing the modifications. This strategy includes an extensive study of both the static and the dynamic aspects of the program to obtain an understanding of both the program structure and any causal interaction among program components. This approach is costly in comprehension time but enables the maintainer to make a more rapid and confident modification.

The as-needed strategy enables the maintainer to minimise on comprehension time by concentrating on the program areas which are likely to require a change. The maintainer will immediately attempt to localise areas of code which may require a change in order to perform the correct maintenance. Once this initial understanding of the code is obtained, the maintainer will typically proceed to perform the maintenance operation. During maintenance the maintainer will typically require additional information and will then investigate further on an as-needed basis. There is thus no guarantee that the maintainer will gain a full understanding of the causal relationships or dependencies between the program components and it is unlikely that they will detect unforeseen impacts of their modifications.

The conclusions which are drawn from the use of these strategies are that the systematic approach requires more time during the comprehension stage of maintenance but results in a strong cognitive model of the program. This model includes static and structural information, but, more importantly it also includes information on the dependencies and causal interactions between program components. In contrast, the as-needed approach requires less comprehension time but results in a weaker and incomplete cognitive model. The model will include static information and some structural information, but will generally lack any knowledge of the dependencies or causal interaction between components. It is obvious that these two strategies can only be compared for use on small programs. Program size can rapidly surpass the capability of a single person to obtain a full understanding of its operation, hence the systematic approach is redundant. However, it may still be possible to subdivide the program into more manageable sections with which the systematic approach may be applied to each section. In the case of large programs, both the as-needed and systematic strategies suffer because of the sheer volume of information.

7.7.6 Soloway, Adelson, Ehrlich and Letovsky

Soloway and Ehrlich (1984) describe a study to evaluate the use of programming plans and rules of discourse in expert programmers. Their view is that programs are composed from programming plans which have been adapted to meet the needs of the specific problem. They also believe that these plans are composed in accordance with the rules of programming discourse. They believe that the ease or difficulty with which comprehension can take place is dependent on the extent to which the rules of discourse are obeyed. Programs in which the rules of discourse have been followed (plan-like programs) will generally be easier to understand or maintain than those in which the rules have been violated (unplan-like programs).

Their study also aimed to investigate the differences between novice and expert programmer performance when confronted with both plan-like and unplan-like programs. They believed that the experts would perform much better than the novices on plan-like programs due to their experience and expectations of the rules of discourse. Conversely, on unplan-like program they expected that the performance of expert programmers would drop to the level of the novices. The reason for this being that the experts would be confused by the rule violations, whereas the novices would be less sensitive to them as they have less knowledge, and hence lower expectations of the rules of discourse. The results of the study supported this theory and highlighted the fact that expert programmers form strong expectations about program structure and style. When these expectations are violated their performance drops greatly.

In some later work, Letovsky and Soloway (1986b) performed a "think aloud" experiment in which a number of expert maintainers were observed adding a new feature to an existing software system. The authors identify the fact that maintainers are typically under pressure to perform a task, and are normally subject to time constraints. They believe that this results in maintainers concentrating their attention on localised areas of the code which they believe are required to perform the maintenance task (similar to the as-needed strategy of Littman *et al.*). When the documentation or the program code do not highlight any remote dependencies these can often be missed by the maintainers' focused attention and thus may result in an inaccurate understanding of the program as a whole. This, in turn, may lead to inaccurate or inefficient modifications to the program.

Letovsky and Soloway describe these "loose" dependencies as delocalised plans. Delocalised plans are programming plans which are implemented in a distributed manner throughout the program. The results of the study highlight the problems which delocalised plans cause in the program comprehension task.

Soloway *et al.* (1988) propose a top-down model of comprehension which is based on the notion of programming plans. This model draws to some degree on the ideas of Brooks (1984) in that the top-down comprehension model is constructed from an overall idea of the program function. This is, however, only feasible if the maintainer has had previous experience with a similar task. The model proposed by the authors uses three types of plans: strategic, tactical, and implementation. Strategic plans specify language-independent actions or algorithms and describe a global strategy used in programs or algorithms. Tactical plans are localised strategies used in problem solving which generally describe a particular algorithm, function or process. Finally, implementation plans contain actual source code segments and provide the mapping from the tactical plans to the source code. They perform the actual implementation. The mental model used in this theory is constructed in a top-down manner using a hierarchy of goals and plans. Beacons and rules of discourse are used in mapping from goals to plans, and in forming lower level plans.

7.7.7 Basili and Mills

Basili and Mills (1982) describe an experiment in which they attempt a program comprehension task upon an unknown program without any form of documentation other than the code itself. Although the authors do not propose a theory or cognitive model, their research is of interest as it describes a study of the comprehension process and places emphasis not on the actual understanding of the code, but in the capturing or recording of this understanding. This is a vital concept particularly in the task of redocumentation or in recording knowledge gained to aid future maintenance. The method used was to simulate a programmer within a maintenance environment using techniques of program design but adapted for program understanding. The programmer was thus given a program and the task of developing a specification and correctness proof from it.

The authors take the view that the actual process of program understanding is of equal importance to being able to capture or record this understanding. Their reasoning is that a lot of the comprehension effort is repeated due to the loss or poor communication of previously found information. The authors believe that being able to derive a program specification, and, in particular, a correctness proof is vitally important to both the comprehension and the maintenance tasks.

The authors' technique follows a bottom-up approach in that the low-level detail of the program is discovered first, with more abstract or high-level functionality being discovered from this. Their technique thus operated at a number of levels. Initially, simpler parts of the program were reduced into primes using direct cognition. Small looping structures were simplified by the identification of loop invariants. At a higher level, these small program primes were organised into functional segments, the operation of which was determined by further analysis. This process was performed a number of times, obtaining a higher level understanding of the program at each stage until a full specification was achieved.

7.8 Conclusions

This chapter has presented a number of key theories developed for program comprehension. These theories vary to different degrees, yet all maintain a high level commonality or structure in the cognitive model. This commonality can be summarised in that all theories subscribe to the idea of the cognitive model being composed of a knowledge base, a mental model and an assimilation process. The interpretation and composition of each of these components is the subject of the various theories.

It is well known that program comprehension plays a major part in the majority of software engineering activities, particularly in software maintenance. The level of program comprehension required can vary greatly depending on the task and the complexity, quality and size of the target system. Similarly, program comprehension is not limited solely to extracting information from the source code. Any form of system documentation or previous maintenance records are used as an integral part. However, more often than not, this documentation will be inaccurate, inconsistent, incomplete or even non-existent. This leaves the maintainer with the complex task of attempting to recover not only the operation and structure of the software system, but many design issues and implicit assumptions made during its implementation. Clearly, this is not an easy task at all. Program comprehension research is thus vital to discover methods or tools which could aid maintainers to recover the intentions behind the code.

7.9 Current Theories and Tool Support

What features should an ideal tool possess in order to support program comprehension? Program comprehension tools play a supporting role in other software engineering activities of design, development, maintenance, and redocumentation. As discussed in the previous section of this chapter, there are many characteristics which influence the cognitive strategies the programmers use and, in turn, influence the requirements for tool support.

7.10 Cognitive Models and Tool Implications

Documentation: Brooks suggests that documentation should be designed to support top-down comprehension strategies (Brooks, 1983). He advocates that it is as important to document the problem domain as it is to document programming concepts. Also, he stresses the importance of explicitly documenting domain knowledge to improve comprehension (Clayton *et al.*, 1998). Brooks suggests that different styles of languages require different styles of documentation. Observations made from work carried out by Laitenberger *et al.* research corroborate that different people read the documentation from different points of view and how they read the documentation will depend on their comprehension goal (Laitenberger, 1995). Prechelt *et al.* (2002) report that from their experiments redundant design pattern documentation i.e., program level documentation, definitely improves the maintenance tasks. The additional documentation results in faster task completion times and fewer errors.

Browsing and navigation support: The top-down process requires browsing from high level abstractions or concepts to lower level details, taking advantage of beacons (Brooks, 1983) in the code. Flexible browsing support also helps to offset the challenges from delocalized plans. Bottom-up comprehension requires following control-flow and data-flow links as well as cross-referencing navigation between elements in the program and situation models defined by Pennington. The Integrated Metamodel suggests that the frequent switching between top-down and bottom-up browsing should be supported (von Mayrhauser, 1993). Since both experts and novices switch between top-down and bottom-up strategies (Burkhardt, 1998), they may both benefit from the tools that support breadth-first and depth-first browsing.

Searching and querying: Tool support may be beneficial for the searching of code snippets by analogy and for iterative searching. Inquiry episodes (Letovsky, 1986a) should be supported by allowing the programmer to query on the role of a variable, function, etc. A program slice is a subcomponent of the program that may potentially impact the value of some variables at another part of the program (Tip, 1995). Weiser conducted empirical research that demonstrated that programmers use slices during debugging (Weiser, 1982). Francel *et al.* (1999) also determined that slicing techniques can be useful during debugging to help the programmers find the location of a program fault. This research suggests that comprehension tools should therefore have query support for program slices, especially for tools that support debugging.

Multiple views: Due to the diversity of comprehension strategies and the variability of questions, programmers need to answer during comprehension, programming environments need to provide different ways of representing programs. One view could show a textual representation of the code in the program, an additional view may show the message call graph providing an insight into the programming plans, while a third view could show a representation of the classes and relationships between them to show an object-centric or data-centric view of the program. These orthogonal views, if easily accessible, should facilitate comprehension, especially if effectively combined and cross-referenced. Petre *et al.* discuss some of the challenges faced when using and bridging between multiple views (Petre, 1998).

Context-driven views: The size of the program and other program metrics influence which view is the preferred one to show how to support a programmer's task. For example, to support the browsing of an unfamiliar object-oriented program, it is usually preferable to show the inheritance hierarchy as the initial view. However, if the inheritance hierarchy is flat, it may be more appropriate to show a call graph as the default view.

Cognitive support: Experts need external devices and scratchpads to support their cognitive tasks, whereas novices need pedagogical support to help them access information about the programming language and the corresponding domain. Robbins' (1996) research indicates the importance of having tool support to manage "to do" activities during design. More cognitive support could also benefit comprehension for sequential tasks such as code inspections and debugging.

7.11 Tool Requirements Explicitly Identified

Several researchers studied expert programmers in industrial settings and consequently recommended specific requirements for improving tools to support comprehension. Others built on their own personal or colleagues' experiences to recommend needed tool features. These efforts and the requirements they determined are summarized here.

Concept assignment problem: Biggerstaff notes that one of the main difficulties in understanding comes from mapping what is in the code to the software requirements – he terms this the concept assignment problem (Biggerstaff, 1983). Although automated techniques can help locate programming concepts and features, it is challenging to automatically detect human-oriented or domain-based concepts. The user may need to indicate a starting point and then use program slicing techniques to find related code. It may also be possible for an intelligent agent (that has domain knowledge) to scan the code and search for candidate starting points. From experimenting with research prototypes, Biggerstaff found that queries, slicing, graphical views and hypertext were important tool features.

Reverse engineering tool needs: von Mayrhauser and Vans (1993), from their research on the Integrated Metamodel, make an explicit recommendation for tool support for reverse engineering. They determined basic information needs according to cognitive tasks and suggested the following tool capabilities to meet those needs:

Top-down model: On-line documents with keyword search across documents; pruned call trees; difference tools; history of browsed locations; entity fan-in.

Situation model: A view showing a list of domain sources including non-code related sources; a view displaying a visual representation of major domain functions.

Program model: Pop-up declarations as well as on-line cross-reference reports and function count. In addition Wong discusses reverse engineering tool features (Wong, 2000). He specifically mentions the benefits of using a "notebook" to support the continuous comprehension processes.

Importance of search and history: Singer *et al.* (1997) also observed the work practices of software engineers. They explored the activities of a single engineer, as well as a group of engineers, and considered company-wide tool use statistics. Their study led to the requirements for a tool that was implemented and successfully adopted by the company. Specifically, they suggested tool features to support "just-in-time comprehension of source code". They noted that engineers, after working on a specific part of the program, quickly forget details when they move to a new location. This forces them to rediscover information at a later time. They suggest that tools need the following features to support rediscovery:

- search capabilities so that the user can search for code artifacts by name or by pattern matching;
- the capabilities to display all relevant attributes of the items retrieved as well as the relationships among items;
- features to keep track of searches and problem-solving sessions to support the navigation of a persistent history.

Information needs for maintainers: Erdos and Sneed designed a tool to support maintenance following many years of experience in the maintenance and reengineering industry. They proposed that a programmer maintaining an unfamiliar program will need to answer the following seven questions (Erdos, 1998):

1. Where exactly is a particular subroutine/procedure invoked?
2. What are the actual arguments and results of a function?
3. How does control flow exactly reach a particular location?
4. Where is a particular variable set, implemented or queried?
5. Where exactly is a particular variable declared?
6. Where exactly is a particular data object accessed?
7. What exactly are the inputs and outputs of a module?

Software visualization tool needs: In (Storey *et al.*, 1999) he presented a cognitive framework of design elements for improving software exploration tools. The framework provides an overview of the various tool features which could provide cognitive support for the various comprehension models such as the top-down, bottom-up and knowledge-based approaches. The emphasis was on tool support for browsing static software structures and architectures.

Pacione *et al.* (2004) provide a more extensive software visualization model to support program comprehension. Although their model was specifically designed to evaluate software visualization tools, it is also usable as a mechanism for evaluating more general purpose program comprehension tool requirements. Their research gives a detailed list of both specific and general comprehension tasks. General tasks include determining how the high-level components of a system interact and determining how interactions occur between objects. More specific tasks include asking how the problem domain functionality is implemented in the software systems. Pacione further maps these tasks to specific activities and determines how the information needs of these activities can be met through static and dynamic software visualizations.

7.12 Discussion

The methods for determining program comprehension tool requirements – that is determining which new features should be added or which features should be replaced or improved in a program comprehension environment – is not trivial. On the one hand, the empirical approach results in the construction of theories about program comprehension strategies and proposed tools. Despite criticism, these predominantly formal experiments nevertheless have contributed to the wide body of knowledge we now have about comprehension theories and tool requirements. Moreover, some researchers, such as von Mayrhauser and Vans (1993) and Singer *et al.* (1997) have conducted more qualitative experiments using professional programmers on industrially-relevant programs. Techniques such as the analysis of think-aloud protocols (Letovsky, 1986a) and contextual inquiry (Beyer, 1997) proved useful in many of these ecologically valid experiments.

In contrast with the empirical approach, some researchers and tool designers may rely on practical experience and intuition to propose what is needed in a comprehension tool. Given the variability in comprehension settings, all these approaches contribute to the required body of knowledge.

7.12.1 Tool Research

The field of program comprehension research has resulted in many diverse tools to assist in program comprehension. Program understanding tool features can be roughly divided into three categories: extraction, analysis and presentation (Tilley, 1996).

The extraction tools include parsers and data gathering tools to collect both static and dynamic data. Static data can be obtained by extracting facts from the existing source code. A fact extractor should be able to determine what artifacts the program defines, uses, imports and exports, as well as the relationships between those artifacts. The technologies underlying fact extractors are based on techniques from compiler construction (Aho, 2000). For example, modern fact extractors include CAN, a fast C/C++ extractor, from the Columbus reverse engineering tool (Ferenc, 2004) and CPPX (Dean, 2001). Moonen *et al.* (2001) discuss the benefits of island grammars for generating parsers that can handle incomplete source code and different language dialects. Dynamic data is obtained by examining and extracting data from the run-time behaviour of the program. Such data can be extracted through a wide variety of trace exploration tools and techniques (Hamou-Lhadj, 2004).

Analysis tools support activities such as clustering, concept assignment, feature identification (Eisenbarth, 2003), transformations, domain analysis, slicing and metrics calculations. There are numerous software clustering techniques that can be used during reverse engineering to identify software components (Koschke, 2000). Frank Tip provides a survey of program slicing techniques (Tip, 1995) and Mathias *et al.* (1999) discuss the role of various software metrics on program comprehension.

Dynamic analysis usually involves the comprehensive instrumentation of the existing source code. With a dynamic analysis, only a subset of the program code may be relevant but dynamic traces can be very large, posing significant challenges during the analysis of the data. Systä *et al.* (2001) describe how static analysis can be used to prune the amount of information looked at during the dynamic analysis.

Presentation tools include code editors, hypertext viewers, visualizations, and browsers. Integrated software development and reverse engineering environments usually have some features from each category. The set of features they support is usually determined by the purpose for the resulting tool or by the focus of the research.

It is possible to examine a selection of these environments and to recover the motivation for the features they provide by tracing back to the tool and to the cognitive theories. For example, the well-known Rigi system (Muller, 1988) has support for multiple views, cross-referencing and queries to support bottom-up comprehension. The Reflexion tool (Murphy, 1995) has support for the top-down approach through hypothesis generation and verification. The Bauhaus tool (Eisenbarth, 2001) has features to support clustering (identification of components), slicing and concept analysis. The SHriMP tool (Storey, 2003) provides navigation support for the Integrated Metamodel, i.e., the frequent switching between strategies in use. And the Codecrawler tool (Lanza, 2001) uses the visualization of metrics to support an understanding of an unfamiliar system and to identify bottlenecks and other architectural features.

7.12.2 Methods for Evaluating Comprehension Tools

Evaluating program comprehension tools can be a formidable task for a researcher. In many cases the comprehension tools are evaluated by researchers using case studies. There have been some usability experiments conducted to evaluate program comprehension tools (Storey *et al.*, 2000). Bellay and Gall conducted a comparative evaluation of five reverse engineering tools using a case study and an evaluation framework (Bellay, 1998).

Tools which fall into the extraction and analysis categories are inherently easier to evaluate if there are well-established benchmarks and associated criteria (Sim, 2003). However, for many of the tools that present information to the user and offer cognitive support, it is not always that easy to determine what to measure and when to take such measurements.

The comprehension theories can definitely play a key role in the evaluation of these environments. They can be used as a first step in performing a heuristic evaluation of the environment and in describing what the environment does and does not do. Secondly, they can be used to help guide evaluations and to assist in presenting results.

7.12.3 Programmer and Program Trends

Any research paper or talk that attempts to predict the future always discusses how risky and difficult such an endeavour is. Fortunately, it is less risky to closely examine current trends and predict what will occur in the very near future. Tilley and Smith (1996) wrote a thought-provoking paper entitled "Coming Attractions in Program Understanding".

7.12.4 Programmer Characteristics

More diversified programmers: The need to use computers and software intersects every walk of life. Programming, and hence program comprehension, are no longer a niche activity. Scientists and knowledge workers in many walks of life have to use and customize software to help them do scientific or other work. Today, scientists are using and developing sophisticated software through web services and other mechanisms despite the fact that they lack a formal education in computer science. Consequently, there is a need for techniques to assist in non-expert and end-user program comprehension. Fortunately, there is much work in this in which they investigate how comprehension can be improved through tool support for spreadsheet and other end-user applications.

Sophisticated users: Currently, advanced visual interfaces are not often used in development environments. A large concern by many tool designers is that these advanced visual interfaces require complex user interactions. However, tomorrow's programmers will be more familiar with game software and other media that displays information rapidly and requires sophisticated user controls. Looking at today's industry trends, many programmers are using larger screens and multiple monitors to help with programming and other complex tasks.

Consequently, the next generation of users will have more skill at interpreting information presented visually and at manipulating and learning how to use complex controls on larger displays and on multiple monitors. Grudin (2001) discusses some of the implications for multiple monitor use for programmers as well as other classes of users. Modern developers are also more likely to have had much exposure to social software such as blogging, wikis and social bookmarking (Hammond, 2005). Such features are expected to be the next generation of development environments.

Globally distributed teams: Advances in communication technologies have enabled globally distributed collaborations in software development. Distributed open source development is having a significant impact on industry. The most notable examples are Linux and Eclipse. Some research has been conducted on studying collaborative processes in open source projects (Mockus, 2002; Gutwin, 2004; German, 2006), but more research is needed to study how distributed collaborations impact comprehension.

7.12.5 Agile Developers

Agile development which incorporates techniques such as test driven development and pair programming has an impact on how programs are comprehended within an organization. To date there have been few studies to investigate how these practices improve or possibly hinder how programmers comprehend programs.

7.12.6 Program Characteristics

Distributed applications and web-based applications are becoming more prevalent with technologies such as .NET, J2EE and web services. One programming challenge that is occurring now and is likely to increase is the combination of different paradigms in distributed applications e.g., when a client side script sends XML to a server application. Service-oriented architectures are also becoming popular and may require different comprehension tool support.

7.12.7 Higher Levels of Abstraction

Visual composition languages for business applications are also on the increase. As the level of abstraction increases, comprehension challenges are shifting from the understanding of source code in a single program to more abstract concepts such as the understanding of the services provided by and the interfaces of components in libraries and how to make use of software frameworks.

7.12.8 Dynamically Configured Systems

The prevalence of model driven development and autonomic systems are leading to complex systems that are dynamically configured at run-time. Such systems will pose significant comprehension challenges in the future. Pluggable frameworks such as Eclipse are also posing development challenges as it is difficult to understand and manage the dependencies resulting from the different versions of many plugins. More advanced tool support for such environments will be required as these technologies mature.

7.12.9 Aspect-oriented Programming

The introduction of aspects as a construct to manage scattered concerns (delocalized plans) in a program has created much excitement in the software engineering community. Aspects have been shown to be effective for managing many programming concerns, such as logging and security. However, it is not clear how aspects written by others will improve program understanding, especially in the long-term. The focus of the work currently is on developing techniques and tools to support aspect-oriented programming and on how to identify aspects in legacy code for future refactorings (Hannemann, 2001; Tonella, 2004). More empirical work is needed to validate and demonstrate the assumed benefits of aspect-oriented programming for the long-term comprehension of software programs.

Improved and newer software engineering practices: The more informed processes that are used for developing software today will hopefully lead to software that is easier to comprehend in the future. Component-based software systems are designed using familiar design patterns, and other conventions. Future software may have traceability links to requirements, and improved documentation such as formal program specifications. Test driven development methods may also lead to code that is easier to comprehend due to the implicit requirements captured by test cases.

Diverse sources of information: The program comprehension community, until quite recently, mostly focused on static and dynamic analysis of source code in conjunction with documentation could facilitate program comprehension. Modern software integrated development environments, such as the Eclipse Java development environment, also manage other kinds of information such as bug tracking, test cases and version control. This information, combined with human activity information such as emails and instant messages, will be more readily available to support the analysis of program comprehension. Domain information should also be more accessible due to the model driven development and the semantic web.

7.13 Future Methods, Theories and Tools

7.13.1 Theories

As the programming workforce and technology change, learning theories (Exton, 2002) will become more relevant to end-users doing programming-like tasks. Theories are currently being developed to describe the social and organizational aspects of program comprehension (Gutwin, 2004).

The impact of open source processes and agile methods have yet to be fully understood. Richer's cognitive theories about how aspect-oriented programming will impact comprehension in the longer term need to be further developed. More theories about the collaborative nature of program comprehension, both co-located and distributed, are needed.

It is becoming clear to many in this research area that developing theories on program comprehension is an ambitious undertaking. This is mostly due to the large variability in the possible conditions for any experiment. It is important as a community to have many data points; this will enable future researchers to do a meta-analysis of results from several experiments so that common trends and issues can be extracted. This phenomenon can be compared to efforts in the clinical trial community in which many studies have to be done to understand how a drug interacts with other drugs, different kinds of individuals and environmental conditions.

In our research community, we need to document and present results in such a way that others can make sense of our data and conclusions. Researchers evaluating presentation tools and user interfaces for program comprehension tools could benefit from the work of Walenstein and Green *et al.* Walenstein proposes a methodology for evaluating cognitive support (Walenstein, 2003) and Green's Cognitive Dimensions provides a language and framework that can be used for evaluating presentation tools (Green, 1996). More work is needed to understand how we can combine results and benefit from collaborative efforts in empirical work.

Faster Tool Innovations: The use of frameworks as an underlying technology for software tools is leading to faster tool innovations as less time needs to be spent on reinventing the wheel. A prime example of how frameworks can improve tool development is the Eclipse framework (see www.eclipse.org). Eclipse was specifically designed with the goal of creating reusable components which would be shared across different tools. The research community benefits from this approach in several ways. Firstly, they are able to spend more time on writing new and innovative features as they can reuse the core underlying features offered by Eclipse and its plugins; and secondly, researchers can evaluate their prototypes in more ecologically valid ways as they can compare their new features against existing industrial tools.

Plug 'n play tools: We have previously described about understanding tools according to three categories: extraction, analysis and presentation. Given a suite of tools that all plug in to the same framework, together with a standard exchange format (such as GXL – http://www.gupro.de/GXL/), researchers will be able to try easily different combinations of tools to meet their research needs. This should result in increased collaborations and more relevant research results. Such integrations will also lead to improved accessibility to repositories of information related to the software, including code, documentation, analysis results, domain information and human activity information. Integrated tools will also lead to fewer disruptions for programmers.

Recommenders and search: Software engineering tools, especially those developed in research, are increasingly leveraging advances in intelligent user interfaces (e.g., tools with some domain or user knowledge). Recommender systems are being proposed to guide navigation in software spaces. Examples of such systems include Mylar (Kersten, 2005) and NavTracks (Singer, 2005). Mylar uses a degree of interest model to filter non-relevant files from the file explorer and other views in Eclipse. NavTracks provides recommendations of which files are related to the currently selected files. Deline *et al.* (2005) also discuss a system to improve navigation. The FEAT tool suggests using concern graphs (explicitly created by the programmer) to improve navigation efficiency and enhance comprehension (Robillard, 2003). This work can be further inspired by research from the HCI (Human Computer Interactionz) community on tracking interaction histories to inform navigation (Chalmers, 1998; Wexelblat, 1998, 1999).

7.14 Tools

Search technologies, such as Google, show much promise at improving the search for relevant components, code snippets and related code. The Hipikat tool (Cubranic, 2006) recommends relevant software artifacts based on the developer's current project context and the development history. The Prospector system recommends the use of relevant code snippets (Mandelin, 2005). It combines a search engine with the content assist in Eclipse to help programmers use complex APIs. Zimmerman developed the eRose tool which generates recommendations on which files should be changed together (Zimmerman, 2004). eRose uses CVS data to find files that have frequently been changed together. Holmes and Murphy (2005) propose using structures to create code recommendations during evolution tasks.

Although this work in search and recommendations is relatively new, it shows much promise and it is expected to improve navigation in large systems while reducing the barriers in reusing components from large libraries.

Adaptive interfaces: Software tools typically have many features which may be overwhelming not only for novice users, but also for expert users. This information overload could be reduced through the use of adaptive interfaces. The idea is that the user interface can be tailored automatically i.e., will self-adapt, to meet the different kinds of users and tasks at hand. Adaptive user interfaces are now common in Windows applications such as Word. Eclipse has several novice views (such as Gild (Storey, 2003) and Penumbra (Mueller, 2003)) and Visual Studio has the Express configuration for new users. However, neither of these mainstream tools currently has the ability to adapt or even manually be adapted to the continuum of novice to expert users.

Visualizations have been, undoubtedly, the subject of much research over the past ten to twenty years. Many visualizations, and in particular graph-based visualizations, have been proposed to support comprehension tasks. Some examples of research tools include Seesoft (Ball, 1996), Bloom (Reiss, 2001), Rigi (Wong, 1995), Landscape views (Penny, 1992), sv3D (Marcus, 2003), and Codecrawler (Lanza, 2001). Graph visualization is used in many advanced commercial tools such as Klocwork, Imagix4D and Together. UML diagrams are also common in mainstream development tools.

Challenges with visualizing software include the large amount of items that can be displayed, knowing at what level of abstraction details should be shown, as well as selecting which view to show. More details about the user's task combined with metrics describing the program's characteristics (such as the inheritance depth) will improve how visualizations are currently presented to the user. A recommender system could suggest relevant views as a starting point. Bull proposes the notion of using a model driven visualization (Bull, 2005). He suggests creating a mechanism for tool designers and expert users that recommends useful views based on characteristics of the model and data.

Collaborative support: As software teams increase in size and become more distributed, collaborative tools to support distributed software development activities become more crucial. In research, there are several collaborative software engineering tools being developed such as Jazz and Augur (Hupfer, 2004; Froehlich, 2004). A review of how these and other tools determine human activities to improve comprehension through visualization is given in (Storey *et al.*, 2005). There are also some collaborative software engineering tools deployed in industry, such as CollabNet, but they tend to have simple tool features to support communication and collaboration, such as version control, email and instant messaging. Current industrial tools lack more advanced collaboration features such as shared editors and awareness visualizations.

Although collaborative tools for software engineering have been a research topic for several years, there has been a lack of adoption of many of the approaches such as shared editors in industry and a lack of empirical work on the benefits of these tools. Another area for research that may prove useful is the use of large screen displays to support collocated comprehension. O'Reilly *et al.* (2005) propose a war room command console to share visualizations for team coordination. There are other research ideas in the CSCW (computer supported collaborative work) field that could be applied to program comprehension.

Domain and pedagogical support: The need to support domain experts who lack formal computer science training will necessarily result in more domain-specific languages and tools. Non-experts will also need more cognitive scaffolding to help them learn new tools and domain-specific languages more rapidly. Tools to support the maintenance of programs written in domain specific languages will also be required. Pedagogical support, such as providing examples by analogy, will likely be an integral part of future software tools. The work discussed above on recommending code examples is also suggested at helping novices and software immigrants (i.e. new programmers to a project). Results from the empirical work also suggest that there is a need for tools to help programmers learn a new language. Technologies such as TXL (Cordy, 2002) can play a role in helping a user see examples of how code constructs in one language would appear in another language.

Large screen and multiple displays: Modern tools should be designed to take advantage of the now ubiquitous use of multiple monitors and large screens. Little is understood about how these multiple monitors impact comprehension and how tool support could be improved to match such display configurations. Larger screens could also improve pair programming and the comprehension strategies used during agile development.

7.15 Discussion: Back to the Future

It is an interesting exercise to travel back and look at Tilley and Smith's research work from 1996 on "Coming Attractions in Program Understanding" (Tilley, 1996). Some of the predictions they made then for technologies which would be available within five years were correct. They suggested that mature technologies would be leveraged, which is now the case with mature off-the-shelf technologies such as Windows components and the Eclipse framework. They also predicted that web interfaces and hypertext would play a pivotal role. Many modern tools today use web interfaces for navigating software resources. Tailorable user interfaces are now common, as are more advanced pattern matching facilities.

Some of their predictions, however, have not been fully realized and indeed overlap the predictions in this chapter. These include:

- computer support for collaborative understanding;
- access to alternative sources of data through natural language processing;
- data filters to allow the programmer to focus on relevant information;
- conceptual and domain modeling techniques;
- the use of intelligent agents in a "maintainer's handbook";
- more advanced visual interfaces.

Keywords

adaptive; perfective; corrective; preventative; comprehension task; comprehension activity; comprehension process; comprehension strategy; maintainer; cognitive model; cognitive support; mental model; mental representation; delocalized plans; coding standards; algorithm implementations; knowledge base; mental model; assimilation process; task-specific knowledge; business rules; control systems; database systems; software structure; opportunistic processors; bottom-up; top-down; semantic constructs; semantic abstractions; syntactic abstractions; slot types; slot fillers; code presentation; naming standards; systematic strategy; needed strategy; chunking process; situation model; causal knowledge; static knowledge; breadth-first; depth-first; reuse task; textual representation; software immigrants

Exercises

1. Define the term program comprehension.
2. Discuss the theories of program comprehension.
3. What methods are available for use in evaluating comprehension tools?
4. What are sophisticated users?
5. Explain the relationship between the knowledge base model and the mental model.
6. What are Letovsky's three main types of conjectures?
7. What are the differences between assimilation and knowledge acquisition?
8. Elaborate on top-down comprehension.
9. Highlight the impact of program characteristics on program comprehension.
10. Explain in detail about Brooks cognition model.

CHAPTER 8

Legacy Systems

Objectives

The objective of this chapter is to introduce the student to legacy systems. We look at how they come into existence, their impact and how they prevent them from causing system failure. When you have read this chapter you will be able to:

- Understand what legacy systems are
- Understand the importance of studying legacy systems
- Understand the legacy system life cycle
- Understand how legacy systems can be assessed

8.0 Legacy Systems

8.0.1 Background

A legacy system is a system approaching the end of its useful life. It is in danger of preventing a group from maintaining its operational objective. Legacy systems may be "massive, long-term business investment[s]", crucial to an organization (Bisbal *et al.*, 1999). They must adapt to the shifting business and technological requirements of an organization to remain operationally ready (Madisetti *et al.*, 2000). For example, if new government legislation mandates that all cars must run on electricity by 2015, the useful life of an automobile may be cut short as this date approaches. Because the car satisfies critical transportation needs, for instance, servicing the commute for a job 40 miles away, an additional investment may be required to deal with the impending obsolescence of the car. Some of the options are buying a new car, converting the current car so that it runs on electricity, or utilizing public transportation. The driver must find a way to address the changing government requirements.

Preventing a legacy system from failing or not performing as desired is a challenging task, being delegated to more decision makers as systems age (Alderson and Shah, 1999). Because these systems affect company revenue streams and fulfill critical needs, their obsolescence cannot be ignored without negatively impacting other organizational functions (Brooke and Ramage, 2001). Researching the various methods utilized for prolonging life and how they can be applied to systems with particular problems will help system engineers and decision makers decide best how to approach system obsolescence and keep systems functioning for years more.

Legacy systems are also important to study because they are often directly linked to a corporation's core competency, performing key tasks which the organization cannot do without. A pizza parlor may be using an authentic wood-burning oven to bake the pizza crust. If the oven should break or require service, the bakery will be unable to make pizza crusts, curtailing their profit. If the oven gives trouble when the pizza parlor first opens for business, the base of customers who are used to the "authentic" taste of the pizza crust would be small and the repair or replacement of the oven would go unnoticed. However, as time passes, it becomes more difficult to halt active systems for service without affecting the business adversely and interrupting the organizations' functioning. The organization becomes more dependent on the legacy system as its importance to business functions grows, increasing the risks of interrupting the system for maintenance and service along with the risk of what will happen if legacy system issues are not addressed properly (Adolph, 1996). Back to the pizza parlor example, if a new oven is bought after the pizza parlor has built up a solid customer base, it may be unable to successfully duplicate the taste and texture of the authentic oven. Customers may not come back as the pizza does not have the authentic taste they have grown accustomed to.

It is important to study the life extension of legacy systems because as a system ages it becomes host to all types of problems. Budgetary constraints and functionary requirements for the system may rise, while the reliability of third party vendors and suppliers decreases (Adolph, 1996). New regulatory changes made by outside organizations may need to be applied to the system (Reinerstein, 1996). Also, vendors may no longer supply the materials or parts needed to repair or maintain elements of the system (Solomon, 2000). Systems dealing with impending obsolescence must find a way to remain responsive and continue to provide valuable products and services to their users (Sage, 1999).

Many companies try to postpone the decline of their systems into legacy territory by concentrating on maintenance and support of the system. Maintenance is part of every system's life cycle and many organizations assume that regular, scheduled maintenance is enough to keep a system going (Bisbal, 1999). However, the techniques used to maintain a system have many concerns that drive the search for reliable, efficient life extension techniques. Continued maintenance and support may not be robust enough to add functionality or incorporate new methodologies successfully. Constant modification and maintenance is thought to contribute to the degradation of the system (Bennett *et al.*, 1999). As Adolph points out, "constant patching makes the system's reliability questionable" (1996). For instance, a car with a flat tyre may have the tyre repaired once so that it is safe to drive on. A car that is being driven with a tyre that has been patched for a second time may not be as reliable.

It also becomes increasingly difficult to find employees with the skills to maintain legacy systems as the system or the employees' age advances (Adolph, 1996). One reason may be the skills required to maintain the system are no longer taught or passed on, reducing the dwindling pool of people who do have the knowledge needed to perform what may or may not be highly specialized procedures. Also, those that do know what was needed to upkeep a system may have retired or moved around in the organization so that there is no one immediately available who can service the system (Adolph, 1996; Mahaffey *et al.*, 2000). The employees who are left and have the skills needed to work on an "older" system may be reluctant to volunteer for the job. Maintenance is often seen as a less desirable job function because people associate job advancement with staying abreast of new skills (Ahrens *et al.*, 1995). Development tasks, associated with learning the latest and greatest information about a system, tend to be rewarded more than maintenance careers, which few employees aspire to (Ahrens *et al.*, 1995). The difficulty associated with finding someone to maintain a system has been a contributing factor in the search to define what other types of life extension techniques can be used for a particular legacy system.

Another issue influencing the study of legacy systems is the costs associated with the life cycle extension of systems. When determining if a system is becoming burdensome to an organization, "the total cost of a system over its intended life cycle" must be taken into account (Blanchard and Fabrycky, 1981). The maintenance and support of a legacy system can consume an enormous amount of its life cycle budget, particularly towards the end of the life cycle when the system is under increasing pressure to keep up with new technologies, upgrades, and replacement of components. As you can observe in Figure 8.1, many systems incur substantial changes in cost during two key phases of their life cycle; the first key phase is when the system is starting up and

Figure 8.1 Estimate costs incurred during lifecycle of a system (Dilts, 2004)

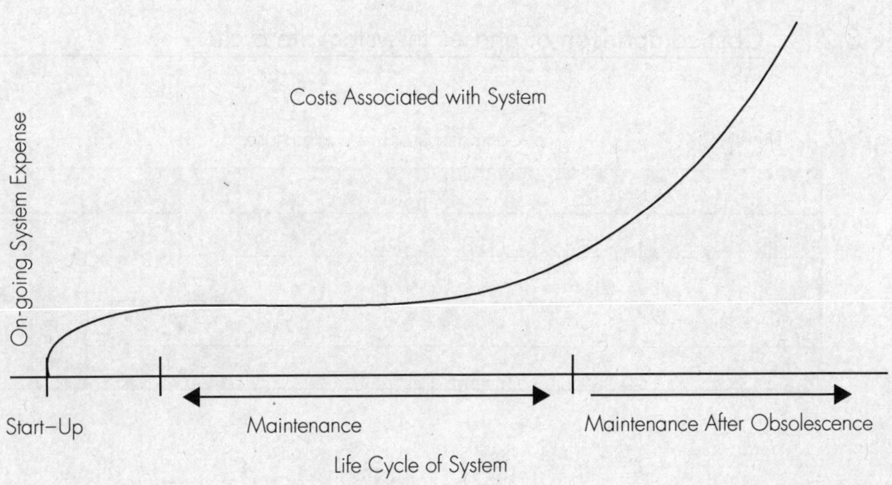

nearing its implementation and the second key phase is towards the end of the system's life (Dilts, 2004). The high cost during the start-up/implementation phase can be attributed to the gathering of materials, testing of the system, and actual implementation costs associated with getting the product up and running. The high costs incurred as the system nears the end of its life are often attributed to the increased maintenance required to keep the system functioning and performing its needed tasks (Dilts, 2004).

Although some legacy systems do not have their maintenance cost as the determining factor of their legacy status and take into account other issues such as physical degradation and age; recent estimates have concluded most companies spend from 70% to 75% of a system's total life cycle cost on support measures designed to keep the system operational (CSTB Report cited in Ahrens *et al.*, 1995). Extending the life of a system may help to curb these support measures and reduce the money spent on the system towards the end if its life as components are upgraded and repaired for further use.

As Figures 8.1 and 8.2 show, one effective way to reduce the life cycle cost is to reduce the maintenance cost of the system. Figure 8.2 shows the relative cost of maintenance compared to other phases of the life cycle using a bar graph. Figure 8.1 shows that the cost of maintaining a system is much greater than any of the costs associated with the development, design, implementation, and testing phases of a system's life cycle. Maintenance costs are rising so much that the percentage of Fortune 1000 companies information systems' budgets dedicated to maintenance has gone "from 40% in the early 1970's to 90% in the early 1990's" (Index Group Survey, 1990 cited in Ahrens *et al.*, 1995). The cost of ensuring that a system does not interfere with the organizations' revenue stream and remains operational is a substantial amount of the total life cycle cost, both financially and time wise (Bennett *et al.*, 1999). Organizations are very interested in other techniques that could be used to treat legacy systems and decrease the maintenance costs associated with keeping them going. "Management must be convinced that the organization is really going to achieve a significant benefit in reduced cost" to utilize a particular life extension method over another (Sneed, 1995). The model hopes to identify those particular methods that may reduce maintenance costs for an organization.

Figure 8.2 Cost comparison of phases in system life cycle

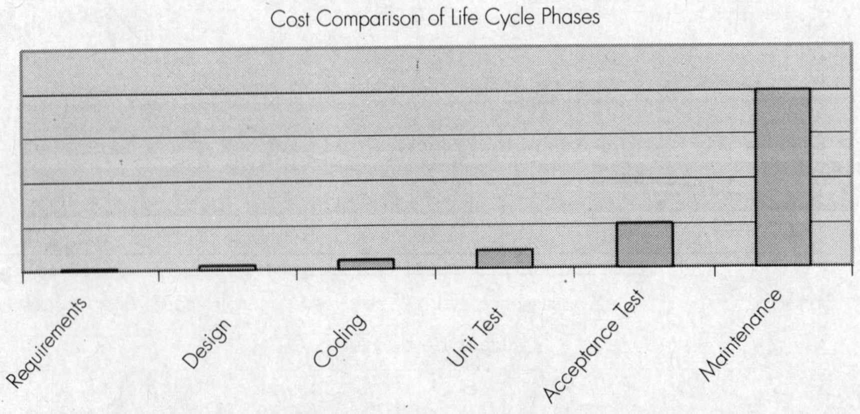

8.1 Legacy System Life Cycle

A system can become a legacy system while in any of the different life cycle phases, including introduction, growth, maturity, decline, phase-out, and obsolescence (Figure 8.3). The introduction stage signifies the beginning of the life cycle and is marked by high production and design costs, low usage, and frequent modifications to the system (Solomon *et al.*, 2000). The 21 Hummer SUV for example was very expensive and designed for military use only during this stage of its life, undergoing frequent modifications to fulfill mission needs. A system could also be classified as a legacy system at this stage if it has a long design time and has not yet been introduced, meaning new requirements of functionality delay its introduction (Madisetti *et al.*, 2000).

Next is the growth stage, which takes place when the product has been accepted into the mainstream market. It is now that the usage increases and the cost of keeping up the system declines (Solomon *et al.*, 2000). The Hummer is at this stage, as it is being sold through commercial automobile dealers and the price and functional requirements have been reduced to fit mainstream needs. The maturity stage lasts for the longest amount of time, as shown on the life cycle curve below. It signifies that the product has sustained heavy use and is probably being offered at its lowest cost (Solomon *et al.*, 2000). Some automobiles make this stage as the ubiquitous Honda Civic has, and some have not, as classic Corvette owners could attest to.

The decline stage is marked by increased maintenance and part replacement, a sure sign of impending obsolescence (Solomon *et al.*, 2000). Many owners of older vehicles find themselves with an automobile at this stage as they try to preserve its functionality. If no method is chosen to address obsolete components and surging maintenance responsibilities, the system will enter the phase-out stage followed by the obsolescence phase. The phase-out stage describes a system that may not be used as much as it has previously been because it requires frequent maintenance and faces declining support by manufacturers and third party vendors (Solomon *et al.*, 2000). The obsolescence stage signals the system is no longer receiving manufacturer's support and the

Figure 8.3 Life cycle of a system (Solomon *et al.*, 2000)

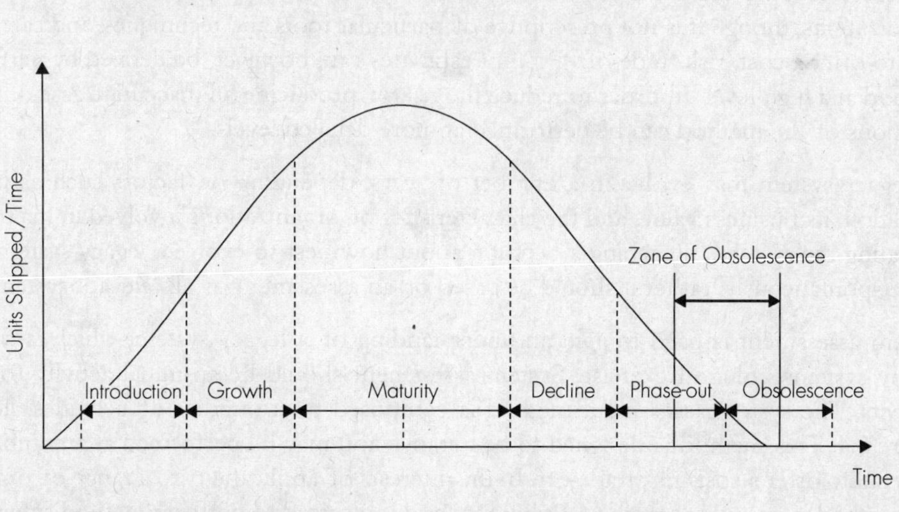

technology responsible for the system is no longer being implemented in the same form and fashion (Solomon *et al.*, 2000). A model-T Ford, the first mass produced car, would now be in the obsolete stage as cars have made great strides in technology and no longer use the same technology as the model-T. Once the system reaches the obsolescence stage, a final decision must be made to extend its life or ignore it.

Solomon's model incorrectly assumes a system can only approach obsolescence during the phase-out and obsolescence stage of the life cycle. Legacy systems can be deemed obsolete before they enter these final stages due to the long design and testing phases associated with their complexity (Madisetti *et al.*, 2000). Advances in technology or changes in materials can spur a system's march to obsolescence during any phase of the life cycle. Life extension methods can be performed concurrently with any phase of system development to ward off a speedy demise towards obsolescence (Solomon *et al.*, 2000). The life extension model developed by researchers examines actions taken to keep the system performing at the levels needed to be viable to the organization during any phase of the life cycle.

The previous sections have defined what a legacy system is and explained the characteristics associated with the system. The life cycle of a system has also been defined along with the various phases a system can pass through during its life cycle. The idea that a system can approach obsolescence and become a legacy system during any phase of the life cycle has also been presented, challenging conventional thought that system designers must only begin to treat aging systems when they near the end of their life cycle (Madisetti *et al.*, 2000).

8.2 Legacy System Assessment

Determining whether legacy systems are worth keeping requires an overall assessment of the system. There is an assessment method that examines a legacy system from its technical, business and organizational perspectives. Assessment characteristics can be selected and values assigned to them by users through assessment of these perspectives. By interpreting the results obtained from the assessment we can use a method to tailor to the needs of particular evolution projects and organizations, though it is not prescriptive of particular tools and techniques, and can be instantiated to offer a cost/risk trade-off. Prompt estimates can, however, be derived by performing the method at a high level. In order to reduce the risk of producing an inaccurate assessment further iterations of the method can be performed at more detailed levels.

"A legacy system may evolve in a number of ways, depending on factors such as its technical condition, its business value, and the characteristics of organizations involved in maintaining and operating the system." Reaching a decision about how best to evolve a legacy system cannot be made spontaneously; rather it should be based on an assessment of all relevant system attributes.

System assessment is used to gain an understanding of a legacy system, which is fundamental to any system evolution exercise. System assessment should be an initial activity for evolution projects. The system assessment method is composed of a number of activities, illustrated in Figure 8.4. This method is designed to be iterative and may be performed at a number of levels of detail to offer a cost/risk trade-off. In the interests of applicability to a range of organizations, this method is not prescriptive of techniques and tools used to perform method activities.

Figure 8.4 Assessment method activities

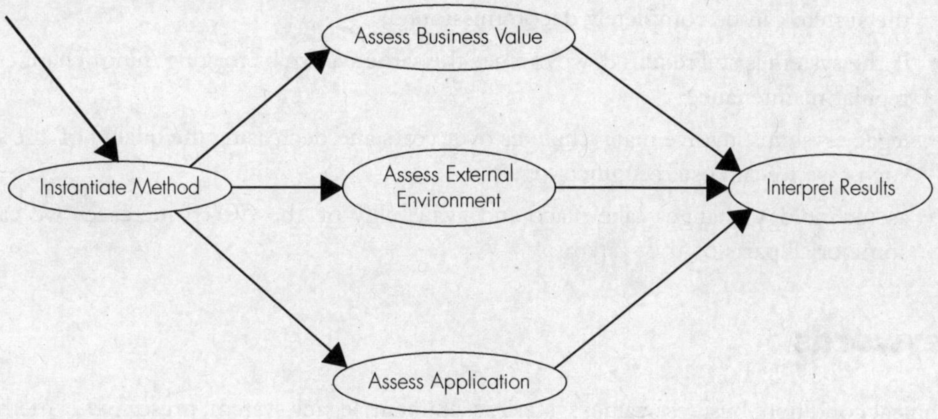

8.2.1 Assessment Activities

We can gain a sufficient depth of understanding of the legacy system from technical, business, and organizational perspectives from which a decision can be made for an appropriate evolution strategy.

The following factors force the legacy system to evolve

- business process redefinition and reorganisation, due to rapidly changing legal requirements;
- redefinition of corporate strategy e.g., from a data processing model to a multichannel service oriented model;
- lack of existence of a corporate information model;
- lack of a well defined architecture; and
- no adequate database system, phasing out of a line of hardware and system software.

8.2.2 Instantiation

An instantiation activity is necessary to tailor the assessment method to the needs of the organization and project. The assessment activities shown in Figure 8.4 may be performed in parallel, and in some cases, particular activities can be omitted. This flexibility is necessary to provide a user-driven method. It involves defining two parameters:

Assessment technique: Either expert opinion or quantitative metrics may be used. This decision is based on the availability of individuals to play expert roles, and the maturity of the organization performing the assessment;

Assessment level: The level of detail at which to carry out the assessment. A decision can be made by examining the varying degrees of granularity.

In order to perform system evolution of legacy systems we need to choose an appropriate strategy for its development. For implementing this, the strategic options give below can be followed:

- when it is found that the system does not make any effective contribution to the business, the system can be completely decommissioned;
- if the system is still required, we can use the same system by making minor changes and with regular maintenance;
- legacy systems involve many changes over years and decreasing the quality of the system. In such case we can use reengineering;
- as technology changes take place and availability of the COTS increases we can replace some or all parts of the system.

Keywords

technical condition; business value; system assessment; legacy system; prescriptive; method activities; information model; user-driven; COTS; design methodologies; implied decisions; obsolete

Exercises

1. What are legacy systems?
2. Discuss the importance of legacy systems.
3. Why is preventing legacy systems from failing or not performing as desired a challenge?
4. Narrate the issues influencing the study of legacy systems.
5. Using a labeled diagram, clearly outline why a system can become a legacy system at any point in its life cycle?
6. Illustrate all the phases in the legacy system life cycle.
7. What is the assessment of legacy systems and what does it entail?
8. Elaborate on all the activities involved in legacy system assessment.

CHAPTER 9

Reverse Engineering

Objectives

The objective of this chapter is to introduce the student to reverse engineering and its associated patterns. When you have read this chapter you will be able to:

- Understand the concept of software reverse engineering
- Understand the reverse engineering procedure
- Identify and distinguish the patterns associated with reverse engineering
- Site examples of situations and conditions governing the existence of each pattern

9.0 Reverse Engineering

Reverse engineering is the process of analyzing a subject system to identify the system's components and their interrelationships and create representations of the system in another form or at a higher level of abstraction – Chikofsky and Cross (1990). In reverse engineering, the requirements and the essential design, structure and content of the legacy system must be recaptured. In addition to capturing technical relationships and interactions, information and rules about the business application and process that have proved useful in running the business must also be retrieved. This involves extracting the design artifacts and building or synthesizing the abstractions that are less implementation dependent. The key objectives in reverse engineering are:

- Cope with complexity;
  - Have a better understanding of voluminous and complex systems,
  - Automatic techniques provide a way to extract relevant information and leave out low-level details.

- Generate alternative views;
  - Reverse engineering tools should provide different views of the systems,
  - So as to enable the designers to analyse the system from different angles.
- Recover lost information;
  - Changes made to the system are often undocumented – this enlarges the gap between the design and the implementation,
  - Reverse engineering techniques retrieve the lost information.
- Detect side effects;
  - Reverse engineering can help detect problems due to the effect some changes may have on the system before they result in the failure of the system.
- Synthesize higher abstractions;
  - Extract high-level abstract views of the system.
- Facilitate reuse;
  - Reverse engineering can help detect candidate system components that can be reused.

The effectiveness of this process will affect the success of the reengineering project. Reverse engineering does not involve changes to the system or the creation of a new system. It is the process of examination without changing its overall functionality.

The reverse engineering process, shown in Figure 9.1, begins by extracting the requirements and detailed design information from the source code and the existing documents. A requirements

Figure 9.1 Reverse engineering procedure

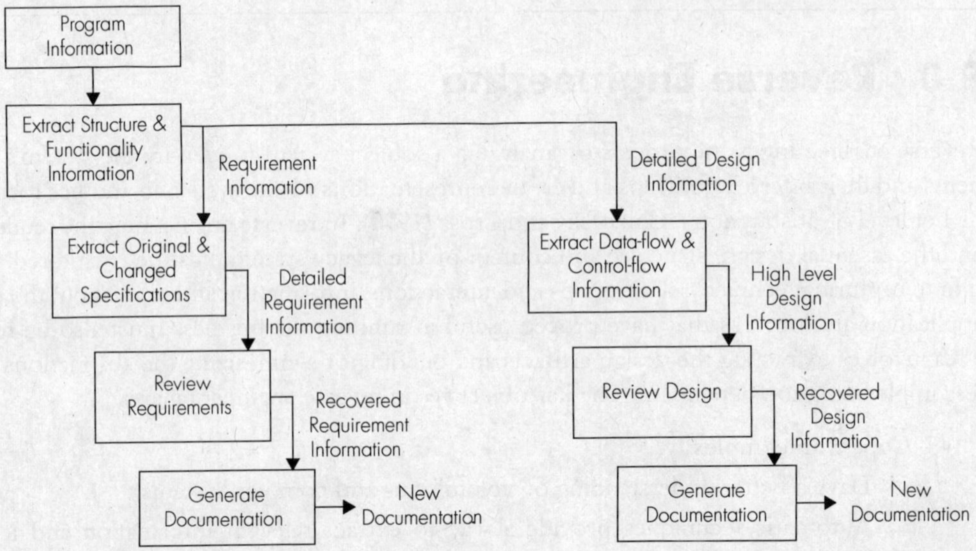

document is created and a high level design abstraction is extracted and expressed using data-flow and control-flow diagrams. The recovered design is reviewed for consistency and correctness.

9.1 Reverse Engineering Procedure

The reverse engineering process begins by extracting detailed design information, and from that extracting a high-level design abstraction. Detailed (low-level) design information can be extracted from existing design documents and the program source code. This information includes structure charts, data descriptions and Public Documentation License (PDL) to describe processing details. A similar approach, but automated, is described elsewhere to recover Jackson and Warnier/Orr documents from code. The high-level design representation is an extraction from the recovered detailed design and is expressed using data-flow and control-flow diagrams. Throughout this chapter the term "recovered design" will be used to denote the extracted design. The steps for this procedure are discussed below. Figure 9.1 gives a summary of this procedure.

Collect information: Collect all the possibly available information about the program. The sources of information include design documents, documentation for system calls and external routines and source code. Personnel experienced with the software should also be identified.

Examine information: Thoroughly review the collected information. This step allows the people working on the recovery to become familiar with the system and its existing components. A plan for dissecting the program and recording the recovered information can be formulated during this stage.

Extract the structure: Identify the structure of the program and use this to create a set of structure charts. Every node in the structure chart corresponds to a particular routine called in the program. Hence, the chart makes a record of the calling hierarchy of the program. For each edge in the chart, the data passed and returned by a node must be recorded.

Record functionality: For every node in the structure chart, record the processing done in the program routine corresponding to that node. A PDL can be used to show the functionality of program routines. For system and library routines the functionality can be described in English or in a more formal notation.

Record data-flow: The recovered program structure and PDL can be analysed to identify data transformations in the software. These transformation steps show the data processing done in the program. This information is used to develop a set of hierarchical data flow diagrams that model the software.

Record control-flow: Identify the high-level control structure of the program and use control-flow diagrams to record it. This refers to high-level control that affects the overall operation of the software, not to low-level processing control.

Review recovered design: Review the recovered design for consistency with available information and correctness. Identify any missing item of information and attempt to locate it. Review the design to verify that it correctly represents the program.

Generate documentation: The final step is to generate complete design documentation. Information explaining the purpose of the program, program-overview, history and so on will need to be recorded. This information will most probably not be contained in the source code and must be recovered from other sources.

9.2 Clean-room Reverse-engineering

Reverse-engineered software is said to be clean-room reverse-engineered if its creators avoid directly examining the software that is emulated. This can be done by the use of published specifications and test programs. Using clean-room reverse-engineering technique prevents the developers from including pieces of the software to be emulated in the emulated software. It does not prevent the developers from infringing on existing registered patents or infringing on look-and-feel copyrights.

Clean-room reverse-engineering can sure be a labour intensive methodology. Any behavior that is either not documented or incorrectly documented can lead the developers into writing, running and analyzing complex tests to determine the true behavior of the system being emulated. Although Apple's Classic Macintosh Operating System is fairly well documented by Apple in the Inside Macintosh series of books, each error and omission has either resulted in an incompatibility in Access to Research for Development and Innovation's (ARDI) software or the expenditure of engineering time searching for better documentation or spent creating new, often esoteric, tests.

9.3 Dirty-room/Clean-room Reverse-engineering

Directly examining the thing to be emulated is dirty-room reverse-engineering. For example, looking at the individual instructions that constitute a computer program, even if only to determine specifications that are not publicly available, is an example of dirty-room reverse engineering. Dirty-room reverse engineering done by the same engineers who create emulation software will always run the risk of deliberate or accidental copyright violations by incorporating portions of the software to be emulated in the emulator. To carefully avoid this kind of risk, dirty-room reverse engineering has to be done in conjunction with clean-room reverse engineering by using two physically and electronically isolated teams so that one team does dirty-room engineering and the other does clean-room engineering.

In strictly clean-room reverse engineering, the moment it is determined that the specification that the clean-room engineers are working from is insufficient to produce the degree of compatibility desired, the only recourse is to search for additional documentation or to write additional tests. In dirty-room/clean-room reverse engineering, the clean-room engineers have to write a description of the portion of the specification that needs to be elaborated or clarified. The dirty-room engineers then have to use that request to create additional functional specifications. These functional specifications should not reveal, in any way, the way in which the emulated software was written as such revelations would defeat the whole purpose of having separate clean-room and dirty-room engineers. One way of preventing such contamination is to disallow direct communication between the clean-room and dirty-room engineers. Instead, all communication between the two teams has to be passed through an intermediary who enforces protocol. Specifically the role of the intermediary is to insure that **only** functional specifications are passed from the dirty-room to the clean-room. Any implementation detail coming from the dirty-room should be intercepted and prevented from ever being seen by the clean-room.

For complex products, it has since been observed that the number of man-hours needed to create an emulation using dirty-room/clean-room reverse engineering may be less than the number of man-hours needed to create an emulation using only clean-room-reverse engineering. This will be the case when it is considerably easier for dirty-room engineers to determine all hidden specifications, than it is for clean-room engineers to determine the same hidden specifications through the construction and analysis of tests.

9.4 Strictly Clean-room Reverse-engineering

Strictly clean-room reverse-engineering is when only a clean-room team is used – without the use of any dirty-room team. To date, ARDI has strictly used clean-room reverse engineering in the construction of its software, even though doing so has been less efficient than using dirty-room/clean-room reverse engineering. The benefit of such a technique to ARDI is that ARDI has constantly avoided the overhead of having separate dirty-room engineers as intermediaries. The significant drawback has been that ARDI's lower operating system layers are not sufficiently compatible to allow Apple's upper operating system layers to work with them. Such compatibility measures have easily provided dirty-room/clean-room reverse engineering more clear goals and compatibility.

9.5 Reverse Engineering Patterns

9.5.1 Introduction

Each pattern in the larger language can – because it is connected to the larger language – help all other patterns to emerge. It can be safely said that patterns can exist at all scales. The patterns are not just mere patterns of relationships, but rather patterns of relationships among other smaller patterns, which themselves have still other patterns hooking them together and we eventually see that the world is entirely made of all these interhooking, interlocking non material patterns.

It can be seen then that patterns are very much alive and continuously evolving. No matter what the asterisks say, the patterns are still hypotheses and are therefore still tentative, free to evolve under the impact of new experiences and observations. But what guarantee can be drawn that this flux, with all its individual acts, will not create chaos? It mainly evolves around the close relationship between the process of creation and the process of repair. It has also been found that different patterns in different languages have underlying similarities, which suggest that they can be reformulated to make them more general, and usable in a greater variety of cases.

So the actual work of any process of design strongly lies in the task of making up the language, from which you can later generate one particular design. The language will evolve in a piecemeal approach, one pattern at a time.

A lot of work to-date on patterns has concentrated on characterizing the recurring functional, structural, and behavioral relationships among objects. Very little attention has been paid to how classes and frameworks emerge and evolve. However, truly reusable objects are a result of an iterative and evolutionary process. It is possible to characterize aspects of this process by using patterns. Kent Beck *et al.* highlighted that an emphasis on the transformations that designers can make to existing objects to improve them can be as helpful to designers as depictions of the resulting artifacts.

Booch and Cunningham (1990) claimed that many of the objects in a system may be found by a simple examination of the grammatical relationships in the system's specification. Quite a number of the remaining objects are uncovered using analysis tools such as Class, Responsibilities, Collaboration cards (CRC). Just a few are found late in the life cycle; however, (they concede) these are often of exceptional value since they embody insights that emerge only from experience and can "make complexity melt away". Adding that would be important while the basic identities of many objects may be discovered early, these objects will change and improve as the system evolves. Truly reusable objects tend to emerge as the result of this evolutionary process. Dennis DeBruler (1994) also noted that it is important to allow for down-stream changes to avoid design paralysis during the early phases.

It may be possible, however, to characterize this process using a four-layer set of patterns. These patterns would be far from a fullfledged pattern language for object-oriented software development. They should instead be treated as a rough, preliminary sketch of where some of the major landmarks in such a language might be located. A full exposition of these potential patterns is beyond the scope of this book. We have decided to focus on five of them in greater detail. Nonetheless, it is expected that these patterns in their complete form, and also the other patterns they give rise to, may begin to discern the outlines of this nascent pattern language to the reader.

A top-layer pattern that develops software that is usable today and reusable tomorrow has forces that are resolved by the second-layer patterns: Prototype a first pass design, Expand the initial prototype and Consolidate the program to support evolution and reuse. In this section, we define each of these second layer patterns. Then, we define two patterns that apply during the consolidation phase. The consolidation aspects of program evolution have been a focus of the research on object evolution, life cycles, reuse and refactoring. Guidelines for design during the consolidation phase have also been documented. Evolve Aggregations from Inheritance Hierarchies, also examined in this section, is one of the third-layer patterns that resolves the forces associated with the consolidation process. It should always be remembered that inheritance models the *is-a* relation, while aggregation models the *has-a* relation.

However, these relations tend to be less distinct than they might be thought to be at first. Can a pixel be considered a point, or does it have a location, which is a point? Is a matrix an array that has extra behavior, or does a matrix consist of a representation, which is an array? Different people give different answers to these questions, and it is common for a person's answer to change over time. Flexibly looking at it, both points of view can lead to working programs. On the contrary, they differ in how the resulting designs will be reused and the kinds of changes that can easily be made to them. It is important to be in a position to change software so that it reflects the ongoing point of view. Although it is possible to convert aggregation to inheritance, converting inheritance to aggregation seems to be more common, for several reasons.

Create Abstract Superclass is another third-layer pattern defined in this section. During the consolidation phase, abstractions common to two or more classes can be moved to a common abstract superclass. This pattern clearly describes what can be done, and what forces must have to be resolved. Finally, there is the fourth layer of refactoring (behavior preserving program transformation) pattern that resolve the forces of this (and similar) patterns. This layered approach has been found helpful in characterizing the program consolidation phase, in understanding how refactorings can be interleaved with additions, and in ensuring that refactorings can be safely applied to object-oriented programs.

9.5.2 Background: Object Evolution

There are three distinct phases in the evolution of object-oriented abstract classes, frameworks and components: a prototype phase, an expansionary phase and a consolidation phase. Closely associated with each of these phases is a complete series of high-level patterns that address the forces that have to be resolved during the phase. Like clockwork these high-level patterns, in turn, are realized by applying lower-level patterns that resolve these forces. The software development process has shown these phases iterated and replicated in and among classes, frameworks and applications. This pattern of self-similarity at different levels is typical of fractal curves; hence we introduce the Fractal Model.

The Fractal Model can be thought of as an object-oriented specialization of Boehm's Spiral Model. The Spiral Model is cast broadly, in such a fashion that it accommodates reuse, iteration, and the independent evolution of subsystems. The Fractal Model puts emphasis on those characteristics of objects that allow them to evolve in ways that traditional software cannot. It is also outstanding in its emphasis on consolidation and refactoring as essential stages in the evolution of truly reusable components.

9.5.3 Pattern: Prototype a First-pass Design

Context: In order to develop software that is usable today and reusable tomorrow, one must first address the problem at hand. Initially, it is mandatory that user requirements be made available. There is both internal and external pressure to produce tangible results relatively in a quick way.

Problem: Building systems from the ground up is expensive and time consuming. Moreover, it is difficult to be sure if they really solve the problems they were expected to solve until they are complete. These days it is now rare to see systems built totally from scratch. Modern software systems now rely more on a variety of domain independent components and tools. However, reusable domain-specific objects and frameworks are still not popular, mainly outside the area of graphical user interfaces.

It should come as no surprise and that is so, since simply designing a system is hard. To design a general, reusable system from the first principles is much more difficult. History has proved that designing a system that addresses both the requirements at hand, as well as a broader range of potential future problems pose nearly insurmountable challenges.

Solution: The initial design of a system should focus on the requirements at hand, with broader applicability as a secondary concern. It is, however, important to get something running relatively in a quick manner, so that feedback regarding the design can be arrived. This initial or first-pass prototype can borrow expediently from existing code. As Brooks notes, software should be grown not built. As a matter of fact, successful large systems begin as successful small systems. A sure way of a good start is to build a prototype. In the case of object-oriented programs, early prototypes always allow designers to get feedback from customers, and enable designers to thoroughly understand the architectural issues they need to confront. In most cases, the prototype is a rather quick, first-pass design, in which the emphasis is on finding a set of objects that embody the surface structure of the problem at hand.

The prototype phase may involve the application of analysis and design methods as well as the development of initial prototype implementation. During the development of a prototype, it is considered common to expediently make use of existing code in order to get something work quickly. Such a strategy does not only depend on the availability of a pre-existing domain-independent reusable components like collections, but also on the infrastructure of domain-specific artifacts. Even in those domains in which such code does not exist, code from a related domain can always be "borrowed". Programming-by-difference involves the leveraging of existing code to create a new application based on an existing one. It is also relatively fair to ask where such reusable code (which serves as the foundation for an initial design) comes from for domains where none previously existed. The next two patterns will address this issue.

Related patterns: While this phase can realize a reasonable first-pass set of objects, the designs of these objects still need to be refined and later may need to be redesigned. Some examples of patterns that apply in this phase are:

- nouns in the specification imply objects, verbs operations (P1);
- build on existing objects using inheritance (P2);
- get it running now, polish it later (P3); and
- avoid premature generality (P4).

(Note that no further effort has been made to develop these patterns here). This phase also sets the stage for exploration and consolidation ready.

9.5.4 Pattern: Expand the Initial Prototype

Context: Successful systems are seldom static, instead, success sets the stage for evolution.

Problem: When software addresses an important need, both users and designers may recognize opportunities to apply the software in new ways. Often, when addressing these new applications you would require some changes to the program that were not envisioned when the software was initially designed. Such software evolution and reuse can undermine a program's structure, and over time, make it more difficult to understand and maintain the software. During the expansion phase, designers often try to reuse parts of a program for purposes that differ from the program's original purpose to varying degrees. In traditional languages, this type of reuse might be undertaken by making copies of the original code, or by introducing flags and conditionals into the original code. Such activity tends to compromise a program's structure, and make it difficult to understand and change the program later.

Solution: In object-oriented programs, inheritance is a powerful and useful mechanism for sharing functionality among objects. An exercise to place new code in subclasses usually helps in maintaining design integrity, because changes are isolated in these subclasses, and the original code in the superclasses remains intact. Objects can evolve more gracefully than traditional functions or procedures because exploratory changes can be connected to subclasses. Such changes are much less potentially disruptive to existing code that has more dependency on a component. What generally results from the expansion phase is a class hierarchy that models a complete history of changes. However, the resulting subclasses are not yet truly general in nature. More desirable, from a software maintenance point of view, would be an inheritance hierarchy that models a type hierarchy.

Related patterns: During expansion, patterns such as these come into play:

- subclass existing code instead of modifying it (E1);
- build on existing objects using inheritance (E2; like P2);
- defer encapsulation for shared resources (E3);
- avoid premature generality (E4; like P4); and
- get it running now, polish it later (E5; like P3).

It should be noted that some of the same patterns that appeared during the prototype phase appear here as well. This reflects the original underlying similarities between these two phases.

9.5.5 Pattern: Consolidate the Program to Support Evolution and Reuse

Context: Initial designs are often loosely structured. As objects evolve, insights as to how they might have been designed begin to emerge clearer.

Problem: As objects evolve, they are subjected to forces that can undermine their structure if they are left unchecked. It should be kept in mind that prototypes are often first-pass designs that are expediently structured. During the expansion phase, the introduction of new requirements, as well as sometimes conflicting requirements, can muddle the clarity of the parts of the original design. Unfortunately, the much needed insight necessary to improve the objects is often not available until later in the life cycle. However, mere traditional life cycle notions do not address the need to exploit this insight at all. As a matter of fact reusable objects seldom emerge fully formed from an initial analysis of a given problem domain. In many cases, they are discovered later in the life cycle, or are polished and generalized as a system evolves. It follows that the objects in the system must be changed to embody this structural insight. Unfortunately, traditional waterfall life cycle models do not accommodate redesign late in the life cycle. Later life cycle models, such as the Spiral Model, embrace iteration, but they do not address the unique properties of evolving objects.

It should be noted that objects evolve differently from traditional programs. This is simply because they can, and do, change within and beyond the applications that spawn them. However, some of these changes add breadth or rather functionality to the system; others improve its structure or future reusability. It is, therefore, easy to understand why the latter are often deferred indefinitely. This is an unfortunate scenario, since it is these changes that can be of the most enduring value. Prototypes are loosely structured for a number of reasons. One being that they are often built to allow the designer to gain an initial sense of the layout of the design space. By definition, the designer's understanding of the given problem is immature at this time. Objects that are found during this phase may reflect the surface structure of the problem adequately, but they will need to be refined to do so more elegantly. In addition, they will also need to be reused in order to become reusable.

There is a second reason for the structural informality of prototypes and it is that they often are constructed in an expedient fashion out of existing reusable parts. This should not be misunderstood for a bad practice. "Get it running first and then polish it later (P3)" can be an effective strategy for learning how to employ existing components to address new requirements. In both these cases, the insight necessary to get the objects right is not really available up-front. In the event that the process does not accommodate it when it does become available, these rough drafts can become the final ones. During the course of expansion, the objects that have proven useful are redeployed in contexts that differ from their original ones. It is worth noting that since the requirements raised in these contexts were not part of the specification for the original objects, they could not, in general, have been anticipated when these objects were designed. Under an object-oriented system, these tend to accumulate around the leaves of the inheritance graph. Over a period of time, the hierarchy can become overgrown with redundant, haphazardly organized code.

Solution: Exploit opportunities to consolidate the system (by refactoring objects) to embody insights that become evident as the system evolves. It should be appreciated that objects can provide opportunities for reuse that are not available to conventional software. However, object-oriented encapsulation encourages more modular initial designs. Inheritance allows the changes made to accommodate new requirements to be made in subclasses, in which they will not undermine the structural integrity of already existing objects. Later on, the insight gained during the prototype and consolidation phases can be employed to refactor the system. Refactorings improve the systems' structure and organization and do not necessarily change the way the system works.

The experience accrued during successive reapplications of an object (during the prototype and expansion phases) should then be applied during a consolidation phase so as to increase its generality and structural integrity. A program's design should be improved; abstract classes and frameworks should emerge or be made more explicit. During the period of expansion, the size of a system typically increases. On the contrary during the consolidation period, it can shrink. As an example, a designer might come to notice that the two methods added during the expansion

Table 9.1 Design rules

	Design rules
DR1	Use consistent names
DR2	Eliminate case analysis
DR3	Reduce the number of arguments
DR4	Reduce the size of methods
DR5	Class hierarchies should be deep and narrow
DR6	The top of the class hierarchy should be abstract
DR7	Minimise access to variables
DR8	Subclasses should be specialisations
DR9	Split large classes
DR10	Factor implementation differences into subcomponents
DR11	Separate methods that do not communicate
DR12	Sent messages to components instead of to self
DR13	Reduce implicit parameter passing

phase contain duplicated code or data. The designer might then factor this common code into a common superclass, or on the other hand a method may have grown larger as the code evolved. A designer might decide to break this code into several methods in an effort to increase the level of abstraction, and to provide new places to override behavior. As an object evolves within a certain timeframe, it is common for new objects to emerge. We attempt to clarify later on the refactoring that addresses this. Each refactoring process can, thus, be seen as addressing and correcting forces that, if left unchecked, would undermine the structural integrity of the objects that comprise the entire system. As a system evolves, disorder and entropy will start taking effect. Consolidation can be considered as an entropy reduction phase.

Related Patterns: Table 9.1 lists 13 design rules that are characteristically employed during consolidation. Table 9.2 lists potential refactorings that can be employed during consolidation phase.

9.5.6 Pattern: Evolve Aggregations from Inheritance Hierarchies

Context: The class hierarchies that emerge during the prototype and expansion phases are often functional, but neither elegant nor reusable. As the consolidation phase progresses, designers take time to exploit opportunities to clean up the system, improve its structure and comprehensibility,

Table 9.2 Refactoring patterns

Category	Refactoring(s)		
High level refactoring	HR1	:	Create abstract superclass
	HR2	:	Subclass and simplify conditionals
	HR3	:	Capture aggregations and components
Supporting refactorings; Create program entity	SR1	:	Create empty class
	SR2	:	Create member variable
	SR3	:	Create member function
Delete program entity	SR4	:	Delete unreferenced class
	SR5	:	Delete unreferenced variable
	SR6	:	Delete a set of member functions
Change program entity	SR7	:	Change class name
	SR8	:	Change variable name
	SR9	:	Change member function name
	SR10	:	Change type of a set of variables and functions
	SR11	:	Change access control mode
	SR12	:	Add function argument
	SR13	:	Delete function argument
	SR14	:	Reorder function arguments
	SR15	:	Add function body
	SR16	:	Delete function body
	SR17	:	Convert instance variables to pointers
	SR18	:	Convert variable references to function calls
	SR19	:	Replace statement list with function call
	SR20	:	In-line function call
	SR21	:	Change superclass
Move member variable	SR22	:	Move member variables to superclass
	SR23	:	Move member variables to subclass
Composite refactorings	SR24	:	Abstract access to member variable
	SR25	:	Convert code segment to function
	SR26	:	Move a class

and increase its reuse potential. Evolving aggregations from inheritance hierarchies can play an equally major role in the entire system consolidation process. This pattern can be used in:

- factoring implementation differences into subcomponents (DR10);
- separate methods that do not communicate (DR11); and
- send messages to components instead of to self (DR12).

Problem: Inheritance sometimes is overused during the early phases of an object's evolution. Changing informal, white-box-based inheritance to black-box style aggregate-component relationships can result in better encapsulated, well structured, more reusable and understandable code.

Designers tend to depend heavily on inheritance during the prototype and expansionary phases of an object's evolution. Inheritance is often used where aggregation would be better because:

- since inheritance is supported at the language level, it is easier to use it than to construct aggregates by hand. The fact that it is a feature of object-oriented languages, programmers are trained to use it as they learn the language. They do not become familiar with design idioms and patterns such as aggregation until they become more experienced;
- it is not obvious that an *is-a* relationship should become a *has-a* relationship until the subclass becomes more mature;
- since inheritance creates a white-box relationship, sharing resources such as operations and variables are made easy. How best to untangle intra-object coupling that may exist only becomes clear when the object has been used and reused for a while, and the fissures along which new object may be cleaved become more evident.

There comes a time (the consolidation phase) when designers may notice that parts of an object exhibit a degree of cohesion that suggests that distinct objects can be factored from the existing hierarchy. The following benefits might be realized if some inheritance relationships were able to be changed into aggregations:

- cohesion and encapsulation could be improved by changing one large class to two smaller classes;
- aggregates have the flexibility to change their components at run-time, while inherited subparts remain static. That is, components are at liberty to exploit dynamic polymorphism. A component might become a member of a different aggregate as well;
- separate classes can be reused independently, and may also independently evolve. Each may spawn subclasses that can be interchangeably used by the other, since they will communicate only by a public interface;
- an aggregate might have one or more instances of a given component class.

A more practical example of an inheritance-based relationship that could be cast as an aggregate might be a matrix class. The first design of such a class might be based on the observation that a Matrix is a TwoDimensionalArray to which a repertoire of arithmetic operations are added. Hence, Matrix might be defined as a subclass of TwoDimensionalArray that adds operations like +, *, and transpose to the inherited methods for accessing and changing array elements. Changing the relationship from an inheritance based relationship to aggregation might take advantage of the fact that the TwoDimensionalArray subpart is being used essentially intact as a state repository for the Matrix abstraction. Making this part of the Matrix, a component can allow alternate representations for this repository, such as SparseArrays or even stateless identity objects, to be used in place of TwoDimensionalArrays.

Solution: Change inheritance-based relationships into aggregate-component relationships by factoring parts of an existing class into a new, component class. Perform these changes in such a way that the program will still work as it did before. Suppose that *A* happens to be a subclass of *C*, *A* can reuse behavior of *C* by:

- adding an instance of *C* as a component variable of *A*;

- replacing references to variables and functions inherited from *C* with references to the component;
- eliminating the inheritance link between *A* and *C*.

For example, the Matrix class is a subclass of the TwoDimensionalArray, with an inherited variable arrayRepr and two inherited functions *get* and *put*. An instance of the class TwoDimensionalArray is added as a component variable of Matrix. References to the inherited members of class TwoDimensionalArray are then replaced by references to members of its newly formed component variable. Then, the superclass Matrix is changed for example, to another class, or to null if Matrix is now a top-level class. Ensuring that the program will still work after the changes are performed is easy for steps 1 and 3, but more difficult for step 2. Where the references to inherited variables and functions must be replaced not only in *A* (or Matrix) but also in its respective clients. One way to make step 2 much easier is by abstract access to the variables inherited by *A* (or Matrix), and change the accessing functions so as to point to the members of the component variable.

Related patterns: Changing inheritance-based relationships to aggregate/component relationships can require that a number of supporting refactorings be applied to a program. Creating an instance of the component class and populating it does employ the pattern create member variable (SR2). Bear in mind that changing the superclass of the aggregate class employs the pattern move class (SR25). Other related patterns include the following create member variable (SR2), create member function (SR3), delete unreferenced variable (SR5), delete a set of member functions (SR6), add function body (SR15), move member variable to superclass (SR22), move member variable to subclass (SR23) and move class (SR25). Changes to argument lists and member names are necessary, employing the patterns change variable name (SR8), change function name (SR9), add function argument (SR12), delete function argument (SR13) and/or reorder function arguments (SR14). Note that the abstracting access to variables employs the pattern abstract access to member variable (SR23).

9.5.7 Pattern: Create Abstract Superclass

Context: As noted for the prior pattern, the class hierarchies that emerge during the prototype and expansion phases are often functional, but neither elegant nor reusable. One way to clean up inheritance hierarchies during the consolidation phase is to simply define abstract classes that capture behavior common to one or more of the existing classes. This pattern should be employed to satisfy the following design rules:

- class hierarchies should be deep and narrow (DR5);
- the top of the class hierarchy should be abstract (DR6); and
- subclasses should be specializations (DR8).

Problem: As programs evolve, abstractions emerge. Abstractions that appear in two or more classes are often implemented differently, and are often intertwined with code that is specific to a class. Unless abstractions are consolidated in one place, code duplication will persist, making it hard to reuse the abstraction. Systems grow with age. As they grow, it has been observed that the same abstraction may appear in more than one place in a program. This may happen because:

- one common programming practice is to extend a program by copying existing code and modifying it. As this happens, code gets duplicated;
- on multi-person projects, different project members may implement the same functionality independently in the parts of a program for which they are responsible.

During the entire consolidation phase, these common abstractions may be discovered. If the abstractions were consolidated in one place, several benefits might be realized:

- defining the abstraction in one place reduces the program's size and possibly its execution time;
- separating out the abstraction makes it easier to understand and reuse;
- if the abstraction (or its implementation) is flawed, it need only be fixed in one place. A simple problem with the copy-and-modify approach to software development is that the errors in the original code get copied along with the code. If the error is subsequently discovered and fixed in one place, it may still persist somewhere else;
- if throughout a program abstractions are separated out and made explicit, it can make the entire program easier to understand and evolve.

A good example of where this pattern might be applied is that of where two classes DenseMatrix and SparseMatrix are defined. Suppose that DenseMatrix was defined first, and then later SparseMatrix was defined by copying DenseMatrix and modifying it. Noticeably, both these classes contain common behavior and duplicated code. An abstract superclass Matrix could then be defined that captures the common behavior between these two classes.

Solution: Factor abstractions common to two or more classes into a common abstract superclass. Perform these changes in such a way that you ensure the program will still work as it did before. Suppose that the classes C1 and C2 share a common abstraction. An abstract superclass can be defined by:

- adding a new class A1, which initially contains no locally defined members;
- making A1 the new superclass of both C1 and C2;
- determined the common behavior (functions, or parts of functions) in C1 and C2;
- changing (as needed) function names, argument lists, function bodies and the attributes of reference variables so that functions that implement common behavior (in C1 and C2) are implemented identically;
- moving the common functions to A1 and then deleting them from the subclasses.

Related patterns: Creating the abstract superclass may employ the patterns create empty class (SR1), create member variable (SR2), create member function (SR3), delete unreferenced variable (SR5), delete a set of member functions (SR6), change variable name (SR8), change member function name (SR9), change type of a set of variables and functions (SR10), change access control mode (SR11), add function argument (SR12), delete function argument (SR13), reorder function arguments (SR14), replace statement list with function call (SR19), and move member variable to superclass.

Keywords

interrelationships; essential design; technical relationships; design artifacts; high-level design; structure charts; data descriptions; public documentation license; design documents; formal notation; high-level control; consistency; correctness; program-overview; published specifications; test programs; incorrectly documented; protocol; intermediary; man-hours; emulation; hidden specifications; design paralysis; preliminary sketch; prototype phase; expansionary phase; consolidation phase; spiral model; fractal model; programming-by-difference; design integrity; waterfall model; future reusability; entropy; refactoring; cohesion; dynamic polymorphism

Exercises

1. Define the term reverse engineering.
2. Outline and discuss the objectives of reverse engineering.
3. Define the following terms with respect to reverse engineering:
   - consistency;
   - correctness;
   - design paralysis.
4. With the aid of a well labeled diagram explain the reverse engineering procedure.
5. Outline the differences between clean-room reverse engineering and dirty-room reverse engineering.
6. Explain the relationship between clean-room reverse engineering and dirty-room reverse engineering.

CHAPTER 10

Forward Engineering

Objectives

The objective of this chapter is to introduce the student to software forward engineering and its respective patterns. When you have read this chapter you will be able to:

- Understand the concept of software forward engineering
- Understand the forward engineering approaches
- Identify and distinguish the patterns associated with forward engineering
- Site examples of situations and conditions governing the existence of each pattern

10.0 Forward Engineering

10.0.1 Introduction

A new target system is created by moving downward through levels of abstraction, by a successive replacement of existing system information with more detailed information. This downward movement is actually a forward movement in the standard software development process, hence it is known as forward engineering. Forward engineering moves from the high level abstractions and the logical implementation independent designs to the physical implementation of the system. A sequence from requirements through design to implementation is followed. In this process, the risks are due to the degree and preparation during reverse engineering. Projects are exposed to more risk with the alteration or addition of new requirements.

10.1 Re-engineering Approaches

There are three different approaches to software re-engineering. The approaches differ in the amount and rate of replacement of the existing system with the target system. Each approach has its own benefits and risks.

10.1.1 Big Bang Approach

The "Big Bang" approach, also known as the "Lump Sum" approach, replaces the entire system at one time, as shown in Figure 10.1. This approach is used by projects that need to solve an immediate problem, such as a migration to a different system architecture.

The advantage of this approach is that the system is brought into a new environment all at once. No interfaces between old and new components must be developed, no mingled environments must be operated on and maintained. The disadvantage of this approach is that the result tends to be a monolithic project that may not always be suitable. For large systems, this approach may consume too many resources or require large amounts of time before the target system is produced. The risk with this approach is high, the system must be functionally intact and work in parallel with the old system to assure functionality. This parallel operation may be difficult and expensive to run. A major difficulty is change control; between the time the new system is started and finished, many changes are likely to be made to the old system, which have to be reflected in the new system. It is difficult to stay abreast and not to lose any capability that has been implemented in the old system. That means what is being reengineered is likely to change.

10.1.2 Incremental Approach

The "Incremental" approach to re-engineering is also known as "Phase-out". In this approach, as shown in Figure 10.2, system sections are re-engineered and added incrementally as new versions of the system are needed to satisfy new goals. The project is broken into re-engineering sections based on the existing system's sections.

The advantages of this approach are that the components of the system are produced faster and it is easier to trace errors since the new components are clearly identified. Since interim versions are released, the customer can see the progress and quickly identify any lost functionality. Another benefit is that changes to the old system can be easier to deal with, since changes to components that are not being re-engineered have no impact on the current component. A disadvantage

Figure 10.1 Big Bang approach

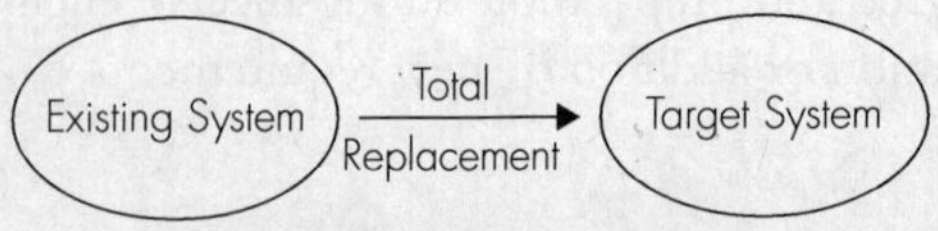

Figure 10.2 Incremental/Phase-out reengineering approach

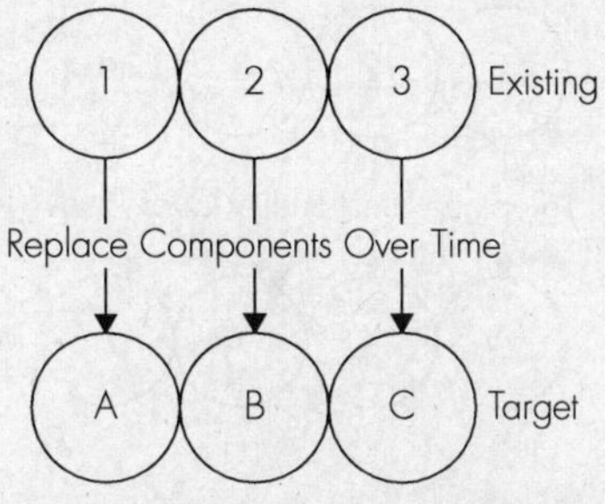

is that the system takes longer to complete with multiple interim versions that require careful configuration control. Another disadvantage is that the entire structure of the system cannot be altered, only the structure within the specific component sections being reengineered.

This requires careful identification of components in the existing system and extensive planning of the structure of the target system. This approach has a lower risk than the Big Bang because as each component is re-engineered, the risks for that portion of the code can be identified and monitored.

10.1.3 Evolutionary Approach

In the "Evolutionary" approach, as in the incremental approach, sections of the original system are replaced with newly re-engineered system sections. In this approach however, the sections are chosen based on their functionality, not on the structure of the existing system. The target system is built using functionally cohesive sections as needed. The Evolutionary approach allows developers to focus re-engineering efforts on identifying functional objects regardless of where the tasks reside in the current system. As shown in Figure 10.3, components of the current system are broken by functions and re-engineered into new components.

The advantages of Evolutionary re-engineering are the resulting modular design and the reduced scope for a single component. This approach works well when converting to object-oriented technology. One disadvantage is that similar functions must be identified throughout the existing system then refined as a single functional unit. There may also be interface problems and response time degradation since functional sections of the original system are being reengineered instead of architectural sections.

10.2 Organizational Patterns for Moving Forward

10.2.1 Background

Change is one of the few "constants" of software engineering. While managing this change is a challenge for all software-intensive organizations, managing change becomes more difficult when

Figure 10.3 Evolutionary reengineering approach

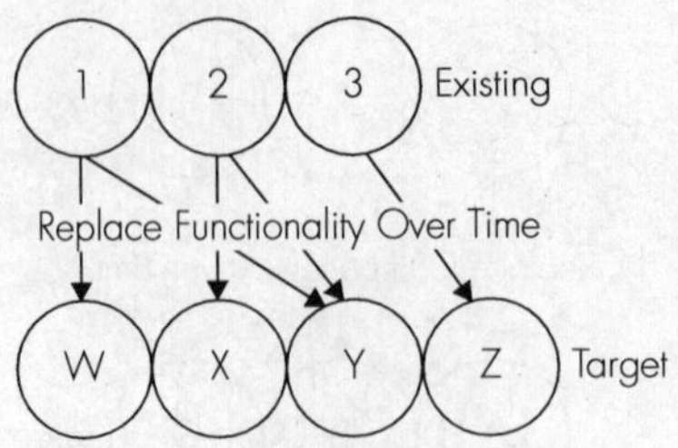

organizations build product-lines. While reuse helps manage change across the product-line more effectively, managing change for specific components becomes more difficult. When organizations undertake software reuse, the need to manage change for components grows due to the expanded usage and results often in an expanded life-cycle of a software asset. These changes need to be managed in a well coordinated fashion. This section describes six organizational patterns that support software reuse and address these concerns.

1. Develop a shared platform;
2. Maintain reuse platform identity;
3. Integrate reuse and tie to the bottom line;
4. Reuse more than just code;
5. Treat reusable components like products; and
6. Merge after cloning.

Some of these patterns focus on organizational issues i.e., on practices that support managing the rhythms of change and managing cloning to maintain a shared code base.

10.2.2 Pattern #1: Develop a Shared Platform

Problem statement: Multiple projects incur redundant development costs by independently implementing identical or similar functionality.

Context: Projects within an organization are loosely coupled, allowing each project to effectively focus on the needs of its customers. However opportunities arise to achieve economise by centralizing some functionality into a common platform.

Forces

1. Multiple implementations of similar functionality are often more expensive than a shared solution;
2. Projects need to minimize their development costs;
3. Projects need to maximize the revenue potential for their products and services;

4. The existing organizational structure may not easily support coordination across projects;
5. The needs among projects, while similar, may not be identical – or at least may not appear to be identical to the project staff; and
6. Expertise in common areas may be spread across projects; such staff members may be in high demand in their projects.

Solution

1. Bring together staff representing multiple projects, to assess common needs;
2. If the areas of common needs are significant, charter the development of a shared platform, funded and staffed either jointly among the application projects, or by a corporate level "core" organization;
3. Define plans for projects to transition onto the common platform; and
4. Maintain close ties between the platform projects and the application projects, to help focus both the platform development and increase the confidence level among application projects that the platform will meet their needs.

Result: A platform is developed to address the shared needs of the application projects. Cost saving (in areas addressed by the shared platform) is realized for the projects, over time. The time to market is also significantly reduced. Opportunities may also arise to share application level components among projects, and to migrate staff among projects given their shared platform understanding.

Consequences: For the benefits of a shared platform to be realized over time, it is important to maintain reuse platform identity. A proper investment plan is required to establish the platform before the benefits can be realized.

10.2.3 Pattern #2: Maintain Reuse Platform Identity

Problem statement: A shared platform has been built, or is envisioned, but potential users, aside from the pilot adopters, are not willing to commit to using the shared platform.

Context: Over time, user needs change, technologies and interfaces change, and designers' insights change. Change is one of the inherent complexities of software and the only constant. Platforms and frameworks have been recognized as a means for managing change and for reducing development costs and development intervals. As a result the organization has decided to develop a shared platform.

New platforms are often introduced with a pilot adopter in place. While it is necessary for the platform and pilot application development groups to work closely together to make the initial use of the platform successful, it is tempting to associate a platform project too closely with the pilot application. This association is sometimes realized by placing platform staff and application development staff in a common organization. This close association may benefit the application developers with access to and control over the platform development staff.

From the application developers' perspective, distinctions between platform and applications are irrelevant to their customers. It may seem expedient to make arbitrary changes to the platform to accommodate application specific needs, in ways that compromise the generality of the platform. A further expedient may be to merge application and development staff; in the process, platform identity and platform support may be lost.

This close collaboration can cause other potential adopters to see the platform as only suitable for the pilot application, or that the pilot application has too much control. As a result of such perceptions, other application groups will not commit to use the platform. A warning sign that the platform identify has not been maintained is that the schedules for platform adoption after the pilot application begin to slip.

Forces

1. Costs can be reduced and economies of scale achieved through the use of common platforms;
2. Change, at all times, is inevitable;
   a. ironically, introducing change is hard;
   b. pilot projects mitigate some of the challenges of introducing new technology;
3. Platform development groups are driven by multiple, conflicting goals;
   a. near-term focus of the application development groups using the platform;
   b. long-term requirements for potential adopters of the platform;
4. Application development groups are focused on near-term deliverables to specific customers and markets. In order to maximize product quality while minimizing product development intervals and development costs, application development groups seek to reduce and eliminate:
   a. unnecessary dependencies between organizations;
   b. unnecessary distractions of their staff;
5. Funding sources often drive the priorities of an organization;
6. Organizations that are closely tied together (e.g., in the same business unit) often have better communication than organizations that are not as close;
7. Potential platform users that are not confident that a platform will be responsive to their needs will not use the platform; and
8. A platform closely tied to a single project may not be seen as responsive to the needs of other users.

Solution

1. Establish a separate organization for the platform;
2. Keep the staff of the platform development organization and the initial application organization separate. There should be good communication, and clear, commonly understood expectations between the two groups;
3. Use stable corporate funding to get the platform started, and then ensure stable funding from the application organizations once the platform is established;

4. There needs to be an advocate for the platform at the corporate level;
5. The platform organization should act like a product organization to engage customers and address customer needs as well.

Result: If platform identity is maintained, applications are better able to have their needs met, and the value of the platform is greater because it can be used by more applications, which results in reductions in cost and market time for a larger portion of the organization.

Consequences: Maintaining platform identify may make achieving success with the initial application more challenging.

10.2.4 Pattern #3: Integrate Reuse and Tie to the Bottom Line

Problem statement: Incentives to establish reuse are not taken seriously.

Context: The organization has multiple improvement efforts going on simultaneously e.g., process improvement, new tools, risk management – as well as an organization wide reuse effort. The reuse effort is being ignored and rejected by the organization as just "one more" activity to distract engineers and managers from meeting the business objectives.

Forces

1. The improvement efforts are related – but staff focusing on a particular improvement effort may be unaware of other, related improvement efforts;
2. Organizations are often under tremendous pressure to meet the business objectives of completing projects on time and on budget;
3. Some level of reuse often happens, even without a formal reuse program;
4. Organizations cannot be motivated by mandate at all.

Solution

1. Reuse leaders should identify fit and ways to serve and be served by other improvement efforts;
2. Coordinate and align the reuse effort with other improvement efforts in order to get the full benefits at an optimum cost. The organizational structure should support shared responsibility among the improvement efforts;
3. Identify and communicate common, coordinated recommendations to practitioners regarding the improvements – emphasizing the value of the improvement efforts to the managers and engineers whose support and actions are needed to make the improvement successful;
4. Manage the coordination among the efforts;
5. Track, on an ongoing basis (and require estimates in budget proposals for) how much reuse has been achieved and how much has been saved;
6. Integrate reuse throughout the life-cycle, not just at coding phase.

Result: The engineers and managers involved with the reuse activity receive consistent, easy-to-understand and follow improvement guidance that shows them how to better achieve their business objectives. The reuse effort is more likely to take hold, and deliver the expected results of reduced costs and reduced time-to-market.

Consequences: Even if reuse is tied to other improvement efforts, the improvement efforts still need to be tied to the bottom-line and other motivations of both managers and engineers. If the value of the improvements to the participants is not clearly communicated, the integrated improvement efforts may be more likely to fail. Even with careful coordination and consolidated "improvement" strategy, the effort may be seen as more complex than each of the efforts individually. The reuse effort could also be canceled if other improvement efforts are deemed more critical (this may not be bad).

10.2.5 Pattern #4: Reuse More than Just Code

Problem statement: Engineers do not reuse already developed code components because the components either do not fit with other components, or do not quite fit the requirements.

Context: Managers and practitioners are beginning to make a dedicated, long-term effort to improve results and customer value. Software reuse is seen as a sure way of achieving these results.

Forces

1. Managers and practitioners often equate reuse with code, not with knowledge capture or organizational learning;
2. If different parts of the organization have very different practices, they may find it more difficult to share assets and share people among different groups;
3. Code components reflect decisions made during requirements and design;
4. Consistently achieving high levels of process maturity requires an understanding and application of sound requirements and design techniques.

Solution

1. Reuse software assets from all phases of the life-cycle including:
   a. processes;
   b. checklists;
   c. project management templates;
   d. requirements;
   e. designs.
2. Establish a repository and other automated tools to share the assets;
3. Tie the complete reuse exercise to knowledge capture activities.

Result: A number of benefits have been attributed to this approach, although not all organizations realize all the benefits. The creation and reuse of non-code assets makes code reuse more likely. Organizations are also better able to bring in and train new staff. Reusing non-code assets also results in more direct benefits such as improved cycle-time, consistency and repeatability and reduced costs, risks and surprises.

10.2.6 Pattern #5: Treat Reusable Components like Products

Problem statement: Application developers typically associate components with "use at your own risk stuff" – they do not trust or use components they do not fully understand.

Context: An internal organization is chartered to introduce a new set of behaviors and/or a new technology through their development and management of reusable components. The goal of this activity is to achieve a significant improvement in delivering higher value and better business results. The target adopters are mainly application software development organizations. The application development organization is under tight deadlines. Those who supply components must support a diverse group of product developers, each with his or her needs. Even though each component has one owner, others may need to make changes to his or her component when he or she is away to meet deadlines.

A warning sign that this problem is occurring is that component owners do not hear about change requests from component users, either because components are not being used at all, or because a configuration management (CM) system is not being utilized to capture and communicate change requests.

Forces

1. If individual developers are not confident that component features critical to their work will not change, and that new component features will be addressed in a timely fashion, developers will probably not use the components;
2. The supplying organization must add new features and feature sets to its components to increase its customer base;
3. Potential adopters will not use a component if they are unsure that it will be maintained and that it will be managed – unexpected defects coming from lack of CM are not cool;
4. With a standard configuration management system, only one component owner has access to a component;
5. A standard configuration management approach focuses on tracking baselines of entire systems e.g., NamedStableBases, and not tracking specific components across multiple systems;
6. Without a product mentality, component suppliers can easily become detached from their customers;
7. Lack of proper information raises the perceived risk of using a component. The perceived risk on the part of (potential) reusers causes them to lose confidence that a component will meet their needs, and hence makes them reluctant to reuse the component;
8. Potential reusers are often willing to forego their desire to know everything about the asset's internals and if they trust the supplier's credentials and know that the supplier has a competent CM tool and process.

Solution: Treat reusable components like products. A lot is known about how to build and market products that go within other products (though reuse efforts still believe they are doing something entirely different). For example, the organization responsible for reuse should gain the confidence of the target customer base through building a high-quality product, tracking and responding to change requests, gaining endorsement from a respected expert and end user, and drawing to your team a group of developers that people trust. The reuse organization shares the developer's risk through specific commitments to deliver the features promised, managing and responding to change requests, and assuring that critical features persist. Unfortunately, the benchmarks are set by product vendors (who certainly are not perfect). Make use of user groups and other communications forums to encourage the platform user community to exchange information and drive consensus regarding proposed platform changes. A flexible CM system and process is only a part, not complete solution. Developers should be able to view version histories, and outstanding change requests. Users should also be able to use the CM to report defects and make other change requests.

Result: Reusable components are presented in a way that developers are more comfortable with. They are willing to try to use components because they have a clearer understanding of who is responsible for what. They see the risk of using a component counteracted with endorsements from their peers and the experts they respect. The use of reusable components grows from small groups within product organizations to a point at which the major product features may depend on the components. The user community is far better informed about the specific reusable components. This knowledge reduces their perceived risk to reusing components, and increases component usage. The flow of information apparently helps in developing relationships between the component owners and the reusers.

Consequence: As use grows, a problem in a component may adversely affect multiple business-critical products.

Example: In the early days of the acceptance of C++ in the AT&T development community, it was determined that the acceptance would go faster if users were supplied with a set of standard "computer science" functions that would make system development using C++ easier. This set came to be known as the C++ Standard Components Library (SCL) and contained functions such as Lists, Maps (associative arrays), String, Blocks (unbounded arrays with memory allocation as needed). The Standards Component Library was very popular and was used by hundreds of projects across AT&T. The components were put under configuration management control and change requests (bug reports and enhancement requests) were tracked in the configuration management system, which associated each source change with specific change requests. Any developer assigned a change request could change a component and an audit trail of the change would be kept by the system.

The C++ hotline used the configuration management system to enter customer change requests, track the quality and change history of the components and support the assembly and packaging of new releases. The project's configuration management was more than just the supporting system. It included the process (e.g., review boards amongst an array of others). Acceptance was generally higher and cloning was not a problem. The success of the Standard Components Library was based on many factors, which helped build confidence among potential users:

1. The quality of people, many of whom had published books and had excellent reputations within the company;

2. The quality of the components and the support that was initially given. The configuration management played a supporting role here in that without it, quality and support would not have been as good as they were.

The releases of reusable components were not much different from the releases of other products that have to run in multiple environments.

10.2.7 Pattern #6: Merge after Cloning

Problem statement: Organizations clone software to add components to quickly respond to customer requests, but the organization does not want to get saddled with the long-term costs associated with cloning.

Context: While cloning offers a means to quickly respond to pressure to develop new features quickly, cloning often has far-reaching consequences. When a developer clones, code is duplicated, complicating product tracking and management. It does not take much time before developers build new and complex extensions on the clones making them incompatible with the actual code base. The final result is that code grows rapidly in size and complexity. This increased the maintenance burden for each product in place. It is imperative that clones are merged periodically.

Forces

1. Rapid response requires that developers have access to and the ability to modify existing source code;
2. It is often easier to change source by "copy and modify" (i.e., by creating clones) rather than by extending or generalizing the original source;
3. White box access to source is necessary to respond rapidly to multiple quick response requests from end-customers;
4. Generalizing existing components may require coordination not just with the component supplier, but also other users of that component.

Solution

1. Merge the clones regularly;
2. Provide application developers with "white box" access to at least selected parts of the platform source;
3. When cloning, encourage developers to duplicate the smallest portion possible;
4. Establish very clear rules for what types of changes can be made through cloning;
5. Identify clones by watching for signs, such as duplicate functionality, email postings etc., and then examine the code to determine if cloning is taking place;
6. Allow only one clone of any given component at the same time;
7. Encourage users (application developers) to submit bug reports, bug fixes and suggestions for extensions and generalizations;
8. Provide comprehensive support to component users so that they can more easily use the generalized software.

Result

1. Code base improves in robustness and reliability; bugs get fixed and stay fixed at any point in time. There is a single point of maintenance, which simplifies the task of building products;
2. Reduced maintenance costs. Every line of shared code in use, means that there are 2 or 3 lines of avoided code somewhere else;
3. Application developers can respond to market pressures more quickly than if generalized components were built or modified initially;
4. Reuse suppliers build trust with users;
5. Code base stays upward compatible at any given phase.

Consequences: Additional effort must be made to reincorporate cloned software. There is also the substantial risk that cloning could get out of hand e.g., cloned chunks are too big, or there are too many clones, making the practice too expensive to sustain. There may be limits to the number of simultaneous clones that an organization can create and still merge them back into the base. An organization may have reached or passed this limit when the time required to merge the clones slows down, or if a merge cannot be completed before the next scheduled merge. Another warning sign is that merges cannot be completed with major changes.

Example: One organization, in order to meet schedule, cloned its product in order to run the application in an additional operating environment. The organization recognized that in doing so, they had effectively doubled their maintenance costs, and that there was no way that they would be able to support all of the operating environments in their plans. They moved back to a common code-base and reduced their cycle-time from 12–24 months to 12–14 months, and they also reduced their maintenance costs.

Keywords

logical implementation; physical implementation; reverse engineering; big bang approach; lump sum approach; system architecture; monolithic projects; change control; new system; incremental approach; phase-out approach; interim versions; extensive planning; evolutionary approach; object-oriented technology; functional unit; change; product-lines; expanded life-cycle; coordinated fashion; common platform; time-to-market; shared platform; pilot adopter; pilot application; application developers; platform identity; platform support; process improvement; risk management; reuse effort; shared responsibility; cycle-time; component suppliers; benchmarks; review boards; cloning

Exercises

1. Define the term forward engineering.
2. List and describe in detail the reengineering approaches.
3. Discuss organisational patterns and their overall impact.
4. Why is it difficult to fix the order for organisational patterns?
5. Why are applications developed using Waterfall Models difficult if not impossible to reuse?
6. Where does the element of risk management come into play within the organisational patterns?

CHAPTER 11

Software Reengineering

Objectives

The objective of this chapter is to introduce the student to the concept of software reengineering and its related environment. When you have read this chapter you will be able to:

- Understand the concept of software reengineering and the activities that take place within it
- Understand the challenges that take place when attempting to reengineer software
- Understand existing reengineering concepts and their applications
- Understand the existing software reliability methods and their nature
- Understand how to deal with software reliability
- Understand reengineering phases and tasks
- Understand the implementation and risks involved during reengineering

11.0 Reengineering

The term reengineering is quickly becoming a favoured buzz word, but what does it mean to software managers and developers? Basically, reengineering involves the process of taking existing legacy software that will have become expensive to maintain or whose system architecture or implementation are now obsolete, and redoing it with current software and/or hardware technology or, technically, it is the examination, analysis, and alteration of an existing software system to reconstitute it in a new and better form, and the subsequent implementation of the new form, thereof. The difficult part lies in understanding the existing system. In most cases the requirements, design and code documentation will no longer be available, or will be out of date, so it is really not clear what functions are to be moved.

Generally the system would contain functions that will no longer be needed, and those functions will not be moved to the new system. This chapter first defines reengineering and looks at why it is necessary, and what its objectives are. The steps, phases and approaches are then discussed. A unique method of reengineering, hybrid reengineering, is also defined and discussed.

11.0.1 What is Reengineering?

Reengineering is a process that involves the examination, analysis and alteration of an existing software system to reconstitute it in a new form, and the subsequent implementation of the new form, thereof. The process typically encompasses a combination of other processes such as:

- reverse engineering,
- redocumentation,
- restructuring,
- translation,
- forward engineering.

The goal is to understand the existing software (specification, design, implementation) and then to re-implement it to improve the system's functionality, performance or implementation. The objective is to maintain the existing functionality and prepare for functionality to be added later.

11.1 Reengineering Objectives

Although objectives of a specific software reengineering task are determined by the goals of the owners and users of a system, there are two general reengineering objectives.

Improve quality: Typically, the existing software system will be of low quality, due to many modifications during the course of time. The user and system documentation will often be out-of-date or no longer available. One of the main objectives of reengineering is to improve software quality and to produce current working documentation. A higher degree of quality is needed in an effort to increase reliability, to improve maintainability, to reduce the cost of maintenance, and to prepare for functional enhancement. Object-oriented technology may be applied as a means to achieve a higher level of maintainability and also to reduce costs.

Migration: Old and working software may still meet the users' needs, but it may be based on hardware platforms, operating systems, or languages that might have become obsolete and thus may need to be reengineered, transporting the software to a newer platform or language. Migration may involve quite extensive redesigning if the new supporting platforms and operating systems are very different from the original, such as the move from a mainframe to a network-based computing environment.

However, the number of large systems being built from scratch is diminishing, while the number of legacy systems in use is very high. While the functionality of existing systems has been observed to remain constant, on the other hand the context of new systems, such as the application environment, system level hardware and software, have proved to be different. Enhancements to the functionality of the existing systems may also be needed, but although the reengineering effort may configured for enhancements, they should not be incorporated until after the reengineering is complete. This facilitates the comparison of functionality between the existing system and the new system.

The root of the problem is that systems currently in use, "legacy" systems, have become lacking in good design structure and code organization, making changes to the software difficult and costly. Corporations do not want to throw away these systems because there are many built in subtle business application processes that have evolved over time that would be lost. In most cases the original developers of the legacy systems are not available to verify or explain this information; the only available source is the current software source code. The original expense of developing the logic and components of the software systems should not be wasted, so reuse through reengineering is desired.

The challenge in software reengineering is to take existing systems and instill good software development methods and properties, generating a new target system that maintains the required functionality while applying new technologies. Although specific objectives of a reengineering task are determined by the goals of the corporations, there are four general reengineering objectives.

Preparation for functional enhancement: The reengineered target system can be built to easily facilitate the enhancements. For example, if the desired system enhancements build on object-oriented design, the target system can be developed using object-oriented technology in preparation to increase the functionality of the legacy system.

Improve maintainability: As systems grow and evolve, maintainability becomes a bottleneck and very time consuming. An objective of reengineering is to re-design the system with more appropriately functional modules and explicit interfaces. Documentation, internal and external, will also be current, hence improving maintainability.

Migration: The computer industry continues to grow at a fast rate; new hardware and software systems include new features, quickly outdating current systems. For these reasons, companies with working software that meets their needs might need to migrate to a new hardware platform, operating system or language.

Improve reliability: Although it is possible that reliability was never very high in the first place, more likely, over time and with multiple changes, there have been problems, one change causing multiple additional problems. As maintenance and changes continue, the reliability of the software steadily decreases to the point of being unacceptable.

Although reengineering should not be done to enhance the functionality of an existing system, it is often used in preparation for enhancement. Legacy systems, through years of modifications due to errors or enhancements, become difficult and expensive to change. The code no longer has a clear, logical structure and documentation may not exist, and if it exists, it is often outdated. Reengineering specifies the characteristics of the existing system that can be compared to the specifications of the characteristics of the desired system. The reengineered target system can be

Figure 11.1 Levels of abstraction

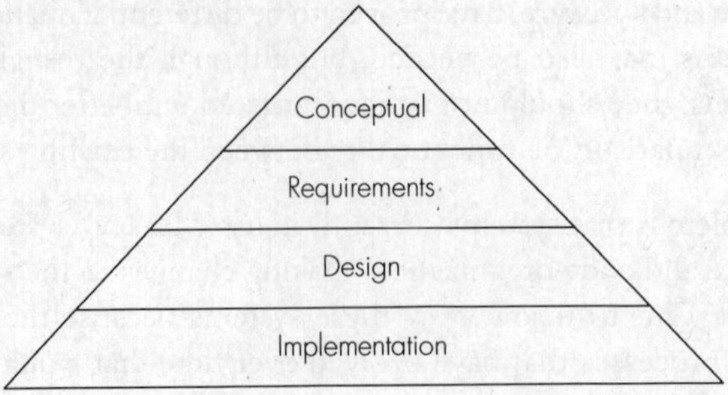

built to easily facilitate the enhancements. For example, if the desired system enhancements build on object-oriented design, the target system can be developed using object-oriented technology in preparation for increasing the functionality of the legacy system. As systems grow and evolve, maintainability costs increase because changes become difficult and time consuming. An objective of reengineering is to re-design the system with more appropriately functional modules and explicit interfaces. Documentation, internal and external, will also be current, hence improving maintainability.

11.2 Reengineering Concepts

11.2.1 Software Development Levels of Abstraction

Levels of Abstraction, Figure 11.1, that underlie the software development process also underlie the reengineering process. Each level corresponds to a phase in the development life cycle and defines the software system at a particular level of detail (or abstraction).

The conceptual abstraction level is the highest level of abstraction. Here the concept of the system – its reason for existence – is described. At this level functional characteristics are described only in general terms. In the requirement abstraction level, functional characteristics of a system are described in detail. In these first two levels, internal system details are not mentioned. In the design abstraction level, system characteristics such as architectural structure, system components, interfaces between components, algorithmic procedures and data structures are described. The implementation abstraction level is the lowest level. Here a system description focuses on implementation characteristics and is represented in a language understood by a computer.

11.3 General Model for Software Reengineering

Reengineering starts with the source code of an existing legacy system and concludes with the source code of a target system. This process may be as simple as using a code translation tool to translate the code from one language to another (FORTRAN to C) or from one operating system to another (UNIX to DOS). On the other hand, the reengineering task may be very complex, using the existing source code to recreate the design, identify the requirements in the existing system then compare them to current requirements, removing those no longer applicable, restructure and redesign the system (using object-oriented design), and finally coding the new target system. Figure 11.2 depicts a general model for software reengineering that indicates the processes for all levels of reengineering based on the levels of abstraction used in software development.

The model in Figure 11.2 applies three principles of reengineering: abstraction, alteration, and refinement. Abstraction is a gradual increase in the abstract level of system. System representation is created by the successive replacement of existing detailed information with information that is more abstract. Abstraction produces a representation that emphasizes certain system characteristics by suppressing information about others. This upward movement is termed reverse engineering and has associated sub-processes, tools and techniques. Alteration is the making of one or more changes to a system representation without changing the degree of abstraction, including addition, deletion and modification of information, but not functionality. Refinement is the gradual decrease in the abstraction level of system representation and is caused by the successive replacement of existing system information with more detailed information. This is termed forward engineering and resembles the software development of a new code, but with some process refinements.

To alter a system characteristic, work is done at the level of abstraction at which information about that characteristic is explicitly expressed. To translate the existing code to a target language no reverse engineering is needed, the alteration (recoding) is done at the implementation level. As the level of abstraction increases, the alteration tasks change and the amount and tasks of reverse engineering change. To re-specify requirements, reverse engineering techniques must be applied to the implementation and to the design to obtain the functional characteristics.

Figure 11.2 General model for software reengineering

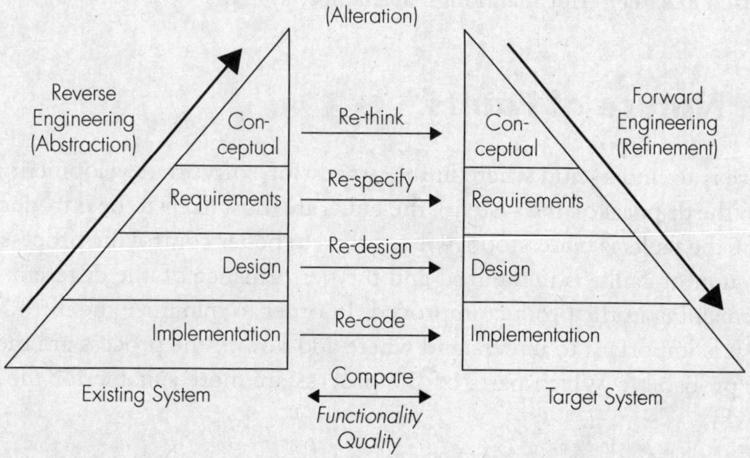

11.4 Software Reliability Methods

"Software reliability is the probability that software will not cause the failure of a system for a specified time under specified conditions. This aforementioned probability is a function of the inputs to and use of the system as well as a function of the existence of faults in the software. The inputs to the system in use determine whether existing faults, if any, are encountered" (ANSI/IEEE Std 729-1983-1). From this definition it is observed that the failure behaviour of a software is a function that depends on:

- the number of faults in the software;
- the execution profile.

Thus, the reliability of a software is a function that combines the number of faults and the probability of these faults to occur to produce a failure state. In other words, the probability that the fault exists and the faulty code is executed. As a consequence, it can be improved by reducing either the number of faults or the probability of a fault to produce a failure (focusing our testing effort on the most frequently used functionality).

"Software reliability refers to the probability of failure-free operation of a computer program for a specified time in a specified environment."

Techniques to improve the reliability of a software by reducing the number of faults are classified into three different groups.

Fault avoidance: is aimed at preventing the introduction of faults during the development of the software. In this group are included all the techniques that look into the process of software development: standards, methodologies, etc. The techniques within this group are process oriented.

Fault detection: is aimed at detecting faults once the code has been developed. These techniques focus on the product obtained rather than on the process. These techniques are product oriented.

Fault tolerance: is aimed at giving a controlled response for those uncovered faults. These techniques are used in safety-critical and high availability systems.

11.4.1 Nature of Faults

The aim here is to understand where in the process of software development (from the concept definition to the disposal of the system), the faults are most likely to be introduced and how. Once the nature of the faults is understood, it is possible to better control the process in such a way that the introduction of faults is minimized and the performance of the different techniques to find the faults remaining in the product improved. In order to minimize the introduction of faults in the system, it is important to understand where and how in the process are the faults introduced with higher probability. Which parts of the process are more suitable for the faults to be introduced and why.

Faults are likely to be introduced in every phase in the project and they are propagated between phases. Whenever the natural language (or any other source of imprecision) is used, ambiguity can be introduced. Fault avoidance techniques focus on finding where the faults are introduced and are aimed at providing standards, methodologies or impositions that prevent the developer from introducing faults.

On the other hand, knowing where the faults are more likely to be introduced increases the probability of success of those techniques and tools that focus on finding defects. Faults can be introduced in the following instances.

During the requirements specification: Good requirements are those that are necessary, verifiable and attainable. A poor requirements elicitation process will not detect many requirements that are not clearly stated and as a consequence will not be properly interpreted by designers, implementers or Independent Verification and Validation (IVV) teams, thus resulting in a failure. Firesmith presents an extensive list of attributes that good quality requirements must exhibit, namely: cohesiveness, completeness, consistency, correctness, currency, customer/user orientation, external observability, feasibility, lack of ambiguity, mandatory, metadata, relevance, usability, validatability and verifiability. Hooks gives some recommendations to specify requirements still using natural language (English) but with some kind of formalism. Hooks also presents the most common problems in writing requirements.

- making bad assumptions;
- writing implementation (how) instead of requirements (what);
- describing operations instead of writing requirements;
- using incorrect terms;
- using incorrect sentence structure or bad grammar;
- missing requirements;
- over-specifying.

High-quality requirements is the first step to produce high-quality software. A good requirement is one that is clearly stated. It is important that the requirement is not misunderstood; it must be unambiguous. If requirement documents are inconsistent, ambiguous, incomplete or subject to misinterpretation, the development (costs, schedules), and the final product will be affected. Reviews are an effective way of finding problems but they may prove to be very expensive because they involve a number of people spending time reading and checking the requirements document. Two approaches to this problem can be followed:

- restrict the language used to specify requirements (restricted subset of English or even formal languages like Z);
- analyse the requirements and identify potential problems in the specification.

The first approach has the advantage of a language without ambiguities but on the other hand, it reduces the freedom to specify requirements. Moreover, the language used to specify must be known across all the involved parties (users, designers, IVV teams) and this is normally not the case. The second approach has the advantage that the user has all the expressiveness from a natural language and the document can be shared and reviewed by all the involved parties. Since reviews are very expensive and often of limited effectiveness, these reviews can be automated by implementing a tool to verify requirements. This tool should check three important aspects of quality attributes:

- **Expressiveness:** Characteristics dealing with the understanding of the meaning of the requirements (ambiguities, readability of the document);
- **Completeness:** Characteristics dealing with the lack of information necessary in the specification;
- **Consistency:** Characteristics dealing with semantic contradictions in the document.

There are some tools available but they only provide expressiveness analysis like ARM (Automated Analysis of Requirement Specifications). Some tools like QuARS provide additional support to consistency and completeness analysis but it still must be performed by the reviewer.

During the design phase: Lack of trade-offs, software budget reports or the use of new technologies are common sources of problems introduced within this phase. Important decisions are taken during the design phase and they should be well founded. It is important to demonstrate the feasibility of the proposed solution before going further in the implementation. A formal specification is a solid approach to validate designs.

During the coding phase: Many faults are introduced during this phase depending on the experience and workload of the staff and the complexity of the algorithms. A first check in this phase is performed by compilers who check for lexical and syntactical consistency. Static analysers of dynamic properties have been implemented but with still important limitations. The idea behind this concept is the static validation of properties exhibited during the run-time like access to areas of memory de-referenced and variables not initialized.

During the maintenance phase: As the software is modified during the maintenance – due to corrective maintenance or due to the implementation of new features – faults can be introduced by reengineering (new requirements, design, coding). Another important source of faults in this stage is a poor configuration control and poor integration testing (regression testing is very important to verify that new bugs have not been introduced). The reliability in this stage varies as faults are removed and new bugs are introduced.

According to the way they manifest, the faults can be classified into three categories:

Transient faults: are those that appear for a short period of time and then disappear after a while. They are mainly produced by the failure of processors or by transient or permanent interference in the communication subsystem (network faults). Against these failures some of the techniques described further on in this chapter can be implemented.

Permanent faults: are those that will remain in the system until the fault has been removed, for example software design defects.

Intermittent faults: appear and disappear from time to time.

Orthogonal Defect Classification (ODC) is a defect classification schema that helps to better understand the problems introduced in every phase of the development. The following attributes are collected either when the defect is identified or when it is fixed – activity, trigger, impact, type, qualifier, source and age. With these attributes it is possible to produce quality metrics that can be used to measure the customer satisfaction.

11.5 Dealing with Software Reliability

Software reliability must be integrated in the whole life cycle and must involve all the staff participating in the project. It cannot be just considered at the end. State of the art techniques to improve the software reliability are described in this section. All these techniques are classified into three different groups: fault avoidance, fault detection and fault tolerance. As introduced before, in order to increase the reliability of the software it is possible to reduce the number of faults and/or reduce the probability of a fault to cause a failure. With the classification here described and aimed at reducing the failure behaviour of the target system, the process can be optimized by:

- avoiding the introduction of faults (standards, methodologies);
- implementing in our process techniques aimed at finding and eliminating the faults (since it is not possible to produce fault free software);
- implementing fault tolerance if the nature of the software requires it (since it is not possible to guarantee that there are no faults remaining in our software);
- using operational profiles as representative as possible to optimize the effort and the effectiveness of our testing process.

11.5.1 Fault Avoidance

The techniques in this category focus on the process. They are aimed at defining methodologies and standards that control the development process and prevent the introduction of faults. All the known methodologies and standards like ISO9000, CMM, ECSS, DO178B are included here. In principle it could be stated that the higher the CMM level the company has, the lower the probability to introduce faults in the software. This refers mainly to those problems introduced for example by poor configuration control, poor requirements elicitation process and so on. The maturity level of the company is an indicator of the control it has over the software development process. There are studies that try to assess the reliability of the final product (a first approximation) based on the development process aided by the use of Bayesian networks. They establish a framework to assess this reliability based on the confidence in the development process. This approach is very subjective but could give a rough indication before the product has been developed.

Here we review several techniques that can be introduced in the development process to prevent the introduction of faults.

Formal methods: are design techniques that use rigorous mathematical models to build software and hardware systems and help to reduce the errors introduced into a system, especially at the earlier stages of design. Formal specifications use mathematical notation to describe in a precise way the properties that a software must have, without constraining the way this is achieved. The notation to be used should allow the representation of both static and dynamic properties of the system to be built.

The static aspects are:

- the states the system can occupy;
- invariant relationships when moving from one state to another state.

And the dynamic aspects are:

- the operations that are allowed;
- the relationship between inputs and outputs;
- the change of the state.

Formal methods are used during the specification, design and construction of software products. The major problem that the formal methods encounter is that they offer a very limited expressiveness compared to the natural language and they are still rather difficult to apply. They provide a precise way to represent the system but require a big effort to use and understand the notation.

Software hardening: It has been demonstrated that the complexity of a software has a direct repercussion in the number of faults introduced. Complex software is not easy to understand and maintain. The more complex a software is, the more the probability of faults to be introduced and to be uncovered during testing. Based on this principle, software hardening tries to limit the complexity of the software by establishing reference values for a set of measurements that provide a quantification of software complexity. Every system in the nature describes a process that can be characterized by a set of measurements quantifying the complexity of the system.

These measurements can be equally applied to characterize the complexity of a software system. After that, limits for these parameters are set in such a way that the complexity of a software does not exceed our ability to handle it. It has been conclamated the limitation to handle software over certain limits of complexity. These limits differ depending on the maturity and specific knowledge of the staff. The following measurements of this complexity that will be later on extrapolated to software systems are:

- volume;
- entropy;
- temperature.

Software aging and rejuvenation: Software also suffers from degradation during its life. This happens because some bugs have not been detected and introduce memory leaks or other problems that are accumulated and will probably produce a failure after a certain execution period. This is known as software aging and is no other than a degradation of the execution of a software mainly by memory corruption. It has been conclamated that many of these failures can be prevented just by restarting the application periodically. This introduces the concept of software rejuvenation. This degradation of the execution grows with the execution time and affects also the reliability of a software. As mentioned before, the reliability of a software has a time component. Even if the fault is still there, the failure intensity can be reduced just by restarting the system and reducing the probability of it becoming a failure. The overall reliability of a system – and therefore the customer satisfaction – will increase.

The system can be totally or partly restarted and this restart can be scheduled according to the specific behaviour of the software and the availability requirements of the different components. The scheduling activity is the heart of this technique and has to be good enough to restart the component before it fails and within the availability constraints of the system (especially difficult in systems with 24×7 availability).

Use and certification of COTS: The use of Commercial Off The Shelf (COTS) applications is very attractive since they can save costs in both development and testing. But an important aspect of this re-use in the context of software reliability is the certification of these COTS for the new software. It is very likely that those COTS that are intended for re-use have been developed to meet different requirements and thus will not meet our specific reliability requirements. Many techniques have been described to improve their reliability by introducing new layers between these COTS and the applications.

These new layers observe the data flowing through the interfaces and modify or reject data likely to cause harm. In many cases, an important effort is necessary to accommodate these products in the new software reducing the benefits of this software re-use. The technique of Generic Software Wrappers can provide a common framework for integrating COTS without modifying the software and in such a way that they are protected (they run in kernel space) and non-bypassable.

11.5.2 Fault Detection

The techniques in this category are aimed at detecting faults once the code has been developed. These techniques focus on the product obtained rather than on the process.

Formal methods and formal verification: If formal methods have been used to specify the system, it is possible to verify different properties that the software should exhibit or not exhibit. This is an important attribute that can be verified with formal methods.

Dynamic analysis: is performed during the execution of a program. This technique usually instruments the code, gets some statistics and looks into the dynamic behaviour of the software at run-time. The problem associated to this analysis is that it is based on the execution paths selected in the test cases.

Semantic analysis: performs a static analysis of the dynamic properties of the software. The idea behind this concept is the static validation of properties exhibited during the run-time like access to areas of memory de-referenced and variables not initialized. PolySpace Technologies has developed a tool detecting run-time errors implementing Semantic Analysis. The following run-time errors can be detected through the use of Semantic Analysis:

- concurrent accesses to shared data;
- pointer de-referencing issues (null, out-of bounds accesses);
- out-of-bounds array accesses;
- read accesses to non-initialized data;
- invalid arithmetic operations (division by zero, square root of negative numbers and so on);
- float, integer overflow/underflow;

- illegal type conversion (for example float → int, long → short);
- dynamically unreachable code;
- non-termination of loops; and
- initialized return values.

Semantic analysis is a mathematical approach that statically analyzes the dynamic properties of software applications at compilation time (no need to execute the code).

11.5.3 Fault Tolerance

Fault tolerance is aimed at providing a controlled response, sometimes at a degraded level, on the uncovered faults in the system. Several levels of fault tolerance can be implemented, namely:

- **Full fault tolerance**, in which the system continues the normal operation when a failure occurs;
- **Graceful degradation**, in which the system operates with reduced functionality or performance;
- **Safe mode**, in which the system operates with a minimum functionality and performance during the time that the system is repaired and can be again fully operational.

Software fault tolerance techniques are divided into two groups – single version and multi-version software techniques. The first focus on improving the fault tolerance of a single software is by adding mechanisms to detect, contain and handle errors caused by the activation of faults whilst multi-version software techniques use multiple versions of a software in such a way that different versions of this software do not cause a failure at the same time i.e., containing different failure profiles.

Software fault tolerance can be applied at any level – software component, full application, whole system including the operating system. Single version fault tolerance has the advantage of developing only one version of a software but with added complexity and an important performance overhead. The disadvantage is that it relies on only one version to determine the output of the system. The critical issue is detecting internal errors based on the different checks implemented.

With multiple-version software the probability of a correct output increases (it remains controversial to what extent a multiple-version software can increase the reliability with respect to the single version) but it is still difficult to implement the decision module which provides the correct output based on the outputs from the different versions (especially difficult when different outputs are valid). Another critical issue in multiple-version software fault tolerance is guaranteeing the independence of failure on multiple versions.

11.5.4 Input Sequence Workarounds

Torres-Pomales defines a fourth technique to deal with software reliability. This is nothing more than accepting that the software has a particular design fault and considering this fault as a "feature" of the software. The operator uses an alternative input sequence that produces the expected results without activating the failure. This way the user works around the fault and the system is still available.

11.5.5 Development of Operational Profiles

It is really important that the testing efforts are concentrated in those functionalities with a higher probability of execution. Operational profiles identify every operation in the system and the probability of these functions. These probabilities are then combined with the criticality of every operation to obtain a distribution of the testing effort between operations. The aim of the development of operational profiles is an effective use of testing resources to effectively increase the software reliability.

11.5.6 Conclusions

Software reliability is in general very immature. Most of the techniques here reviewed are still difficult to apply or have a limited applicability. Software complexity is growing very fast and there is an urgent need for tools supporting the validation of systems with high reliability requirements. Software reliability is still to be integrated in the normal development cycle as any other integral process and cannot be just considered at the end.

Formal methods are promising in the avoidance of faults and provide support to verification but are still difficult to apply and suffer from state space explosion which limits its applicability. They are suitable for critical parts of a software and for embedded applications of a limited size. Natural language or semi-formal specifications are still preferred because they can be easily shared among the different parties involved in the development – users, designers, developers, customers.

The development of operational profiles effectively helps to:

- focus resources on the most used and/or most critical functions;
- maximize the test effectiveness by making the tests highly representative of the operational field.

The benefits obtained by the development of operational profiles are worth the effort. An important issue in software reliability is the lack of tools supporting reviews.

- Requirements Verification tools can highly improve the quality of requirements document without limiting the freedom when specifying requirements. The available implementations are very immature but still provide a great support to the user;
- Static analysis of dynamic properties is very promising in the detection of run-time errors. However, this technique is still of limited applicability and demands lots of resources. The current implementations report very good results at the commercial level.

In general there is an important niche for the development of tools capable of supporting the analysis of commercial software and helping the developers in the expensive and tedious process of requirements specification reviews. The implementation of Automated Requirements

Verification Tools capable of checking the consistency and completeness of the requirements seems to be an important line of research. Such a tool could improve the quality of the specifications and, at the same time, reduce the costs due to reviews and defects escaping the reviews and detected at later stages with increased impact.

With systems getting more and more complex, especially safety critical and high availability systems, the fault tolerance should evolve in order to be able to solve the problem of design diversity. Two issues remain critical in the area of fault tolerance systems:

- design of output selection algorithm;
- failure independence in multiple-version software.

The important areas of research within fault tolerant systems are:

- the evaluation of independence between designs;
- the semi-automatic generation of fault tolerant systems;
- the validation of fault tolerant systems (path coverage).

A lot of work is still to be done to guarantee versions independence. Design diversity effectiveness still remains a controversial issue. Software reliability can be highly improved with the available techniques but as the software complexity grows, there is an increasing need of tools supporting the development of safety critical and high availability systems.

Several techniques have been presented in this section that allow improving the software reliability.

- **Defining restrictions** in the architecture to limit the complexity and thus the probability of introducing faults.
- **Optimizing the test efforts** to detect the most critical and probable failures (and thus increasing customer satisfaction).
- **Implementing automated verification** tools to highly improve the efficiency of reviews and testing activities.

All these techniques are very valid and without doubt they considerably improve the reliability, though there is still a compromise between the effectiveness and the ease to apply. A selection or a combination of them is dependent on the reliability targets, the experience of the staff involved in the project and the nature of the project. Bearing in mind that software reliability has to be considered during the whole life cycle and integrated in the development as any other integral process (quality assurance, project management), the selection must include a combination of fault avoidance techniques, fault detection techniques and if required, fault tolerance.

11.6 Reengineering Phases and Tasks

There is a core process that every organization should follow when reengineering. Reengineering poses its own technical challenges and without a comprehensive development process will waste time and money. Automation and tools can only support this process, not preempt it. The reengineering process can be broken into five phases and associated tasks, starting with the initial phase of determining the feasibility and cost effectiveness of reengineering, and concluding with the transition to the new target system. These five reengineering development phases are:

- reengineering team formation;
- project feasibility analysis;
- analysis and planning;
- reengineering implementation;
- transition and testing.

11.6.1 Reengineering Team Formation

This team will manage the reengineering effort from start to conclusion and will need comprehensive training in how to manage the technological change, the basics of reengineering, and the use of target development and maintenance processes. Their tasks will be diverse, starting with establishing goals, strategies and an action plan within the current environment and based on the identified business needs including cost justifications. Although team members must have the "standard" software development skills, they will need additional, specific skills. They will be responsible for identifying, testing and purchasing new tools, then making sure personnel are properly trained to use the tools and the tools are being effectively used. The team will need to provide internal marketing of the reengineering work, consulting with personnel to verify that the process is correctly applied. These tasks will require team members to have good interpersonal skills to resolve the rejection of new concepts and perceptions of software ownership. Since the field of reengineering continues to evolve, the team members will also need to continue research in this technology.

11.6.2 Project Feasibility Analysis

The initial task of the reengineering team is to evaluate the organizational needs and goals that the existing system meets. It is important that the reengineering strategy fits with the organization's cultural norms. Software products currently in use must be analyzed in terms of problem specification including objectives, motivation, constraints and business rules. The value of the applications must be investigated to determine what is the expected return on investment from the reengineering effort: the degree to which the software quality is expected to increase, the maintenance process efficiency improvements, and the business value enhanced. Once the expectations are established, they must be expressed in a measurable way – the reduction cost of sustaining engineering, the reduction of operations, the improvement in performance. Then the costs of reengineering must be compared to the expected cost savings and the increase in value of the system.

11.6.3 Analysis and Planning

This reengineering phase has three steps – analyze the legacy system, specify the characteristics of the target system, and create a standard testbed or validation suite to validate the correct transfer of functionality. The analysis step begins by locating all available code and documentation, including user manuals, design documents and requirement specifications. Once all the information on the legacy system is collected, it is analyzed to identify its unique aspects. The current condition of the existing system, its maintainability and operability, must be specified in order to show a return on investment with the target system. A set of software metrics should be selected to assist in identifying the quality problems with the current system and the prioritization of applications that are candidates for reengineering according to their technical quality and business value. The metrics should include the measurements of the costs of changes to the software, if an increase in maintainability is one of the goals of the reengineering process. At the conclusion of the reengineering effort the same metrics should be used to identify the quality of the new system and the return on investment. The collection of metrics on the new system should continue throughout the development to identify if what is happening is normal or expected and in order to react quickly to abnormal signs.

Once the legacy system and its quality characteristics have been specified, the step of stating the desired characteristics and specification of the target system begins. The characteristics of the existing system that must be changed are specified, such as its operating system, hardware platform, design structure, and language. Finally, a standard testbed and validation suite must be created. These will be used to prove that the new system is functionally equivalent to the legacy system and to demonstrate that the functionality has remained unchanged after reengineering. The testbed for the target system may be implemented incrementally if necessary, but traceability to the functions of the legacy system is important.

11.7 Reengineering Implementation

Now that the reengineering objectives have been specified, the approach has been defined, and the legacy system analyzed, the reverse and forward engineering are started. Using the levels of abstraction, the actual functions of the legacy system are unraveled by reverse engineering. Quite a number of tools are available for this task. These tools must be examined for usability in the context of the objectives of the reengineering process. They must integrate easily into the process with minimum massaging.

After the desired level of abstraction is reached, forward engineering can begin. Forward engineering corresponds exactly to the normal software development process, starting from the abstraction level reached in the reverse engineering process. That is, if the software is to be redesigned to fit a new overall system architecture, the reverse engineering process should extract the software requirements, and the forward engineering process would start with the development of a new design. In forward engineering, any change or increase in functionality must be avoided since this complicates the validation process. Throughout this phase, quality assurance and configuration management disciplines and techniques must be applied. Measurement techniques use should continue to assess the improvement in the software and to identify potential areas of risk.

11.7.1 Testing and Transition

As the functionality of the new system grows, testing must be done to detect errors introduced during reengineering. The testing techniques and methods are the same as those used during a "from scratch" system development. Assuming that the requirements for the new system are the same as those for the legacy system the test suite and test bed developed in the planning phase can be used. The same test cases can be applied to both the legacy system and the target system, comparing the results to validate the functionality of the target system. The software documentation on the legacy must be updated, rewritten or replaced during this phase so that they apply to the new system, and contain the information needed to operate and maintain it.

11.7.2 Hybrid Reengineering

The Software Assurance Technology Center (SATC) has coined the phrase "Hybrid Reengineering" to mean a reengineering process that uses not just a single, but a combination of abstraction levels and alteration methods to transit an existing system to a target system. Projects doing hybrid reengineering choose a combination of abstraction levels based on the condition of the legacy system, the needs of the project and its budget and schedule.

In hybrid reengineering, the legacy systems are reengineered using the approach shown in Figure 11.3, an adaptation of the general model for software reengineering. In Figure 11.3, three development tracks are utilized. The first track is a translation from existing code to a new language, operating system or hardware platform with no abstraction. The second track uses the existing code to identify requirements that can be satisfied by the application of COTS packages. The third track is the more standard reengineering process, the development of new code for project requirements that cannot be satisfied by either of the other tracks, and to "glue" together the translated and COTS components.

Reengineering as a development methodology has inherent risks, such as schedule, functionality, cost, and quality. Hybrid reengineering was developed to decrease some of these risks since COTS packages are expected to have high reliability and require minimal development time. Another method of decreasing time and cost through hybrid reengineering while maintaining functionality is through a straight translation of part of the current code to the new language or operating system.

Figure 11.3 Hybrid reengineering tracks

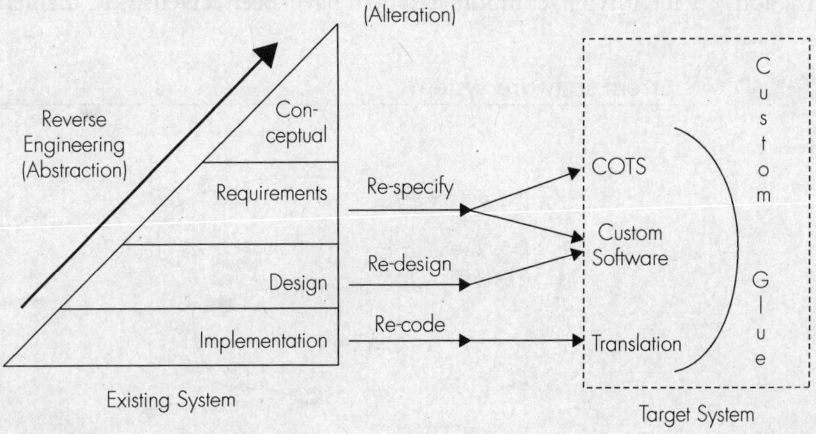

Hybrid reengineering is innovative, combining three distinct reengineering efforts, hence the risks generally associated with reengineering can increase by combining the risks inherent to each track. Since hybrid reengineering is combining products from different development tracks (COTS, custom software and translated software), one new risk is the interface and interoperability of the products. For example, data transfer between products can cause compatibility and timing problems; COTS packages may not work exactly as anticipated. In general metrics can be used by the management to improve software development efforts and minimize the risks. Metrics can help in indicating how well a project will be meeting its defined goals. In hybrid reengineering, metrics can support the justification for decisions on track selection for different software functions and components.

11.7.3 Hybrid Reengineering Tracks

The following sections describe the three hybrid reengineering tracks. After each track is described, the risks associated with the track are identified and appropriate metrics are defined.

11.7.3.1 Translation Track Hybrid Reengineering

Figure 11.4 is a diagram of a "typical" software system that has been in use for some time. In this reengineering example, it is assumed that the project is moving from FORTRAN to C++ (but not necessarily to an object-oriented design).

In looking at the current software system, the manager sees two classifications of code – a stable code that has had minimal modifications and whose requirements have remained unchanged, and some code that has under-gone multiple changes and has become unstable, unreliable, and costly to maintain. Reengineering the stable code may not require total reverse engineering; it might be feasible to simply re-code this portion into the new language or new environment. This process constitutes the translation track of hybrid reengineering. In this track the code in the existing system that is relatively stable, having had minimal changes to the original design and architecture, must be identified. This can be accomplished by an analysis of the code and of change reports. Prior to reengineering, in identifying candidates for translation, metrics such as the logical and calling complexities provide valuable information on structure and coupling and suggest candidates for translation. In identifying components that have been extensively maintained, change or

Figure 11.4 Current software system

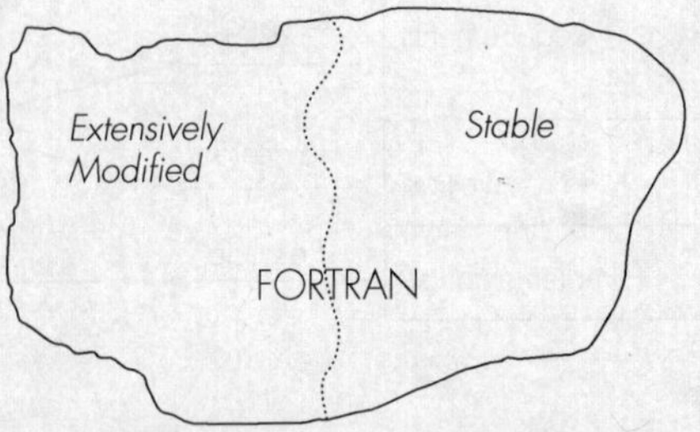

Figure 11.5 Transaction track hybrid reengineering

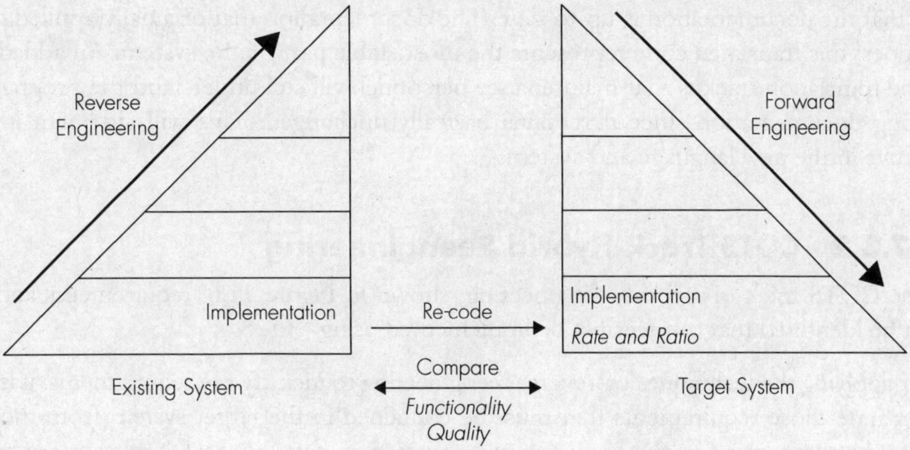

problem reports supply this crucial data. Tracking the criticality of functions will help in making professional tradeoff decisions.

In the translation track, the primary risk is the quality of the resulting code. When transitioning from one language to another, the code can have the syntax of the new language but none of the structures or new features. Nowadays, many source code translators are available to support the transport of code from one language or operating system to another. Source code translators may not solve this problem, since line-by-line translators do not take advantage of target language semantics, constructs, often resulting in a code known as "C-TRAN" – C syntax on FORTRAN structures.

The initial legacy code being of adequate quality does not guarantee that the resulting code will have the same quality. If the quality is not adequate, code may have to be improved. If 20–30% of the translated code must be changed to improve its quality or to meet standards, the code should not be used and those functions or components should be reengineered using another track.

Quantifying the functionality of the legacy system will provide a basis for estimating how complete the new system is during development and provide estimations as to when the target system will be complete. One method being tested by the SATC and other companies to track progress in reengineering uses function points as a measure of functionality. In this application, using the basic function point counting method described by Albrecht (1983), an approximate estimate can be gleaned as to the type and count of tasks. This can be used as a starting point in comparing the progress in transferring functionality between the original system and the target system. Tools are available to count function points from the COBOL code and the SATC is working to develop a tool for FORTRAN and C. In evaluating the progress of the translation, one measure might be the rate at which functionality, approximated through function points, is moving from the existing system to the target system. The ratio of code translated can also serve as a measure of progress.

Once the reengineering is complete, it is important to verify that the functionality is retained in the new system, as well as the quality of the code has improved, hence implying improved maintainability. There is no simple method to ensure that the functionality has transitioned between systems. The most commonly used method involves running test cases on the original system and then repeating the tests on the completed target system. It is also important to make sure that the documentation is up-to-date. The documentation that originally applied presumably still does; this translated code represents the most stable part of the system. An added advantage of the translation track is that maintenance personnel will still understand the program flow and existing documentation since it remains basically unchanged. This will aid them in becoming effective in the new language and system.

11.7.3.2 COTS Track Hybrid Reengineering

In the COTS track of hybrid reengineering, shown in Figure 11.6, requirements and functions must be identified that can feasibly be implemented using COTS.

After applying the techniques of reverse reengineering to identify the requirements, it is important to separate those requirements that must be contained in the target system from those requirements that users want in the new system because they have become habits or are comfortable with those features. The separation of requirements into "necessary" and "nice" is critical to the COTS selection.

The advantage to using COTS is decreased development time and increased reliability. Testing is still needed during integration, but less than for code developed from scratch. The disadvantage can be the number of requirements satisfied by the package. For example, if in the existing system a specific field has 10 characters and the COTS package only allows 8, is this acceptable? Was the 10 character field arbitrary or does it represents a "hidden" business requirement that should not be altered? In addition, users are often resist to change, even change that has little impact, such as different icons or keystrokes to call a function. This must be taken into account for the package to have comparable usability and functionality.

Figure 11.6 COTS track hybrid reengineering

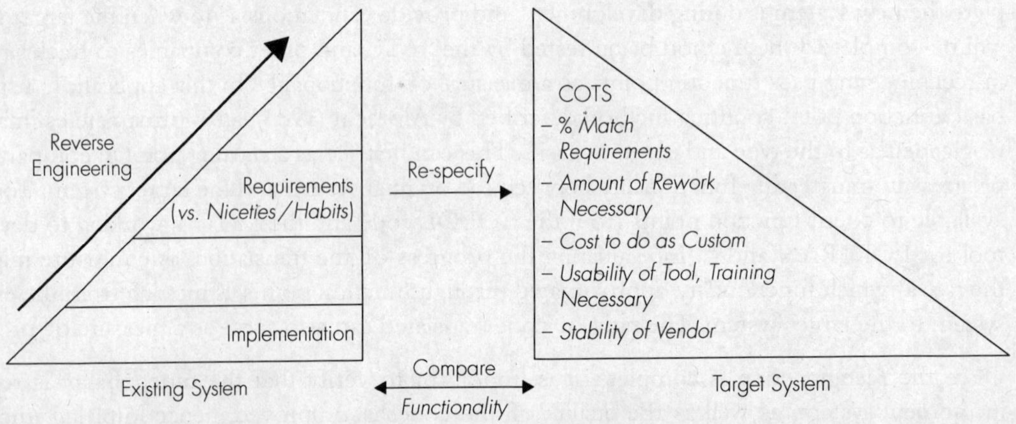

Although the use of COTS software decreases the development time and increases the reliability, COTS also introduces additional risks. A major risk is that the package will not perform as anticipated or advertised, that it is unreliable, immature or incomplete. The package may also, under certain conditions, undergo frequent manufacturer version enhancements requiring constant upgrading. In the worse case, changes may alter or remove functions needed for the system. The COTS software may require improvements, changes or supplementation to match the requirements, causing increase in schedule and, thereby, decreasing reliability. In addition, the use of a COTS software may limit further enhancements to the system, since changes in it provided functions may not be possible due to legal issues.

The stability of the vendor should also be part of the evaluation process since it may be necessary for them to make later required changes. An additional cost may be incurred due to the unfamiliarity with COTS. Simple changes to usability, such as new icons, will require additional training time.

Some metrics are applicable to assist in decreasing the risks associated with the selection of COTS packages. It is important to first identify what percentage of the desired requirements the package totally meets, and which requirements the package partially meets. This information can then be used in determining how much rework or supplementation the package requires in order to totally fulfill the system requirements. Modification or supplementation will impact the schedule and budget, and may well impact maintainability and reliability. After all these evaluations are complete, the cost to develop from scratch should also be estimated, including testing time, and compared to the total costs of COTS.

In this track, once COTS software has been implemented, the functionality of the existing system must be compared to the functionality of the target system. The process of comparison must be based on testing, as was done for translated code functions.

11.7.3.3 Custom Track Hybrid Reengineering

The custom track of hybrid reengineering, shown in Figure 11.7, is similar to traditional reengineering since new code is derived from the existing legacy system.

In this track, reverse engineering is first performed. Those functions that are not satisfied by COTS packages or through translated code must be identified, and their requirements and design extracted. Forward engineering is then executed beginning with the requirements analysis, with the objective of identifying requirements that are not needed. The process is then similar to any development process, beginning with developing a new design, with an object-oriented structure if desired, then implementing the code and doing comprehensive testing.

The advantages to the custom track is that the resulting code should meet its requirements exactly. The developed code should be of high quality and well structured, requiring little corrective maintenance. The disadvantages are similar to standard software development in that the code might not be reliable, requiring additional testing, and that the development/testing process may exceed time and cost budgets. The custom code has the same inherent risks that any code has quality, reliability, schedule.

Since most functions of the legacy system identified as unique to the system will be done with the custom code, the risk is that one of the unique features will not be identified and hence the

Figure 11.7 Custom Track Hybrid Reengineering

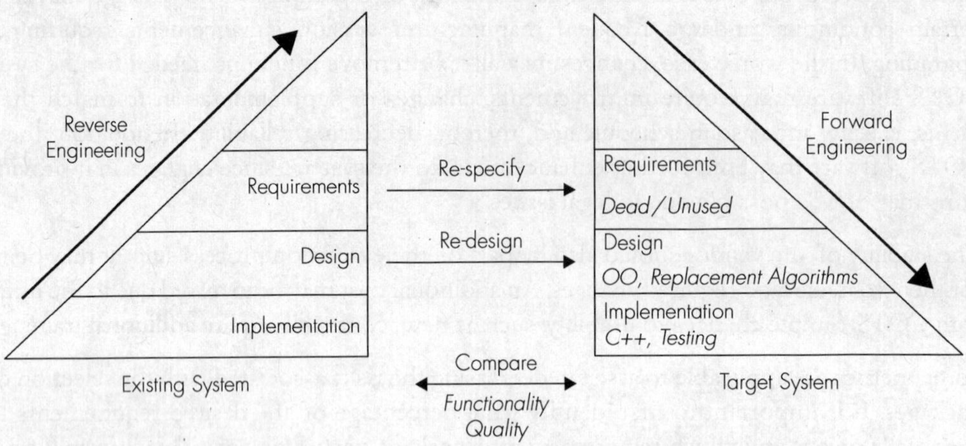

functionality of the new system will be incomplete. All the features identified as critical to the system that are accomplished with custom code will require extensive testing.

The metrics for this track are a combination of both process and product metrics. Prior to reverse engineering, the degree of quality of the existing system should be evaluated for later comparison to the target system (as discussed previously). Effort expended should also be tracked to assist in the evaluation of the ultimate cost to reengineer. This can also be used to approximate schedule completion using the estimate that 60% of the time is in reverse engineering. Once the requirements are respecified, their quality can be evaluated to determine testability. Also discussed previously was the use of function points as a means of calculating the rate of functionality transfer to the target system. Code analysis tools can be used to evaluate the quality of the code as it is being developed and identify the risks. In the testing phase, discrepancy or error rates also help in evaluating reliability. In this track, both the functionality and the quality are compared between the existing system and the target system.

11.7.3.4 Hybrid Reengineering Approach

Hybrid reengineering requires an approach similar to traditional reengineering, but with additional considerations. When starting to reengineer it is important that initial justifications for reengineering such as costs and quality are developed and expectations, such as the return on investment, be stated. An analysis of the legacy system should be done to determine the feasibility of hybrid reengineering.

The analysis of the legacy system should provide a guideline in identifying optimal strategies (translation, COTS, etc.), and projecting the cost of the target system. Once the decision on using a hybrid reengineering approach is made, additional analysis is needed. The first step in a hybrid reengineering approach is to investigate the requirements and constraints of the development. These factors include setting a time table for reverse and forward engineering. Time must be factored in so as to be able to investigate available COTS, including hands-on testing of the COTS. While forward engineering development time should decrease with the use of COTS and the translation of code, additional time will be needed for testing the integration and interface of the products of the three tracks. Budget constraints must be clearly considered; how much can be spent on COTS that provide required features versus those that provide desired features. Management mandates and organization needs must also be identified. As the three tracks are developed, tradeoffs will be important so it is important to prioritize requirements.

An in-depth analysis of the legacy system is important at this stage, focusing on functionalities and code segments suitable for each of the three tracks (Translation, Custom, COTS). In generic reengineering, an analysis of the existing system is usually done to provide an evaluation of the quality of the existing system and the maintenance costs. This information will be used in justifying the costs and improvements at the end of the reengineering effort. In as much as these reasons are still relevant in hybrid reengineering, additional features of the legacy system need to be investigated. During the assessment of the legacy system, sections and functionalities must be identified. These must be further assessed to determine what documentation is available to identify the required features versus what is no longer needed or what users have become accustomed to. It is important that code sections be ordered by the cost of maintenance, and the quality of the current structure. Functions that are unique to this project must be identified. All these components will be used to identify which hybrid reengineering track will be applied to the code section.

Once the code has been divided into the development tracks, each track will proceed independently as discussed. The schedule for track completion will differ based on tasks. As the tracks conclude various tasks, the merging of the final products can begin. For example, the custom glue can be initiated once the COTS have been selected. Training on these packages can also begin.

Once the system is complete and all tracks merged, two tasks remain: testing and justification. First, comprehensive system and integration testing must be performed to ensure that all components work together as a cohesive unit and to ensure that all the functionality of the existing system was transferred to the new system. Second, a justification for the reengineering exercise is usually required – do the benefits gained justify the cost. Some anticipated benefits, such as improved maintenance and operational costs, can only be demonstrated indirectly through the improved quality. Improved quality can initially be demonstrated by a metric analysis of the legacy system compared to the new system. As the new system is commissioned for operation, additional metrics can be used to verify the improvements.

11.7.3.5 Hybrid Reengineering Risks

All software development has inherent risks to schedule and cost and hybrid reengineering, as a software development methodology, is no exception. Hybrid reengineering, because of its composition of the three diverse development tracks, is subject to all the risks that were discussed within each track description. Also, Hybrid reengineering as a unique software reengineering methodology has additional risks to functionality and quality; the functionality of the existing system must be preserved in the new system, and the quality must improve, implying a decrease in operational and maintenance costs. With all the risks in hybrid reengineering, why bother, why not just treat it as a new software development effort and omit the reengineering all together?

11.7.3.6 Hybrid Reengineering Benefits

In general, reengineering is performed as opposed to building a new system because of the invisible business application procedures and logic that are built into the software. These processes might be deeply embedded in business procedures as simple as a field length or as complicated as a mathematical algorithm; the only source of this information is in the legacy code. A second justification for reengineering versus building from scratch are the development and maintenance costs of the legacy system; the time spent developing logic and components should not be wasted. In a reengineering exercise, the existing system is re-implemented and instilled with good software development methodologies, properties, and new technology while maintaining existing functionality, maintainability and reliability are concurrently improved.

Hybrid reengineering has the additional benefits of a reduced development schedule, hence reduced costs. The development schedule is shortened first by minimizing the amount of reverse engineering (recall, reverse engineering is 60% of the effort). The translation track uses minimal reverse engineering time since work is done in the lowest level. The use of COTS decreases the forward engineering development and test time and thus the costs. The use of properly selected COTS also increases the reliability since these packages have been extensively tested.

11.7.3.7 Hybrid Reengineering Metrics

Metrics, when properly applied, provide managers with information about their project to help mitigate risks. It is logical, therefore, to discuss some of the reengineering phases where metrics provide valuable information. Previously we identified metrics applicable for each track in hybrid reengineering, now here, we discuss metrics applicable to the entire project, not just to one track. Metrics provide information on the quality, functionality, and on track selection, a prime area of risk.

At the very beginning of the reengineering effort, it is important to quantify the legacy system. There are only two objectives:

- Identify the amount of functionality;
- The actual quality of the existing system.

By simply quantifying the functionality, we make our scheduling estimates more accurate; during development, completion can be estimated by the percentage of functionality transferred to the new system. Functionality is very important at the conclusion of the project, measuring exactly how much functionality is contained within the new system. Work by SATC and others on working with function points as a means of estimating functionality is currently underway. Function points are quite comparable across languages, and time estimates based on function points are available. In the case of COTS packages, functionality might be measured by the number of requirements satisfied.

Quality is very difficult to measure and, quite a handful of software developers agree, totally on the appropriate metrics. The SATC has a group of metrics it applies to projects to evaluate the quality. These metrics help in evaluating the project at the module level (procedure, function, class or method). The size is measured by counting the number of executable statements. The readability is measured by the comment percentage. The complexity is measured by the cyclomatic complexity (McCabe). The coupling is measured by the calling complexity (fan in/fan out). One final measure of quality is the reliability, the number of errors found, and the projected number of errors remaining. These metrics are quite flexible and can therefore be used for both the translation track and the custom code track, without any side effect. When the components are combined, the number of errors found and the projected number of errors remaining can be applied to the whole system.

Keywords

legacy software; reconstitute; objectives; working documentation; reliability; maintainability; functional enhancement; bottleneck; time consuming; explicit interfaces; conceptual abstraction; system components; components; algorithmic procedures; data structures; testing effort; faults; ambiguity; fault avoidance; defects; inconsistent; ambiguous; incomplete; expressiveness; consistency; completeness; workload; lexical; syntactical; classification schema; software reliability; fault avoidance; fault detection; fault tolerance; translation track; software rejuvenation; hybrid reengineering; testing; justification; cyclomatic complexity

Exercises

1. Define the term reengineering with respect to software.
2. What other processes are encompassed in software reengineering?
3. What is the goal of software reengineering?
4. Discuss the objectives of software reengineering.
5. Explain the general model for software reengineering with the aid of diagrams.
6. At what level should reengineering work be done so as to alter a system?
7. Narrate the software reliability methods.
8. Explain the differences, in detail, between
    - fault avoidance;
    - fault detection;
    - fault tolerance.
9. Discuss the hybrid reengineering approach in detail.
10. Enumerate the potential risks of software reengineering.

CHAPTER 12

Code Slicing

Objectives

The objective of this chapter is to introduce the student to code slicing using relevant examples. When you have read this chapter you will be able to:

- Understand what code slicing is
- Understand the types of code slicing available
- Be in a position to compare and contrast existing slicing techniques
- Know the application areas of code slicing
- Understand the actual implementation of code slicing

12.0 Code Slicing

12.0.1 A Brief History

Here we look at a brief history of program slicing and introduce the key terminology. A slice is taken with respect to a *slicing criterion* <*s, v*>, which specifies a location statement (*s*) and a variable (*v*). This can be easily extended to slicing with respect to a collection of locations and a collection of variables at each location by taking the union of the individual slices. However, to simplify the exposition, we present definitions for the single statement and single variable case.

Program slices, as originally introduced by Weiser, are now called *executable backward static slices*. *Executable* because the basic requirement is that they be in the form of executable programs. *Backwards* because of the direction of edges that are traversed when the slice is computed using a *dependence graph*. And finally, *static* because they are computed as the solution to a static analysis problem (i.e., not taking into consideration of the program's input).

Weiser's requirement that a slice be executable provided an empirical validation of the concept. Although this seems reasonable, many applications of program slicing (e.g., debugging) do not require executable slices. Weiser originally used a Control-Flow Graph (CFG) as an intermediate representation for his slicing algorithm. Ottenstein *et al.* later noted that backward slices could be efficiently computed using the program dependence graph as an intermediate representation by traversing the dependence edges backwards (from target to source). A forward slice might be considered to be informally answering the question ("What statements are affected by the value of variable *v* at statement *s*?")

Laski and Korel (1988) introduced the notion of dynamic slicing: a slice computed for a fixed input. Though the availability of run-time information makes dynamic slices smaller than static slices, it limits their applicability to that particular input only. As with Weiser's algorithm, Korel and Laski's algorithm use a control-flow graph as an intermediate representation. Agrawal and Horgan (1989) later presented a dynamic slicing algorithm that used the program dependence graph (PDG) as an intermediate representation.

12.0.2 Introduction

Program slicing can be defined as a technique for simplifying programs by focusing only on selected aspects of semantics. During the slicing process those parts of the program which can be determined to have no effect upon the semantics of interest are deleted. Slicing has various application areas including testing and debugging, re-engineering, program comprehension and software measurement. For example, during debugging, there is little point in the (human) debugger analysing sections of the source code which cannot have caused the bug. Slicing avoids this situation by simply removing these parts of the program, and focusing attention on those parts which may contain a fault.

This section reviews five semantic paradigms for slicing: static, forward, backward, dynamic and conditioned and two syntactic paradigms: syntax-preserving and amorphous. Over the years, slicing has been successfully applied to many software development problems including testing, reuse, maintenance and evolution. This section describes the main forms of program slicing and some of the applications to which slicing has been put.

Slicing contains two dimensions, namely – the syntactic dimension and the semantic dimension. The semantic dimension focuses on describing that which is to be preserved. The program's static behaviour is preserved by static slicing criteria and its dynamic bevahiour is preserved by dynamic criteria.

However, in the syntactic dimension there is comparatively less choice. However, only two possibilities are available. Firstly, the slice can preserve the program's original syntax wherever possible, merely removing parts of the program which can be found to have no effect on the semantics of interest. This is referred to as a syntax-observing slice. Secondly, the slice is free to perform any syntactic transformation which preserves the semantic constraints desired. This is referred to as amorphous slicing.

12.1 Static Slicing

There are many forms of a slice, so it will be helpful to start off with a simple form of a slice; the static slice. The other forms of slices can be thought of as augmentations of this initial static form. A slice is constructed by deleting those parts of the program that are irrelevant to the values stored in the chosen set of variables at the chosen point. The chosen points of interest are usually identified by annotating the program with line numbers which identify each primitive statement and each branch node.

The point of interest is usually indicated by adding a line comment to the program. In general slices are constructed for a set of variables, but in this chapter only slices constructed for a single variable will be considered. Thus, assuming that you have been given a variable *v* and a point of interest *n*, a slice will be constructed for *v* at *n*. This is not restrictive, since the slice with respect to a set of variables *V* can be formed from the union of the slices on each variable in *V*.

Having chosen a slicing criterion, we can construct one of the two forms of slice: a backward slice or a forward slice. A backward slice contains the statements of the program which can have some effect on the slicing criterion, unlike a forward slice which contains those statements of the program which are affected by the slicing criterion. From now on, we will consider only backward slicing. However, the reader should bear in mind that all the forms of slices which will be discussed here will have their "forward" counterparts.

12.2 Dynamic Slicing

When we debug a program, we would usually have executed it, and presumably found that it produced an unexpected value. We do construct a dynamic slice with respect to three pieces of information. Two of these are just the same as we find in static slicing - the variable whose value appears to be wrong and the point of interest within the program. The third is a mere sequence of input values for which the program was executed. Collectively, this information is referred to as the "dynamic slicing criterion". We shall then say that we can construct a dynamic slice for a variable *v*, at a point *n*, on an input *i*. In order to describe the input sequence *i*, we shall enclose the sequence of values in angled brackets. Thus *<1, 4, 6>* represents a sequence of three input values the first of which is *1*, the second of which is *4* and the last of which is *6*.

12.2.1 Is Dynamic Always Better than Static Slicing?

Dynamic slices are very attractive as an aid to debugging, and in particular, they are superior to static slices for this application. We would forgive the reader for concluding that static slicing is rendered obsolete by dynamic slicing. However, there is still the need to have static slicing for some applications in which the slice has to be found for every possible execution.

For example, assume we are interested in reusing the part of a program which implements a particularly efficient and well-tested approach to some problem. More often than not, in such situations (particularly with legacy code), the code we want to reuse will be intermingled with all sorts of other unrelated code which we do not obviously want. In this situation then static slicing becomes ideal as a technique for extracting the part of the program we require, while leaving behind the part of the program we are not interested in.

This observation highlights the inherent trade-off between the static and dynamic paradigms. Static slices are typically larger, but will definitely cater for every possible execution of the original program. Dynamic slices are typically much smaller, but they will only cater for a single input.

12.3 Conditioned Slicing

The static and dynamic paradigms represent two extremes – either we say nothing about the input to the program (static slicing) or we say everything (dynamic slicing). Conditioned slicing then allows us to bridge this gap.

Fortunately, we can provide information to the slicing tool about the input without giving precise values. Any slice constructed with respect to this condition can therefore omit that statement. This approach to slicing is called the "conditioned approach", because the slice is conditioned by knowledge about the condition in which the program is to be executed. Conditioned slicing addresses the kind of problems the maintainers face when trying to understand the large legacy systems. Often, in this situation, we find ourselves asking questions like "suppose we know that x is greater than y and that z is equal to 4, then which statements would affect the value of the variable v at line 38 in the program".

By using conditioned slicing, we can, therefore, obtain an answer to these kind of questions automatically. By building up a collage of conditioned slices which isolate different aspects of the program's behaviour, we can quickly obtain a picture of how the program behaves under various conditions. Conditioned slicing is a tool-assisted form of the familiar approach – divide and conquer – to understand programs.

12.4 Forward Slicing

Forward slicing uses functions that normally process input values. The objective of this method is to find all areas of code that depend on the values of the input variables. Ripple effect analysis is applied; given a variable and slicing range, the statements in that range that can be potentially affected by the variable are defined. Statements can be affected in terms of data flow, control dependency, or the recursive process; variables on the left and right of the statement are included.

12.5 Backward Slicing

In backward slicing, the process starts with the results of the existing program. Areas of code that contribute to values of output variables are a part of the slice. Given a variable and range, this method of slicing returns statements that can potentially affect the value of the variable; variables only on the right side of the equation are used. Tools are available to facilitate slicing, but the process is still difficult and time consuming.

12.6 Amorphous Slicing

All approaches to slicing discussed so far have been "syntax preserving". This means, they are constructed by the sole transformation of statement deletion. The statements which happen to remain in the slice are therefore a syntactic subset of the original program from which the slice was originally constructed. By contrast, amorphous slices are constructed using any program transformation which simplifies the program and which preserves the effect of the program with respect to the slicing criterion.

This syntactic freedom facilitates amorphous slicing's ability to perform greater simplifications with the result that amorphous slices are never larger than their syntax-preserving counterparts. In most cases they are considerably smaller. Amorphous slicing allows a slicing tool to "wring out" the semantics of interest, thus aiding analysis, program comprehension and reuse. As a matter of fact, it actually does this correctly. However, the syntax preserving slice does not appear to make this very clear. This is because all that can be achieved by statement deletion is the removal of the final statement.

12.7 Applications of Program Slicing

Slicing has quite an array of applications. Any area of software engineering and software development in which it is useful to extract subprograms based upon arbitrary semantic criteria are candidate applications of slicing. We will describe the following four application – debugging, software measurement (specifically cohesion measurement), program comprehension and software maintenance. Slicing is an ever evolving and demanding field. We start with a discussion of debugging, which was the original motivation for program slicing. Now, slicing is applied to many other problem areas.

12.7.1 Debugging

The original motivation for program slicing was to help in locating the faults during debugging activities. The main idea behind was that the slice would contain the fault, but would not contain the lines of code which could not have caused the failure observed. This is relatively achieved by setting the slicing criterion to be the variable for which an incorrect value is observed. Weiser investigated the potential ways in which programmers mentally slice a program when attempting to understand and debug it, which subsequently helped him form a motivation for the consideration of techniques for automated slicing.

In the strictest sense, this approach will only work where the fault is an "error of commission" rather than an error of omission. Slicing cannot be used to identify bugs such as "missing initialisation of variables". If the original program does not contain a particular line of code then the slice will not contain it either. Although slicing is not in a position to identify errors of omission, it has been argued that slicing can be used to aid the detection of such errors.

The application of debugging also motivated and eventually led to the introduction of dynamic slicing. The basic idea here was that slices were typically constructed once a program had produced a failure. In such a situation, the input to the program that caused the fault is available and can be used to narrow the search for the fault, by including only those statements which could have caused the fault on the particular execution of interest.

Dynamic slicing was an important step forward, since static slices for many interesting slicing criteria tend to be rather large. The observation that static slices were large also stimulated the interest in slicing as a means of measuring program cohesion. This meant, in a cohesive program it should be relatively hard to slice the program up into separate components. Bieman and Ott investigated the hypothesis in detail, thus leading to several source level software metrics for cohesion measurement.

Program slicing was discovered as an operation performed by experienced programmers when debugging the code. Programmers, given a piece of code with a bug in it, were asked to describe the code after removing the bug. They could reproduce certain "parts" of the code almost exactly, while others they could not. These parts were not continuous blocks of text (e.g., files, procedures, or functions), but they were rather what we now call program slices. Formalization of this debugging activity lead to the first algorithms for program slicing. Turning this around it should be appreciated that a tool that computes program slices is a valuable aid in debugging. It allows the programmer to focus attention on those statements that contribute to a fault. In addition, highlighting a slice assists in uncovering faults caused by a statement that should be in a slice but is not.

Several types of slices are very useful in debugging. First, dynamic slicing is one variation of program slicing introduced to assist in debugging. When debugging, a programmer normally has a test case on which the program fails. A dynamic slice, which normally contains less of the program than a static slice, is better suited to assist the programmer in locating a bug exhibited on a particular execution of the program. Dynamic slicing can even assist in finding bugs caused by invalid pointers or array subscripts.

Slicing is also useful in algorithmic debugging, which applies the following algorithm to the debugging process – starting from an external point of failure (e.g., an array output value), the debugging algorithm localizes the bug to within a procedure by asking the programmer a series of questions. These questions directly relate to the expected behavior of a procedure. For example, "should the procedure or function add (4, 2) return 6". Since procedures which produce desired results are treated as working, this means that the debugger will attempt to determine if the calls in the procedure produce expected results, otherwise the procedure will be considered as "opened". Algorithmic debugging ends at a procedure with no calls or in a procedure in which all the calls produce the expected output.

One drawback of algorithmic debugging is the questions it asks about procedures that do not effect a buggy result. Program slicing can be of assistance here. Any call not in the slice with respect to the buggy output can be ignored; as it cannot affect the buggy result. Further, parameters that are not in the slice, even for a call that is, can also be ignored.

Apparently, debugging was also the motivation for *program dicing* and latter *program chopping.* Dicing, uses the information that some variables fail some tests, while other variables pass all tests, to automatically identify a set of statements likely to contain the bug. A program dice is obtained using set operations on one or more backward program slices. Some dices are more interesting than others. The interesting ones include the intersection of two slices, and the intersection of slice *A* with complement of slice *B*. The first dice, which identifies common code, is helpful in locating bugs when two computations are both incorrect assuming all incorrectly computed variables are identified and no program bug masks another bug. This dice is also useful in ensuring software diversity in safety critical systems. If for example, the computation of *trip-over-temperature-sensor* and *trip-over-pressure-sensor* include the same computation (often a function call) then this computation is in the dice taken with respect to the two trip signals. Such a computation is of interest in safety critical systems because a bug in this computation may cause both sensors to fail.

The second dice, which yields code unique to *A*, is helpful in locating bugs in computation of *A* if computation of *B* is correct. For example, consider a program that counts the number of words and characters in a file. If the final value of **character_count** is correct, but the final value of **word_count** is not, then the second kind of dice could be applied. In this case, it contains statements that affect the value of **word_count** but not, the value of **character_count**. This implies the looping and reading of characters from the file need not be considered.

Previously only backward slices were considered but of late it has proved that incorporating forward slices increases the usefulness of dicing. For example, the notion of *program chopping* identifies the statement that transmits values from a statement *t* to a statement *s* :*chop(t, s)* and includes those program points affected by the computation at program point *t* that affect the computation at program point *s*. A program chop is useful in debugging when a change at *t* causes an incorrect result to be produced at *s*. The statements in *chop(t, s)* are the statements that transmit the effect of the change at *t* to *s*. Most of the debugging attention should be directly focused there. In the absence of procedures, *chop(t, s)* and is simply the intersection of the forward slice taken with respect to *t* and the backward slice taken with respect to *s* and can be viewed as a generalized kind of program dice. However, the same is not true for interprocedural chopping.

When initially introduced, *s* and *t* were necessarily be in the same procedure, *P*, and only components from *P* were reported. This has been generalized to allow *s* and *t* to be in different procedures and to contain components from procedures other than *P*. It is interesting to note that for interprocedural chopping, the dicing idea of the intersection of a forward and backward slice is imprecise.

12.7.2 Cohesion Measurement

This section presents a brief overview on the application of syntax-preserving static program slicing to the problem of measuring programs for cohesiveness.

It should be known that a cohesive program is one in which the modularisation of the program is performed “correctly”. A cohesive function or procedure should be in a position to perform related tasks. A cohesive function may calculate the result and its remainder arising from the division of one number by another. A less cohesive function is one that will return the largest of two numbers together with the product of the two numbers. In the first case, the two actions are closely related, whereas in the second they are not.

The motivation for assessing the cohesiveness of a program or a part of it solely rests upon observations and claims that highly cohesive programs are easier to maintain, modify and reuse. Cohesion was a product of the endless efforts to define principles for programming, turning the activity from a mere craft into a complete engineering discipline. A recent development on the "cohesion theme" is the idea of encapsulation in object-oriented programming. A well encapsulated object will contain all the relevant data and function members associated with that object.

A slice will capture a thread through a program, which is concerned with the computation of some variable. The basic idea behind functional cohesion is that a function should perform related tasks. If several slices are extracted from a function, each for a different variable, and we find that these slices have a lot of code in common, then we are justified in thinking that the variables were related in some way. We might go further, and decide that the function's "tasks" are captured by the computations it performs on these variables, and therefore we would conclude that the function's tasks are strongly related and that the function is cohesive.

12.7.3 Functional Cohesion

Cohesion is an attribute of a software unit that purports to measure the "relatedness" of the unit. Cohesion has been qualitatively characterized as coincidental, logical, procedural, communicational, sequential and functional, with coincidental being the weakest and functional being the strongest. Yourdon and Constantine noted that functional cohesion " is an integral part of, and is essential to, the performance of a single function."

To construct a slicing-based measure of functional cohesion, Bieman and Ott (1989) defined *data slices*, as a backward and forward static slice that uses data tokens (variable and constant definitions and references) rather than statements as the unit of decomposition. This definition ensures that any change will impact at least one slice and leads to a *slice abstraction* model of the procedure under consideration: one can regard the slice as the sequence of variable tokens that are contained in it.

The tokens that are in every data slice are referred to as *super-glue*; tokens that are in more than one data slice are referred to as *glue*. The metrics are based on the ratios of the appearance of *glue* and *super-glue* tokens in a slice. *Strong functional cohesion* is the ratio of super-glue tokens in the slice to the number of tokens in the slice. *Weak functional cohesion* is the ratio of glue tokens in the slice to the number of tokens in the slice.

Another method for measuring cohesion is to measure the *adhesiveness* of the individual tokens. A token that glues five data slices together is more adhesive than a token that glues only two data slices together. Thus, the adhesion of an individual token is the ratio of number of slices in which the token appears to the number of data slices in a procedure. Bieman and Ott show that these metrics form a well-defined, ordinal measure of the functional cohesion of a program. These measures are, however, not additive.

12.7.4 Program Comprehension

It is widely believed that the maintenance and evolution phases of the software development lifecycle require about 70% of the total costs and so tools which speed up this part of the process are important keys to improved productivity. Often, the maintenance phase starts with program comprehension. This is always the case when legacy systems are concerned, in which documentation may be sparse and the original developers may no longer be available.

Slicing can be of great help within the comprehension phase of maintenance. DeLucia *et al.*, 2001 used conditioned slicing in order to facilitate program comprehension. Field *et al.*, 1995 independently introduced a similar technique they called constrained slicing. Both tend to share the property that a slice is constructed with respect to a condition in addition to the traditional static slicing criterion. The condition can thus be used in identifying the cases of interest in slicing. Harman and Danicic (1996) outlined how this notion of a conditioned slice could be combined with the notion of an amorphous slice in an effort to further assist program comprehension. A program is essentially understood in terms of a set of cases, each of which is captured by a condition. A set of conditions is used to construct a set of cases.

A combination of conditioned slicing and amorphous slicing, can provide the programmer with a convenient tool for program comprehension and analysis. The conditions can thus be used to capture certain cases of interest allowing the program to be broken up into fragments, each relevant to a particular form of computation. The amorphous slicing with respect to the condition, removes parts of the program which are considered irrelevant, focusing attention on the conditions of interest – a software focus.

12.7.5 Differencing Techniques

Programmers are often faced with the problem of finding the differences between two programs. Algorithms for finding *textual* differences between programs (or arbitrary files) are often insufficient. Program slicing can be used to identify *semantic* differences between two programs.

There are two programs related to differencing problems:

- find all the components of two programs that have different behavior;
- produce a program that captures the semantic differences between two programs.

Dependence graph solutions to both problems have also been given. The only reason for not using the data-flow approach is efficiency; the solutions require multiple slices of the same program, which can be done in linear time using dependence graphs.

For programs *old* and *new*, a straightforward solution to Problem 1 is obtained by comparing the backward slices of the vertices in both dependence graphs G_{old} and $G_{new.}$ Components with vertices in G_{new} and G_{old} that have isomorphic slices, have the same behavior in *old* and *new*. The set of vertices from G_{new} which have no vertex in G_{old} which an isomorphic slice safely *approximates*, is the set of components in *new* with changed behavior. This set is safe as it is guaranteed to contain all the components with different behavior. It is (necessarily) an approximation because the exact differencing problem is unsolvable.

We call the vertices in G_{new} with different behavior than in G_{old} the set of *affected points*. The complexity of the straight-forward solution for finding affected points outlined above is cubic to the size of G_{new} (slice isomorphism can be determined in linear time). This set can be efficiently computed in linear time using a single forward slice starting from the set of *directly affected points*. It is the set of vertices of G_{new} with different incoming dependence edges than in G_{old}.

12.7.6 Program Integration

The program integration operation concerns the problem of merging program variants. Given a program named *Base* and two variants namely, *A* and *B*, each created by modifying separate copies of *Base*, we first determine if the modifications interfere. If they do not, our goal is to create an integrated program that incorporates both sets of changes as well as the portions of *Base* preserved in both variants. The need for program integration arises when a system is "customized" by a user and simultaneously upgraded by a maintainer, and the user desires a customized, upgraded version; or when several versions of a program exist and the same enhancement or bug-fix is to be made to all of them.

The integration algorithm uses program differencing to identify the changes in variants *A* and *B* with respect to *Base*. Preserved components are those components that are not affected in *A* or *B*. This set is safely approximated as the set of components with isomorphic slices in *Base*, *A*, and *B*. A merged program is obtained by taking the graph union of (the dependence graph for) the differences between *A* and *Base*, the differences between *B* and *Base*, and the preserved components. This program is also checked for any interference. Interference exists if the changes in Variant *A* and Variant *B* are incompatible. If there is no interference a merged program is produced that captures the changed behavior of *A* and *B* along with the preserved behavior of all three programs.

While it is NP-hard, an important property of the algorithm is that it is semantics-based. An integration tool makes use of the knowledge of the programming language to determine whether the changes made to *Base* to create the two variants have undesirable semantic interactions; only if there is no such interference will the tool produce an integrated program. The algorithm guarantees that the execution behavior of the integrated program relates to the execution behaviors of the base program and the two variants.

12.7.7 Software Maintenance

Software maintainers are faced with the upkeep of programs after their initial release and face the same problems as program integrators – understanding existing software and making changes without having a negative impact on the unchanged part. A new kind of slice, called a decomposition slice, is useful in making a change to a piece of software without unwanted side effects.

While a slice captures the value of a variable at a particular program point (statement), a decomposition slice captures all computations of a variable and is independent of program location. A decomposition slice is useful to a maintainer when, for example, variable *v* is determined to have a value to be changed. A differencing tool based on decomposition slicing, called the Surgeon's

Assistant, partitions a program into three parts (assume the computation of variable *v* is to be changed).

Independent part: Statements in the decomposition slice taken with respect to *v* that **are not** in any other decomposition slice.

Dependent part: Statements in the decomposition slice taken with respect to *v* that **are** in another decomposition slice.

Compliment: Statements that are not independent (i.e., statements in some other decomposition slice, but not *v's*).

Variables can be similarly categorized as follows:

Changeable: All assignments related to the variable are within the independent part.

Unchangeable: At least a single assignment to the variable is in a dependent part. If the maintainer modifies this statement, the new value will flow out of the decomposition.

Used: Variables used in the complement and not in the independent or dependent parts. The maintainer may not declare new variables with these names.

For a maintainer trying to change the code, only independent and dependent statements (i.e., the decomposition slice taken with respect to *v*) are of interest. Furthermore, the Surgeon's Assistant only allows modifications of the independent part and changeable variables (and newly declared variables). The advantage of this approach is that after making a modification only the independent and dependent parts need be tested. The complement is guaranteed to be unaffected by the change; so testing on the complement is unnecessary. Finally, a program is formed by merging the modified independent part and the unchanged complement. This can be done in linear time, without adverse side affects to computations in the complement. The result is a modified and tested program.

12.7.8 Testing

Software maintainers, are also faced with the task of regression testing – retesting software after a modification. This process may involve running the modified program over a large number of test cases, even after the smallest of changes. Although the effort required to make a small change may be minimal, the effort required to retest a program after such a change may be substantial. Several algorithms based on program slicing have been proposed to reduce the cost of regression testing. While decomposition slicing eliminates the need for regression testing on the complement, there still may be a substantial number of tests to be run on the dependent, independent and changed parts. Slicing can be used to help reduce the number of these tests.

The following algorithms assume that the programs are tested using test data adequacy criterion: a minimum standard that a test suite (a set of test cases) must satisfy. An example is the *all-statements* criterion, which requires that all statements in a program be executed by at least one test case in the test suite. Satisfying an adequacy criterion provides some confidence that the test suite does a reasonable job of testing the program.

Gupta *et al.* (1991) proposed an algorithm for reducing the cost of regression testing that uses slicing to determine components affected transitively by an edit at point *p*. They considered a variety of different types of edits (statement addition, statement deletion, modification of the variables used in a statement and so on). While some of these require simplified versions of the following procedure, in general two slices are used. The first slice is a backward slice from *p*. Definitions in this slice of variables used at *p* are recorded. The second slice is a forward slice also starting from *p*. Uses in this slice of variables defined at *p* are recorded.

Bates and Horwitz (1993) present test case selection algorithms for the all-vertices and all-flow edges test data adequacy criterion. The key to their algorithm is the notion of *equivalent execution patterns*. Two program components with equivalent execution patterns are executed by the same test cases. Consider, for example, a component *old* from a tested program and a component *new* from a modified version of the program. If test case *t* tests *old*, and *old* and *new* have equivalent execution patterns then test case *t* is guaranteed to test *new*. No new test case need be devised (even if *new*, does not exist in the original program). The algorithms only select tests that test changed portions of the modified program.

Components with equivalent execution patterns are identified using a new kind of slice called a *control slice*. A *control slice*, which is essentially a slice taken with respect to the control predecessors of a vertex, includes the statements necessary to capture "when" a statement is executed without capturing the computation carried out by the statement.

The notion of equivalent execution patterns is too strong in the presence of procedures and procedure calls because it does not separate different calling contexts (i.e., different chains of call sites). Consider a program with two procedures *main* and *P* where *main* calls *P*. If another call to *P* is added to *main*, then the control slice for any component in *P* will include this new call and therefore cannot be isomorphic with any control slice from the original program. Consequently two such components cannot have the same execution patterns.

Calling context is more accurately accounted for by replacing equivalent execution patterns with the weaker notions of *common execution patterns*. Components with common execution patterns have equivalent execution patterns in some calling context. These components are identified using another kind of slice called a *calling-context slice*, which applies the second pass of backward slicing algorithm "back" through the sequence of call-sites that make up a calling context.

Program differencing can be used to further reduce the cost of regression by decreasing the size of the program that the tests must be run on. For a small change, the program producing the program differencing techniques is considerably smaller and consequently requires fewer resources to retest, especially when run on the reduced test set produced by any of the above named algorithms.

12.7.9 Software Quality Assurance

Software quality assurance auditors are faced with myriad difficulties, ranging from inadequate time to inadequate Computer-Aided Software Engineering (CASE) tools. One particular problem is the location of safety critical code that may be interleaved throughout the entire system. Moreover, once this code is located, its effects throughout the system are difficult to ascertain.

Program slicing is applied to mitigate these difficulties in two ways. First, program slicing can be used to locate all code that contributes to the value of variables that might be part of a safety critical component. Second, slicing-based techniques can be used to validate *functional diversity* (i.e., that there are no interactions of one safety critical component with another safety critical component and that there are no interactions of non safety critical components with the safety-components).

A design error in hardware or software, or an implementation error in software may result in a *Common Mode Failure* of redundant equipment. A common mode failure is a failure as a result of a common cause, such as the failure of a system caused by the incorrect computation of an algorithm. For example, suppose that *X* and *Y* are distinct critical outputs and that *X* measures the rate of increase while *Y* measures the rate of decrease. If the computation of both of the rates depends on a call to a common numerical differentiator, then a failure in the differentiator can cause a common mode failure of *X* and *Y*.

One technique to defend against common mode failure uses *functional diversity*. Functional diversity in design is a method of addressing the common mode failure problem in software that uses multiple algorithms on independent inputs. Functional diversity allows the same function to be executed along two or more independent paths.

One technique to solve this problem combines *Fault Tree Analysis* and program slicing. Once the system hazards have been identified, the objective of fault tree analysis is to mitigate the risk that they will occur. One approach to achieve this objective is to use system fault tree analysis. Under the assumption that there are relatively few unacceptable system states and that each of these hazards has been determined, the analysis procedure is as follows. The auditor assumes that a hazard has occurred and constructs a tree with the hazardous condition as the root. The next level of the tree is an enumeration of all the necessary preconditions for the hazard to occur. These conditions are then combined with logical *and* and *or* as appropriate. Then each new node is expanded similarly until all leaves have calculable probability or cannot be expanded for some reason.

System fault tree analysis gives the auditor the sub-components of the system that must be carefully examined. Part of this examination is the validation that there are no interactions with non-critical functions. The determination of the specific components that will be examined is up to the auditor. This kind of information can be obtained from the design documentation.

Slicing is used as an aid to validate safety is highlighted further. First, the auditor uses system fault tree analysis to locate critical components. The software that is invoked when a hazardous condition occurs is identified in the system. The auditor then locates the software variables that are the indicators of unsafe conditions. Program slices are often extracted on these "Interesting" variables. These slices can be used to validate that there are no interactions between critical components or with non-critical components using program dicing.

Program slices can also be used to assure diversity. Computed from the outputs of individual hazards, they can be examined to determine the logical independence of the events. For instance, if *A* and *B* are two critical conditions, the dice computed by intersecting the program slices on these two conditions provides partial information on whether or not both conditions call simultaneously. If the dice is empty then there is no way that the software can guarantee that both will not occur simultaneously (there may be other ways to verify that both will not occur). If the dice is not empty, inspection of the overlap *may* prove that both conditions cannot occur together (although the functional diversity of such computations is suspect).

These program projections can also be highlighted for more vigorous analysis, inspection and testing. A static program slice can be further refined by examining the trajectory of specific inputs through the program. Dynamic slices are used to observe individual instances of the computation. This simplifies the task of the auditor and permits him to focus on the analytic portions of the audit.

The utility of a slicing tool comes from automating the task of finding statements that are relevant to a computation. Without any tool, the software quality assurance auditor evaluating functional diversity would examine the program under consideration until outputs were identified that should be computed independently. The auditor would then try to verify independence by reading code.

Unravel is a static program slicer developed at the National Institute of Standards and Technology as part of a research project. It also slices ANSI-C programs as well. Its only limitations are in the treatment of **unions**, **forks**, and **pointers** to functions. The tool is divided into three main components:

- a source code analysis component to collect information necessary for the computation of program slices;
- a link component to link flow information from separate source files together;
- an interactive slicing component that the software quality assurance auditor can use to extract program components and statements for answering questions about the software being audited

12.7.10 Reverse Engineering

Reverse engineering concerns the problem of comprehending the current design of a program and the way this design differs from the original design. This involves abstracting out of the source code the design decisions and rationale from the initial development (design recognition) and understanding the algorithms chosen (algorithm recognition).

Program slicing assists in providing a toolset for this type of re-abstraction. For example, a program can be displayed as a lattice of slices ordered by the *is-a-slice-of-relation*. Comparing the original lattice and the lattice after years of maintenance can guide an engineer towards areas in which reverse engineering energy should be spent. Because slices are not necessarily contiguous blocks of code they are well suited for identifying differences in algorithms that may be span multiple blocks or procedures.

Beck *et al.* (1993) observed that elements "towards the bottom" of this lattice are often clichés. For example, in the word count program the slice that reads the characters from a file is contained in three other slices. These slices count the number of words, lines, and characters in the input. The common slice is the read-a-file cliché.

Beck *et al.* (1993) also proposed the notion of interface slicing for use in reverse engineering. In order to understand a program it requires identifying its major abstractions and their interfaces. An interface slice is essentially a forward slice taken with respect to the entry vertices in a collection of procedures. This projection of a general software module (e.g., a set, list, or window widget), captures the particular behaviours required for a particular use.

An interface slice is computed from an interface dependence graph as a forward graph traversal. The dual of this operation uses a backward graph traversal (i.e., traverses the dependence edges from target to source). Starting from all calls on procedure *P*, this "backward" interface slice includes the public interfaces for those procedures (from other modules) that require *P*.

While interface slicing is useful in reverse engineering, it seems more useful in reshaping the development process. In particular, as Beck *et al.* (1993) observed, a programmer with access to a large repository of software modules often wants only part of the functionality of a module in the repository. The programmer will be faced with two unsatisfactory options:

- to create a special copy of the module;
- to include unwanted code.

The first option requires access to the source code, which may not be possible. It also creates multiple copies of some functions from the module, which complicates later updates. The second option increases the code size and may degrade the performance of the compiler when optimizing the code.

Interface slicing can be used to provide a third alternative that has neither of these deficiencies. The complete module is made available to the interface slicer. A programmer, desiring partial functionality from a module, tells the interface slicer which exported functions if requires. The interface slicer then produces the public interface for the required functions without releasing the source for their implementation. Thus, a specialized version of the original is made available to the programmer without introducing a new copy or releasing proprietary source code.

12.8 Slicing Sequential Programs

A slice extracts those statements from a program that potentially have an influence on a specific statement of interest, the slicing criterion. Originally, when slicing was defined by Weiser (1979), he presented an approach to compute slices based on iterative data flow analysis. The other main approach to slicing uses reachability analysis in program dependence graphs. Program dependence graphs mainly consist of nodes representing the statements of a program as well as control and data dependence edges:

Control dependence: between two statement nodes exists if one statement controls the execution of the other (e.g., if or while statements);

Data dependence: between two statement nodes exists if a definition of a variable in one statement might reach the usage of the same variable in another statement.

A slice can now be computed simply in three steps:

1. Map the slicing criterion on a node;
2. Find all backward reachable nodes;
3. Map the reached nodes back on the statements.

Slicing has indeed found its way into various applications. Nowadays it is mostly used in the area of software maintenance and reengineering. It is specifically applied to debugging, testing, program differencing and integration, impact analysis, function extraction and restructuring, or cohesion measurement. It has even been used for debugging and testing spreadsheets or type-checking programs.

12.8.1 Example 1 (Slicing without Procedures)

Figure 12.1 shows an example in which a program without procedures is sliced. To compute the slice for the statement **print a**, we have to follow the shown dependences backwards. This example contains two data dependences and the slice includes the assignment to **a** and the read statement for **b**. In all examples, we will ignore control dependence and just focus on data dependence for the simplicity of presentation. Also, we will always slice backwards from the print a statement. To perform slicing without procedures is trivial: Just find reachable nodes in the PDG. The underlying assumption is that all paths are realisable. This means that a possible execution of the program exists for any path that executes the statements in the same order.

12.8.2 Example 2 (Slicing with Procedures)

Now, the example is extended by adding procedures in Figure 12.2. If we ignore the calling context and just do a traversal of the data dependences, we would add the read a statement into

Figure 12.1 A procedure-less program

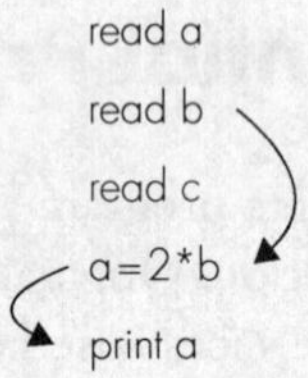

Figure 12.2 A program with 2 procedures

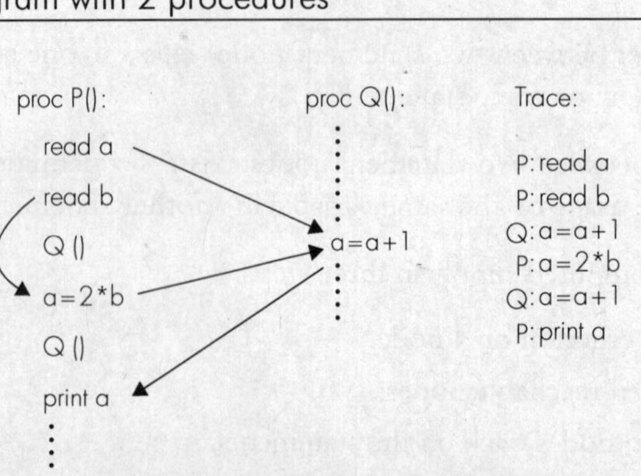

the slice for print a. This is wrong because this statement clearly has no influence on the print a statement. The **read a** statement only has an influence on the first call of procedure Q but *a* is redefined before the second call to procedure Q through the assignment a=2*b in procedure P.

Such an analysis is called context-insensitive because the calling context is ignored. Paths are now considered realisable only if they obey the calling context. Thus, slicing is context-sensitive if and only if realizable paths are traversed. Context-sensitive slicing is solvable efficiently when one has to generate summary edges at call sites. Summary edges represent the transitive dependences of called procedures at call sites.

Within the implemented infrastructure to compute PDGs for ANSI C programs, various slicing algorithms have been implemented and evaluated. Context-insensitive slicing is very imprecise in comparison to context-sensitive slicing. On average, slices computed by the context insensitive algorithm are 67% larger than the ones computed by the context-sensitive algorithms. This shows that context-sensitive slicing is preferable as the loss of precision is not acceptable. A surprising result is that the simple context-insensitive slicing is slower than the more complex context-sensitive slicing (23% on average). The reason is that the context-sensitive algorithm has to visit many fewer nodes during traversal due to its higher precision. Both algorithms usually visit a node or an edge only once, but the context-sensitive algorithm has to visit a few nodes twice.

12.8.3 Slicing Concurrent Programs

Let us move on to concurrent programs. In concurrent programs that share variables, another type of dependence arises: **interference**. Interference occurs when a variable is defined in one thread and used in a concurrently executing thread.

12.8.4 Example 3 (Slicing Concurrent Programs)

In the example in Figure 12.3 we have two threads P and Q that execute in parallel. In this example, there are two interference dependences: One is due to a definition and a usage of variable d, the other is due to accesses to variable c. A simple traversal of interference during slicing will make the slice

Figure 12.3 A program with 2 threads

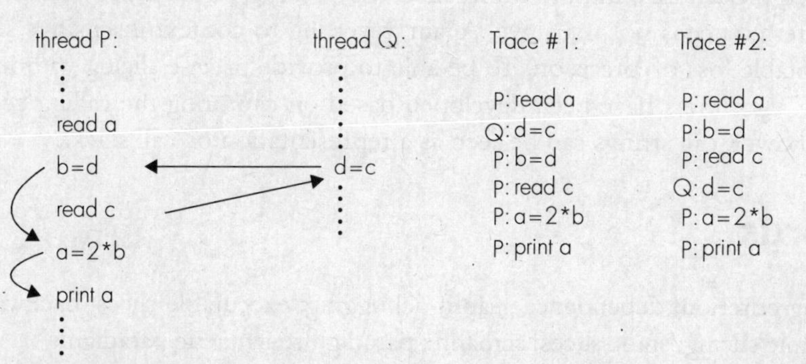

Figure12.4 Another program with 2 threads

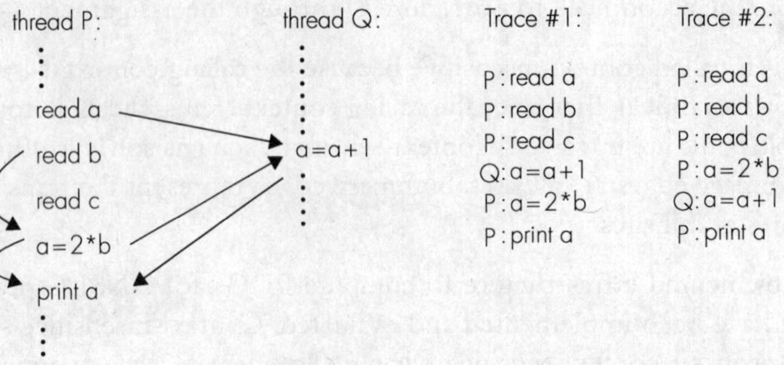

imprecise because interference may lead to unrealizable paths again. In the example in Figure 12.3, a simple traversal will include the **read c** statement into the slice. But there is no possible execution where the **read c** statement has an influence on the assignment b=d. A matching execution would require time travel because the assignment b=d is always executed before the **read c** statement. A path through multiple threads is now realizable if it contains a valid execution chronology. However, even when only realizable paths are considered, the slice will not be as precise as possible. The reason for this imprecision is that concurrently executing threads may kill definitions of other threads.

12.8.5 Example 4

In the example in Figure 12.4, the **read a** statement is reachable from the print a statement via a realizable path. But there is no possible execution where the read statement has an influence on the print statement when assuming that statements are atomic. Either the read statement reaches the usage in thread Q but is redefined afterwards through the assignment a=2*b in thread P, or the read statement is immediately redefined by the assignment a=2*b before it can reach the usage in thread Q. Precise context-sensitive slicing of concurrent programs is undecidable in general. Therefore, we have to use conservative approximations to analyze concurrent programs. A naive approximation would allow time travel, causing an unacceptable loss of precision.
Also, we cannot use summary edges to be context-sensitive because summary edges would ignore the effects of parallel executing threads. Summary edges represent the transitive dependences of the called procedure without interference; they cannot be extended to represent interference, because interference is not transitive. Again, reverting to context-insensitive slicing would cause an unacceptable loss of precision. To be able to provide precise slicing without summary edges, new slicing algorithms have been developed based on capturing the calling context through call strings. However, call strings can be seen as a representation of call stacks.

Keywords

slice; slicing criterion; dependence graph; debugging; executable slices; backward slices; forward slice; dynamic slicing; static slices; semantic paradigms; syntactic paradigms

Exercises

1. Define the term code slicing.
2. List and explain the five major semantic paradigms for code slicing.
3. Discuss the two dimensions of code slicing.
4. What are the potential application areas of program slicing?
5. Describe in detail what cohesion measurement is and how it relates to program slicing.
6. Explain the relevance of program comprehension to program slicing.
7. What are referred to as differencing techniques?
8. Discuss with the aid of examples how you can slice programs.
9. Explain clearly the difference between control and data dependence.

CHAPTER 13

Code Refactoring

Objectives

The objective of this chapter is to introduce the student to software refactoring and its immediate environment. When you have read this chapter, you will be able to:

- Understand the concept of software refactoring
- Understand the types of refactoring and their feasibility
- Compare and contrast existing refactoring techniques
- Know available refactoring tools and their strengths
- Understand refactoring implications on software reuse

13.0 Code Refactoring

13.0.1 Introduction

Programs change and usually they change because of changing requirements or because the context in which they exist changes. But in some cases, the changes to a program do not affect its behavior; only they affect its internal structure. For example, a programmer might change the interface of a function to make it more reusable, change the name of the functions or replace duplicate codes with calls to a function. Sometimes, programmers might have to rewrite part of a program so that they can understand it or make it more aesthetically pleasing. In object-oriented programming, behavior-preserving source-to-source transformations such as these are generally referred to as refactoring.

Refactoring is not a new discipline altogether. Programmers have done it for years in many different languages, although it has been called by different names. It has been carried out manually or with the help of primitive tools like text editors using search and replace. Experienced programmers tend to recognize that the source code should be 'cleaned up' before submission to any system. This cleanup, involves the addition of comments, renaming entities, and clarification of algorithms. However, manually performing these tasks is fairly time consuming, and programmers under time pressure will not do it. Similarly, experienced programmers will not touch an existing source code that works well for fear of introducing an error.

This situation leads to a number of problems in the software: unclear code that leads to corrupted designs, which in turn leads to high maintenance costs and unclear code always arises as a result of the original developer considering 'obvious' what happens to be not so obvious to the next programmer. As requirements change over a certain period of time with regard to the software lifecycle, the design is unfortunately not equally updated to encompass the new requirements since changing the design would involve refactoring large amounts of code. Therefore, these results lead to changes being made in the most expedient means possible, and the design of the system becomes increasingly corrupt and brittle.

These effects are a result of the fact that manual refactoring is tedious and error prone and very expensive. Like all other tedious and error prone manual processes, it should be automated. It is clear that tool support for refactoring will reduce maintenance costs by allowing the programmers to adjust the design to accommodate new and better features. But what is less obvious is its impact on the entire software development process.

State-of-the art software analysis and design methodologies assume that it is rather expensive to change the design once it has been realized in the code. As the rearrangement of the structure of the code becomes cheaper, it will become less expensive to change the design of the software. As a matter of fact, it makes a lot of sense to spend less money on up-front design since shortcomings in the design can be corrected by refactoring the code later. This leads to a qualitatively different form of software development, where the software is designed to support the immediate need and refactored later to add flexibility to support future requirements. One of the red flags that signals an inadequate design is actually the complexity of the code necessary to realize it. Apparently, if a particular design requires awkward coding or convoluted control flow for implementation, its quality is definitely questionable.

However, considering traditional software development methodologies, it is generally too late to correct the design once a significant amount of code is already written. However, the late-design approach creates designs that are no more or less complex than necessary to meet the current set of requirements. Given that the designers do not need to attempt to predict the way in which the system might evolve in the future, they tend to create systems that are more maintainable and cheaper to build. Among the first proponents of this approach was Carl Hewitt (1977), who referred to this style of design as incremental perpetual development. Just a couple of years back, this has been incorporated into a commercial development methodology known as Extreme Programming.

Refactoring generally occurs at all levels. It should be kept in mind that there is high-level refactoring with major design changes and there is low-level refactoring such as renaming a variable.

It was Opdyke (1992) who took the approach towards high-level refactoring, which could be implemented in terms of several low-level refactoring, the fundamental logic being that if we can implement the low-level refactoring correctly, then the high-level refactoring will be correct.

13.1 Refactoring

In object-oriented systems, behavior-preserving transformations are referred to as refactoring. This term probably has its origin from a quote by Peter Deutch (1989): 'interface design and functional factoring constitute the key intellectual content of software and are far more difficult to create or recreate than code'. If the process of separating functions into objects is factoring, then that of changing where the function exists must be refactoring.

It has been recognized, over time, that reusable components are not designed correctly the first time, but rather come about by creating concrete applications and then abstracting the common parts. The reason for this is that people tend to think concretely much better than they think abstractly. When an attempt is made to create abstractions from scratch, people will somehow make some parts more general than necessary and fail to generalize other parts that should have been. An examination of several concrete applications reveals that common parts become apparent quickly even if the common parts are not identical. When they are not identical, the programmer can quickly observe how and where they vary and generalize to support that variance. Quite a handful of researchers have developed program manipulation techniques to support this activity.

The Demeter system was a tool used to facilitate the evolution of class hierarchy. However, this system sought to intimately enforce a notion of good object-oriented style, which has come to be known today as the Law of Demeter. The system had an embedded algorithm that would transform programs that did not conform to the law to ones that did. It was further agreed and proven that any program that is written in a fashion that does not conform to the Law of Demeter can be rewritten to conform to it.

In support of this algorithm, the Demeter system introduced a new data structure known as the class dictionary graph. The vertices of the graph relate to classes and members. Two types of edges that represent the relationships between two vertices do exist and are alternation edges, which represent inheritance relationships, and construction edges, which represent class/member relationships. Bergstein used the class dictionary graphs to define a set of object-preserving class transformations. He clearly defined a complete set of primitive, object-preserving transformations and then derived many higher-level transformations based on them. His transformations were based solely on inheritance. Eduardo Casais identified four categories of support for evolution within object-oriented systems:

1. Tailoring is a process of slightly adapting a class definition without subclassing. This category includes manipulations such as renaming, redefinition of attributes or access privileges.
2. Surgery is a process that involves the addition or removal of entities from a program. Surgery includes adding or deleting classes and/or adding or deleting attributes.

3. Versioning is the process of tracking the changes in the individual entities within the system.
4. Reorganization is a process that involves making large changes to the class library. During the course of this process, the programmers are free to try alternative designs.

Refactoring does support all these behaviors with the possible exception of versioning. Eduardo Casais (1994) developed an algorithm that would introduce new classes into a hierarchy to hold common attributes. Ivan Moore (1996) also took a similar approach; only he did it at a finer granularity level. Moore worked with Self Language and developed a tool called **Guru**, which extracts common portions of methods into a new method that was then rewritten into a newly introduced class. His approach, however, ignored the existing inheritance structure and then recreated an inheritance structure by finding common portions of methods, creating new methods that contained the common code and then creating an inheritance hierarchy that allowed the common code to be inherited.

Correctness is a difficult property to prove. William Opdyke (1992) did identify seven program properties that his refactoring preserved:

1. **Unique superclass:** It dictates that every class must have one superclass. Even though his research was heavily focused on C++, he only considered single inheritance systems.
2. **Distinct class names:** It is important that every class in the system should have a unique identifier; even in the presence of nested scopes or namespaces, this property has to be true at all costs.
3. **Distinct member names:** This property enforces distinct member names within a single class. This gives the method the flexibility to still be redefined in either superclasses or subclasses.
4. **Inherited member variables not redefined:** Classes cannot define variables that are inherited from their superclasses.
5. **Compatible signatures within member function redefinition:** In C++ it is of critical importance that overriding methods should have the same signature as the overridden method.
6. **Type-safe assignments:** After a refactoring exercise, the left-hand side of each and every assignment must be of the type or a subtype of the type of the variable on the right-hand side.
7. **Semantically equivalent references and operations:** Semantic equivalence was defined operationally. It is mandatory that the program produces the same value for a given set of inputs both before and after a refactoring.

13.1.1 Definition of Refactoring

Therefore, in the context of this chapter we will define refactoring as program transformations that have particular preconditions that must be satisfied before the transformation can be legally performed. As an example, the remove class refactoring has the preconditions that the class must exist in the system and should be unreferenced. Our definition incorporates both behavior-preserving transformations as well as non-behavior-preserving transformations.

Table 13.1 Primitive refactoring

Creating an empty class
Creating a member variable
Creating a member function
Deleting an unreferred class
Deleting an unreferred variable
Deleting a set of member functions
Changing a class name
Changing a variable name
Changing a member function name
Changing the type of a set of variables and functions
Changing access control mode
Adding a function argument
Deleting a function argument
Reordering function arguments
Adding a function body
Deleting a function body
Convert an instance variable to a variable that points to an instance
Convert variable references to function calls
Replacing statement list with function call
Inlining a function call
Changing the superclass of a class
Moving a member variable to a superclass
Moving a member variable to a subclass

13.1.1.1 Class Refactoring

These refactoring will change the relationships existing between the classes in the system. AddClass(className; superclass; subclasses) adds a new, unreferenced class to the system. It can also be used to insert a class into the middle of the inheritance hierarchy.

Therefore, one must specify not only its new superclass, but also the set of classes that were subclasses of the original superclass that are now its subclasses.

RenameClass(class; newName): This will rename a class and update all references to it. No other class or globally named newName should exist for this to be a legal refactoring.

RemoveClass(class): This will remove a class from the system. There are two cases where this is applicable:

1. If the class, in question, is unreferenced and has no subclasses.
2. If the class is unreferenced and has subclasses but has no methods or instance variables; in this case, the class is removed and all its subclasses become subclasses of the original class's superclass. See Figure 13.1.

13.1.1.2 Method Refactoring

These refactoring can change the methods existing within the system. Most of them happen to be analogous to operations that can be performed in most non-object-oriented languages. The added complexity that object-oriented languages bring is encapsulation and polymorphism.

1. **AddMethod(class; selector; body):** This adds a new and unreferenced method to the system. This is legal as long as class and all superclasses of class do not attempt to define a method with the same name. Methods with the same name are free to be added to a subclass as long as it is semantically equivalent to the method defined in the superclass. By merely adding an equivalent method to a subclass and removing the method from the superclass, we have managed to effectively push the method downwards into the subclass.
2. **RenameMethod(classes; selector; newName):** Changes the name of a set of existing methods and updates all calls to them. In the event that the method being renamed is used polymorphically in any of the classes in the set, then all the classes that are polymorphic with respect to the method being renamed must also be in the set. It should be noted that it would not be a refactoring to rename a single method that is used polymorphically with another. As an example, to use this refactoring to rename the add method on any of the collection classes, would mean you have to include all of the subclasses of the collection, since they can be used polymorphically with respect to this method.

Figure 13.1 Remove class refactoring using an empty class.

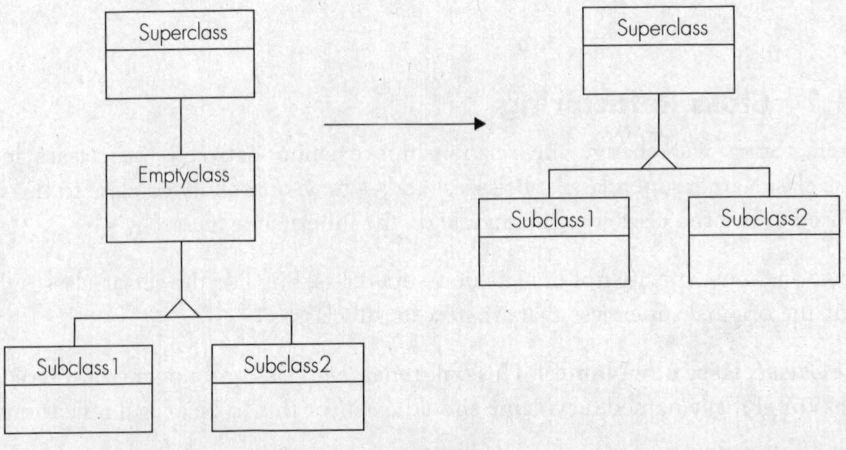

3. **RemoveMethod(class; selector):** This will remove an unreferenced method from the system. This refactoring happens to be legal only if the method is semantically equivalent to the method with the same name implemented in some superclass.
4. **MoveMethod(class; selector; destVarName; newSelector):** Move this method from its defining class to the class of destVarName and give it the name newSelector. This move is a little bit more complex. Essentially, the original method is replaced with a forwarding method that simply calls newSelector on destVarName. To allow the moved method to refer to the members of its original class, newSelector must take an additional parameter that contains the original object.

13.1.1.3 Variable Refactoring

1. **AddInstanceVariable(class; varName; initClass):** Adds a new, unreferenced instance variable to class which is initialized to initClass.
2. **RemoveInstanceVariable(class; varName):** Remove an instance variable from a class. This can only be legal if there are no references to the variable in the class or any of its subclasses.
3. **RenameInstanceVariable(class; varName; newName):** Here you rename an instance variable and update all references related to it.
4. **PullUpInstanceVariable(class; varName):** Removes an instance variable from all subclasses that define it and adds it to class. However, this does add an additional instance variable to classes that did not define it. This is still a refactoring since the added variable is clearly unreferenced.
5. **PushDownInstanceVariable(class; varName):** This removes an instance variable from the class and adds to it the immediate subclasses of class. This can only be legal if there are no references to the variable in class.
6. **AbstractInstanceVariable(class; varName; getter; setter):** Replace all direct references to an instance variable with calls to all accessor functions. All reads of the variable are replaced with a call to getter and all writes of the variable are replaced with a call to setter.
7. **MoveInstanceVariable(class; varName; destVarName):** Simply remove an instance variable and then add it to the class of the object stored in destVarName. This is only legal if the relationship between all instances of class and the instances stored in destVarName is always one-to-one. In a case like this, destVarName is known as an exclusive component.

13.2 Dependencies between Refactoring

The refactoring specified in this chapter is very simple. However, small the refactoring, if it is to preserve behavior, it can then be composed into larger behavior-preserving refactoring, with earlier refactoring changing the program so it meets the prerequisites of later refactoring. If one refactoring happens to 'set up' the preconditions for a second refactoring, then, the latter refactoring is said to be dependent upon the first.

It is very rare to have atomic refactoring performed in isolation. They are too small and hence accomplish very little in their individual capacity. At times they are just part of a group of refactoring intended to cause a design change. Interestingly, there are properties that can be computed from this group. Therefore, this collection of refactoring applied sequentially will need to be formalized.

A chain of refactoring is a sequence of legal refactoring, $< R_1; R_2; \ldots; R_n >$, that are applied to a program sequentially with no intervening changes to the program. Since, each refactoring is legal; the program must satisfy the preconditions of each refactoring when it is applied.

13.3 Eliminating Analysis with Post Conditions

Given the context in which most refactoring are performed, namely within chains, we can reduce the amount of program analysis that must be performed, if we can formally specify how each refactoring affects all of the analysis functions that are used in evaluating the preconditions of the refactoring. Analysis functions are usually computed lazily. A program analysis framework rarely computes the entire function, but only those values that are actually requested from it. For instance, it will not compute the function Senders(class; selector) for all classes and selectors, but only those classes and selectors that affect a particular refactoring. So, by merely incrementally updating these functions as the refactoring are applied, we can thus avoid analyzing the program to find values for analysis functions that were asserted by earlier refactoring.

Therefore, we will augment the definition of a refactoring with post conditions. The new definition inherently includes a third term that specifies how the interpretation of the assertions will change as a result of this refactoring. We, therefore, will choose to refer to this third term as the post conditions of the refactoring, although it is a transformation on assertions and not an assertion by itself. By doing so, we will have moved the domain of discourse of the refactoring from programs to the language used to specify the preconditions. This language is typically easier to reason with than programs.

A refactoring is considered an ordered triple $R = (pre; T; P)$ *where pre is an assertion that must be true on a program for* R *to be legal, T is the program transformation, and P is a function from assertions to assertions that transforms legal assertions whenever* T *transforms programs.*

13.4 Why Developers are Reluctant to Refactor Their Programs?

Let us suppose that you are a software developer. If your project is a new, 'fresh start' (with no backward compatibility concerns); and if you understand the problem your system is supposed to solve; and if your project funding agency is willing to pay until you are satisfied with the results! Such a scenario may be the ideal case for applying object-oriented techniques, for most such a scenario is only a dream.

More often than not, you are asked to extend an existing piece of software. You have a way less-than-complete understanding of what exactly you are doing. You are under a very tight schedule and pressure to produce. What then do you do in such a case? You could re-write the program from scratch or you could leverage your design experience, and correct the ills of the past – and be creative and have fun! However, by the end of the day who will foot the bill? How can you be so sure that the new system will do everything the old system did?

You could simply copy and modify parts of the existing system in an effort to extend its capabilities. This may seem a quicker way, and may even be viewed as a way to demonstrate reuse – without really understanding what you are reusing! However, with time, errors start propagating, programs start getting bloated, program design gets corrupted and the incremental cost of change starts escalating. Refactoring becomes a middle ground between these two extremes. It is a way to restructure software, so as to make design insights more explicit, to develop frameworks and extract all the reusable components, to clarify the software architecture, and prepare to make additions much easier. Refactoring, can seriously help in leveraging your past investment, reduce duplication and streamline a program.

Suppose as a developer you buy into these advantages, you agree with Fred Brooks that dealing with change is definitely one of the 'essential complexities' of developing software. You completely agree, refactoring could finally provide the stated advantages. Why then might you still not consider refactoring your programs? Here are four possible reasons:

1. You might not understand how to refactor
2. If the benefits are long-term, why then exert the effort now? In the long-term, you might not be with the project to enjoy the benefits
3. Refactoring code is an overhead activity, you are paid to write new features
4. Refactoring might give rise problems to the existing program

They are all valid concerns and have been expressed by staff in software development companies. Some are technical concerns, while others are management concerns. All these must be addressed before developers consider refactoring the software in question.

13.5 Dynamic Refactoring

One way to eliminate expensive static analysis is to defer the analysis until runtime. At runtime, it can be observed which program elements are we interested in and then record their values. This section will look at the advantages and disadvantages of refactoring with this type of analysis.

13.5.1 Using Runtime Information for Refactoring

The standard and, arguably, the most preferred method of refactoring code is to statically analyze a program to determine if the preconditions of the refactoring are true. If they appear to be, then refactor the code, otherwise, abort the refactoring. In general, every property of any given program happens to be difficult to decide. Static analyses must therefore, use conservative approximations of the actual functions. Usually, this approach tends to be very successful.

Two common cases that cause this approach to fail are when the approximation takes a long time to compute and when the approximation is extremely poor. The refactoring tool should be designed to be used interactively; so long delays are not acceptable. If an analysis takes too long to compute, the programmer will not use a refactoring based on it, but will rather refactor the code manually and rely on the test suite to catch errors. If, an approximation happens to be particularly poor, in such a case, where it only detects the most degenerate cases, any refactoring based on it will rarely work. Bill Opdyke's approximation for the *IsExclusive* analysis falls into this category. His approximation stated that a component was exclusive if and only if it was created and assigned to an instance variable only in the constructor of the object and never assigned anywhere else.

An alternative approach is to use runtime information to perform this analysis. In this approach, the program is refactored, and the code is instrumented to verify that the preconditions of the refactoring hold true. However, in the event that the instrumentation detects that the assumed preconditions are invalid, then the refactoring must be undone. To ensure the preconditions are true, the program has to undergo testing. After the code is sufficiently tested, the instrumentation can be removed.

There are two types of information that are provided by dynamic analysis, namely – predicates and functions. With dynamic predicates, the predicate is assumed to be true unless if the instrumentation detects otherwise, at which point it then signals its client. As an example, the *IsExclusive* analysis assumes that the component being analyzed is exclusively owned until it is proven otherwise. Predicates are used in the preconditions of refactoring so as to ensure that they are legal. Yet, another type of analysis is dynamic functions. As the program is under execution, the analysis provides its client with the values of the function that occur during the execution.

Consider the following example, the *ClassOfanalysis* function will return the classes that are assigned to a particular variable. This information is usually completes a refactoring. For instance, the *rename* method refactoring has to determine which senders of the particular selector being renamed actually refer to the method that is being renamed. In order to do this dynamically, the *sendersAnalysis* function has to provide the call nodes that actually refer to the method at runtime. The refactoring will therefore have to update these nodes while the program runs.

13.5.2 Definition of Correctness

Most refactoring are program transformations that are intended to be behavior-preserving. Therefore, informally, a refactoring is correct if the program behaves exactly the same after the transformation as it did before the transformation. However, we have to clarify what is meant when we say 'behaves exactly the same'. We have to identify the potential properties of the program that we consider as interesting behavior. For example, in quite a number of systems a transformation is considered to be behavior preserving even if it makes the system a millisecond faster or slower. In the case that the same transformation is made on a real-time system, then the resulting system can break down if it violates specified timing constraints.

Therefore, every program is inherently assumed to have a specification. A refactoring is considered to be correct if a program that meets its specification continues to meet its specification after the refactoring has been applied. Properties of the program that are outside the specification are considered artifacts that will not necessarily be preserved. Test suites as program specifications declaratively state the properties that a program should exhibit. Under normal circumstances, specifications are given to programmers to compare with the program as it is written. A program is considered correct with respect to a specification if it meets the requirements stated in that specification. Balzer and Goldman (1989) suggested eight principles of good program specifications:

1. Separate functionality from implementation clearly
2. A process-oriented systems specification language is definitely required
3. A specification has to encompass the system of which the software is a component
4. A specification has to encompass the environment in which the system operates
5. A system specification must be a cognitive model thereof
6. A specification has to be operational
7. The system specification must be tolerant of incompleteness and augmentable
8. A specification must definitely be localized and loosely coupled

Yet, another form of specification of program behavior is the test suite. Test suites have to satisfy all of the eight principles mentioned:

1. Test suites can be best described as input, result pairs without specifying how the result is obtained. In a real-time environment the result will have to include timing constraints.
2. Roger Pressman (2005) defines a process-oriented description as, 'the what specification achieved by specifying a model of the desired behavior in terms of functional responses to various stimuli from the environment,' test suites can be considered as perfect examples.
3. Good test suites are assumed to verify the interaction between various subsystems within the software. Since, these interactions are complex and dynamic by nature, they are also subject to errors.
4. Good test suites should also account for the interaction of the environment with the software, be it user input or some other form of data acquisition.
5. The cognitive model presented by a test suite is that of a black-box. Anything can and will happen within the box as long as the outputs for a given set of inputs remain constant. This model meshes very well with the maintenance phase of software development since the primary concern of anyone doing maintenance programming is to avoid introducing new errors into the system.
6. Test suites can be considered the ultimate operational specification. The inputs are fed into the program and the results compared against the expected results.
7. Test suites are never complete in any way and yet they continue to eliminate many bugs from the system. Whenever users discover bugs in a running system, they augment the test suite by adding tests that will catch the error that slipped through.
8. Individual tests within the test suite do not depend entirely on each other for results. Therefore, as requirements change, tests can be easily added or removed from the test suite whichever is applicable at the time.

One of the basic requirements that must be met when any change is made to a system is that the system can continue to pass the original test suite. If an extension is made to the system, then it must not only pass the original set of tests, but also any other additional tests to determine if the extension is correct. Despite meeting the requirements for a program specification, test suites do have several drawbacks. First of all, they tend to be quite large. Even though it is practically not possible to test every path through a program, good test suites try to exercise each code segment at least once. To achieve this, it is mandatory that the program must be executed on large sets of inputs.

Test designers try to combine as many tests as possible into a single input set. This leads to the second problem, namely, duplication. These two forces do oppose each other. The less duplication there is, then the larger the test suite and the smaller the test suite there is, then the greater the duplication present. Both of these tend to make changing the specification difficult. One more problem with this type of specification is that it is not generative. We would not want to specify a new system mainly by its test suite. In the degenerate scenario, one could choose to write a program that simply looks up the input value and returns the output value.

The definition of correctness that we will be using when discussing dynamic refactoring is simply based on test suites. A refactoring can be said to be correct if a program that passes a test suite continues to pass the test suite after the refactoring has been applied. With this definition of correctness in mind, refactoring that require runtime analysis can be shown to be correct over a particular set of executions, namely the test suite.

13.6 Dynamic Analysis *vs.* Static Analysis

The standard and arguably, the most preferred method of analyzing code is to do it statically. A static analysis can be said, to examine the source code of the program and compute its appropriate functions. The analysis typically uses a data-flow framework and then computes the fixed-point. The main advantage of static analysis is that it does not depend on any particular execution of the program, but can provide information about all executions of the program.

There are basically two fundamental shortcomings of the static analysis approach. Firstly, all of the interesting properties of programs cannot be decided – they can be reduced to the halting problem. Therefore, static analyses must compute decidable and conservative approximations of the desired properties. Depending upon the application, a conservative approximation can be satisfactory, but there are several situations where static approximations are inadequate. You can consider the example of *IsExclusive*. There are several number of refactoring that can only be performed if one object is stored in an instance variable of one other object at any given time. Detecting this situation is a difficult task since, detecting if two variables contain the same object at any point in their lifetime cannot be decided.

The approximation that was used by Opdyke was to detect degenerate cases that guarantee that a component is exclusive. The most common case that can be detected is that of an instance variable that is only assigned to a newly created object. This is simply to detect whenever a language contains explicit constructors such as C++. However, in a dynamic language such as Smalltalk without explicit constructors, even this crude approximation defies static analysis.

A potential solution to the problem is to make a liberal approximation. This can be accomplished by gathering information while the program is running. The analysis then consists of the data that was observed in a running program. Since, it is not possible to observe each and every possible run of the program the result therefore remains an approximation. However, this approximation is not adequate on the side of incomplete information. As an example, a static type analysis may contain more types than those actually assumed by the program element, but a dynamic type analysis may contain certainly fewer types than the actual type of the program element. Until a path through the program is completely executed, the analyses depending on that path are not computed, therefore, if there are paths that are never executed, they will therefore never be considered by the analyses.

One quite interesting property of the liberal approximation of dynamic analysis is that when coupling it with conservative, static analysis can sometimes lead to the exact information. If, the liberal analysis and the static analysis are the same, then the exact value has been implementation of Dynamic Refactoring. There are two ways to implement dynamic refactoring – an online and an online approach. The online approach instruments a program and collects the information. At some point in the future, this information is used by a tool in an effort to transform the source code based on the observed information. The online approach collects the information and transforms the program while it is in execution mode. While both of these techniques are reflective, choice of language and environment have a great effect on which approach is most feasible. Dynamic environments such as Smalltalk or Lisp lend themselves to the online approach, whereas statically-compiled environments such as C++ or Java are easier to refactor online. The analysis functions for which we have examined dynamic analyses are namely *Senders*, *ClassOf*, and *IsExclusive*.

The Refactoring Browser makes use of a reflective technique known as method wrappers to implement the online form of dynamic refactoring. Method wrappers will allow the code to be executed before and after the invocation of a method. The analysis has to be implemented in this before and after the code. One more benefit of this technique is that every wrapper in the system has the same code, so recompilation is not necessary to install the wrapper. To have a wrapper installed on a method, the wrapper has to be given a reference to the original method, and the wrapped method has to be installed in the method dictionary in place of the original method. The implementation of techniques like this one does not require the recompilation of the method being wrapped. This is a very important consideration when instrumenting a large number of methods.

In order to dynamically compute the senders of a particular method, we put a wrapper on the method we are interested in. At runtime, when the method is called, the wrapper's before code is executed. This code examines the call stack to find the class, selector, and call node of the sender and passes this information to its client. When the analysis is complete and any actions are taken by the client, the wrapper passes the execution on to the original method.

IsExclusive is similar to *ClassOf* in that a variable is constantly monitored. Since this is a predicate rather than a function, it will only notify its client whenever the condition is detected to be false. The client assumes that the function is true unless the analysis reports show otherwise at runtime. This analysis will maintain a table of exclusively-owned objects. If an object is assigned to the variable and already exists in the table, the analysis signals its client that the test is false. Otherwise, the old value of the variable will be removed from the table and the new value is subsequently added.

13.7 The Feasibility of Dynamic Refactoring

It is generally accepted that every software development process should have a test suite to ensure correctness. Moreover, recent discussions about integrating refactoring into a commercial development process, stress the importance of having a test suite before attempting any refactoring, whether manual or automatic. Therefore, it is not unreasonable to assume the presence of a test suite. Projects that do not use test suites probably have problems that will not be solved by refactoring.

Dynamic refactoring is not in any way worse than manual refactoring in fact it is often better. When refactoring is done manually, the programmer has to update all the references manually. If, the programmer happens to miss any, the test suite will certainly fail. The programmer will have to correct the error and run the test suite again. With dynamic refactoring scenario, the test suite must still be executed to perform the analysis, but it will complete successfully and will not have to be rerun for this refactoring. If, later, a customer finds an error in the program that was introduced by the refactoring, it is then evident that the refactoring was incorrect or incomplete and that the test suite was inadequate. In both manual and dynamic cases, the test suite should be sophisticated to catch the error. With the dynamic approach, the quality of the analysis can be measured by quality metrics tests such as coverage. To show that this approach is no worse than the manual approach, consider the following scenario.

A programmer would refactor the program using a dynamic refactoring and then runs the test suite. He then makes sure the program is released. After the release, a user finds an error. Now, was the error introduced by refactoring or was it always present? The test suite would not have caught it if it was always present, so it is not possible to determine if it was preexisting or not. Either way, the test suite has to be extended in an effort to trap the particular error. Manual refactoring will also have the same possibility of error along with the added routine of having to perform the refactoring manually.

The dynamic approach to refactoring has not yet been officially incorporated into the publicly available tools. We feel that the testing tool must be better integrated with the refactoring tool so as to make this approach acceptable to commercial programmers.

13.8 Refactoring Tools

13.8.1 The Refactoring Browser

This presents a practical refactoring tool that could be used in commercial software development since many of the ideas of evolutionary software development, such as continual refactoring and designing to the current set of requirements, would not be fully realized until such a tool has been developed. Also provides a framework with which to test many of the newer refactoring ideas available.

13.8.1.1 History

The first introduction of the Refactoring Browser, then known simply as the Refactory, was as a stand-alone tool separate from any other tools available in the Smalltalk environment. It implemented many of the refactoring that exist in the current tool but in a cruder fashion.

While, technically an interesting tool, it was rarely used. This led to the examination of what the real criteria were to get programmers to use this tool. As a result, the Refactoring Browser was created.

Currently, the Refactoring Browser is being used on several commercial programming projects worldwide, in areas such as public health, telecommunications, insurance and banking. The tool has been performing well in many different contexts. Programmers have begun to realize the inherent power that even simple automated refactoring gives them. Nearly, all feedback has been positive and most of the requests have been for additional features. Figure 13.2 shows a screen-shot of the publicly-available tool.

13.8.2 Technical Criteria for a Refactoring Tool

The main purpose of a refactoring tool is to allow programmers to easily refactor code. The first thing that a programmer notices about automatic refactoring is that it reduces the amount of editing necessary to change the code. The programmer specifies the change that he wants to make, and the refactoring changes the code quickly. When refactoring is done manually, the programmer

Figure 13.2 The refactoring browser

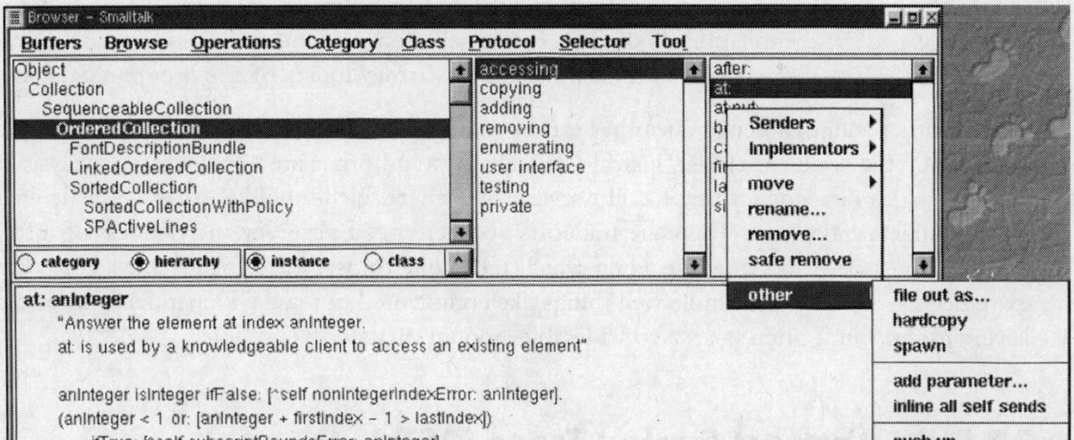

must run the test suite after each small change to ensure that the program behaves the same way as before the refactoring. Testing is time-consuming, even if it is automated. Correct, automatic refactoring appears to reduce the need for that step, and can also accelerate the refactoring process significantly.

The technical requirements for a refactoring tool are those unique properties that allow it to transform a program while making sure its behavior is preserved. This guarantees that the test suite will not have to be rerun after every little change. Even dynamic refactoring, which apparently requires running the test suite, reduces testing. Unfortunately, with manual refactoring, the programmer makes a small change in the code, and runs the test suite. If the test happens to fail, he will have to correct the error and rerun the test suite. Dynamic refactoring will only run the test suite once. Therefore, time is saved by both eliminating the updating of cross-references manually, and only running the test suite once.

13.8.3 Program Database

An important requirement is to have the ability to search for various program entities across the entire program. As an example, a program might want to find all calls that can potentially refer to a particular method. Tightly integrated environments like Smalltalk constantly maintain such databases. At any time, the programmer is free to perform a search to find cross references. Maintenance of this database is thus, facilitated by the dynamic compilation of the code. As soon as a change is effected to any class, it is immediately compiled into bytecodes and the database is updated accordingly. Updates to the database have to be performed explicitly. These updates are quite similar to the compilation of the Java code itself. Some of the more modern environments such as IBM's VisualAge for Java mimic Smalltalk's dynamic update of the program database.

There exists a range of techniques that can be used in the construction of this information. At one end of the scale exists fast, lexical tools like *grep* and other are sophisticated analysis techniques such as dependency graphs. However, somewhere in the middle exists syntactic analysis using abstract syntax trees. There are tradeoffs between speed, accuracy and richness of information that must be made when deciding which technique to use. Take for instance, *grep* which is extremely fast but cannot handle well things like commented-out code. Dependency information is very useful, but it often takes a considerable amount of time to compute.

13.8.4 Abstract Syntax Trees (ASTs)

In most cases refactoring has to manipulate portions of the system that are below the method level. These are generally references to program elements that are being changed. Consider, for example, if an instance variable is renamed (simply a definition change), all other references within the methods of that class and its subclasses must be updated accordingly. Some refactoring are by nature entirely below the method level, such as extracting a portion of a method into its own, stand-alone method, or assigning a common subexpression to a temporary variable and replacing all occurrences of the expression with the temporary variable. Any update to a method needs to be in a position to manipulate the structure of the method. To do this requires the use of abstract syntax trees.

There are more sophisticated program representations that contain more information about the program such as Control Flow Graphs and Program Dependency Graphs. However, we have found the ASTs contain sufficient information to implement powerful refactoring and are created extremely quickly. Morgenthaler found that the information that was contained in CFGs and PDGs could be extracted from ASTs as it was needed rather than having to create the additional graphs. If there is need for more sophisticated information in the future, it may be wise to adopt some of his techniques.

13.8.5 Accuracy

The refactoring that a tool implements must reasonably preserve the behavior of programs. Total behavior-preservation is an impossible state to achieve. For example, a refactoring might make a program faster or slower by a few milliseconds. Usually, this would not have an effect on a program, but if the program requirements include hard real-time constraints, this could cause a program to be incorrect. Even more traditional programs can run into difficulties. For example, if a program constructs a string, then uses the language's reflective facilities to execute the method that the string names, then renaming the method will cause the program to have errors.

It has also been noted that, refactoring can be made reasonably accurate for most programs. A lot of programs do not rely extensively on techniques that defy our analysis and most do not have hard timing constraints. In the documentation of the tool, there are cases that will break a refactoring so programmers that use those techniques can either avoid the refactoring or manually fix the parts of the program that the refactoring tool cannot fix. One of the techniques used to increase the accuracy of the tool is to let the programmer provide information that would be difficult to compute. For example, in the publicly available version of the tool, when a type of a variable is required, you can perform a quick-and-dirty type analysis based simply on the set of messages sent to the variable. At times this list might contain extraneous classes and at times does not include the correct class. It allows the user to select the correct classes from the list and to add classes if necessary. This technique shows the possibility that the programmer can be wrong and will therefore introduce an error into the program. This approach is much safer than manual refactoring, since the tool handles the nonlocal edits. Additionally, the tool provides an *undo* facility that allows the programmer to correct flawed refactoring quickly. Another benefit of this approach is that programmers tend to feel that they have more control over the process and thereby will tend trust the tool more.

13.9 Practical Criteria to Refactoring a Tool

The reason why tools are created is to support humans in a given task. Always remember that if a tool does not fit the way people work, they will simply not use it. The most important criteria are usually the ones that integrate the refactoring process with other available tools.

13.9.1 Speed

It should be borne in mind that the analysis and transformations that are usually required to perform refactoring can be time consuming if they are very sophisticated. It is mandatory that the relative costs of time and accuracy is always considered. If a refactoring apparently takes too long, a programmer will never use the automatic refactoring, but will just perform it manually. 'Too long' is simply a delay a programmer is generally used to. For example, in Smalltalk, compilation of a method takes less than a second when a method is accepted. Therefore, programmers are not always keen on waiting for extended periods of time for a refactoring, since they could perform it and test it in a matter of minutes. C++ programmers are generally use to compilations taking several minutes. We believe that C++ programmers would be more willing to accept refactoring tools that were slower, as long as it was faster to refactor the program with the tool than manually.

When you implement a refactoring, you should always put into consideration the element of speed. The Refactoring Browser has several refactoring, such as Move Instance Variable to Component and Common Subexpression Elimination that have not been implemented because not much about how to implement them safely in a reasonable amount of time is known. Yet, another approach to put into consideration if an analysis would be too time-consuming is to simply ask the programmer to provide the information. This gives responsibility for accuracy back to the programmer while still allowing the refactoring to be performed quickly.

13.9.2 Undo

As mentioned earlier, automatic refactoring tend to allow an exploratory approach to design. You can move the code around over and over again and see how it looks under the new design. Since, a refactoring is defined as basically behavior-preserving, then it follows that the inverse refactoring, which undoes the original, is also a refactoring and behavior-preserving. Earlier version of the Refactoring Browser did not incorporate the *undo* feature. This made refactoring a little more tentative since undoing some refactoring, while behavior-preserving, was difficult. Quite often you would have to go and find an old version of the program and start again. This was annoying. With the addition of undo function, yet another fetter was scrapped off. Now, you can explore with impunity, knowing that you can roll back to any prior version. You can create classes, move methods into them to see how the code will look, change your mind and go in a completely different direction, all very quickly.

13.9.3 Integrated with the Environment

In the past decade, the Integrated Development Environment (IDE) has been at the core of most development projects. The IDE integrates the editor, compiler, linker, debugger and any other tools necessary for developing programs. An early implementation of the refactoring tool for Smalltalk was a stand-alone tool and was rarely used until refactoring was integrated into the Smalltalk Browser.

13.9.4 Understanding How and Where to Refactor

How can you learn how to refactor? What are the available tools and techniques and how can they be combined to accomplish something useful and when should they be applied? This section defines several refactoring.

The Software Refactory project, at the University of Illinois, used a more minimalist approach. They defined a smaller set of refactoring and showed how they could be applied. They based their collection of refactoring on own programming experiences, by evaluating the structural evolution of several object-oriented frameworks (mostly in C++), and by talking with and reading the retrospectives of several experienced Smalltalk developers. Most of their refactoring were low-level, e.g., creating or deleting a class, variable or function; changing attributes of variables and functions such as their access permissions (e.g., public or protected) and function arguments or moving variables and functions between different classes. A smaller set of high-level refactoring perform simple operations such as creating an abstract superclass, simplifying a class by subclassing and simplifying conditionals, or splitting off part of an existing class to create a new, reusable component class (often converting between inheritance and delegation or aggregation). However, the more complex refactoring are defined in terms of the low-level refactoring.

Given an existing program, what refactoring can you decide on applying? That depends, of course, on what you intend to achieve and how. One common reason is to restructure a program to make it easier to add (near-term) a new feature. There are, however, several other reasons why you might decide on applying refactoring. Experienced object-oriented programmers and those who have acquired training in design patterns have learned that there are several desirable structural qualities and characteristics of programs that have been shown to support extensibility and reuse. Object-oriented design techniques such as CRC focus on defining classes and their protocols; while their focus is upon up-front design, there are ways to evaluate existing programs against such guidelines.

An automated tool can have the ability to identify structural weaknesses in a program, such as functions that have an excessively large number of arguments or are excessively long. These are indeed potential candidates for refactoring. Similarly, an automated tool can identify structural similarities that may indicate the presence of redundancies. For example, if two functions are nearly the same (which is often the case when a copy-and-modify process was applied to the first function to produce the second), such similarities can be detected and refactoring suggested that can move common code to a single location. Assuming, that two variables in different parts of a program have the same name, they can sometimes be replaced by a single variable that is inherited in both places. These are few very simple examples – there are many other, more complex cases that can be detected and corrected by an automated tool. These structural abnormalities or structural similarities do not always mean that you would want to apply a refactoring, though they often do.

More recently, much of the work on design patterns has focused on good programming style, and on useful patterns of interactions among parts of a program that can be mapped into structural characteristics and to refactoring. More recently, John Brant and Don Roberts have managed to create a tool that applies an extensive set of heuristics to automatically analyze Smalltalk programs and suggest what refactoring might improve in the program design and where to apply the tool exactly.

Applying, such a tool to analyze your program amounts to applying 'lint' to a C or C++ program. The tool is not smart enough to understand the meaning of the program. Just a few of the suggestions it makes, based on structural program analysis, may indicate changes you would like to make. As a programmer, you make the decision to apply it or not. You make decisions as to which recommendations you actually want to apply to your program. Those changes should improve the structure of your program and, in general, better support changes in the future.

In a nutshell, before programmers convince themselves that they ought to refactor their code they need to understand how and where to refactor. There is no substitute for experience. Automated tools usually analyze the structure of a program and suggest refactoring that might improve the structure. As with most disciplines, tools and techniques are of great help, but only if you use them and use them properly. As programmers engage in refactoring their code, their understanding grows as well.

13.9.5 Refactoring to Achieve Near-term Benefits

It is relatively easy to describe the mid-to-long range benefits of refactoring. However, most organizations are increasingly judged (by the investment community and by others) on their short-term performance. Can refactoring indeed make a difference in the near-term or short-term?

Refactoring has been successfully applied for over ten years by professionals and experienced object-oriented developers. Many of these developers and programmers 'cut their teeth' in a Smalltalk culture that valued clarity and simplicity of code, and embraced reuse. In such a culture, developers and programmers use to invest time to refactor because it was 'the right thing to do'. The Smalltalk language and its implementations are accredited with making refactoring possible in ways that had not been true for most prior languages and software development environments. Pretty much of the early Smalltalk programming was done in research groups such as XeroX PARC or in small programming teams at leading-edge companies and consulting firms. Apparently, the values of these groups were somewhat different from the values of many industrial software groups.

For refactoring to be embraced by the more mainstream software development community, at least some of its benefits must be near-term or short-term. One example is the Choices file system framework. In the initial days, the framework implemented the BSD UNIX file system format. Later on, it was extended to support System V UNIX, MS/DOS, persistent and other distributed file systems. As a matter of fact, System V file systems bear many similarities to BSD UNIX file systems. The approach used by the framework developer was to first clone parts of BSD UNIX implementation, and then modify that clone to support System V. The resultant implementation worked but there were lots of duplicate code. After adding the new code, the framework developer then refactored the code, creating abstract superclasses to contain the behavior common to the two UNIX file system implementations. Common variables and functions were then moved to superclasses. In cases where corresponding functions were nearly but not completely the same for the two file system implementations, new functions were defined in each subclass to contain the differences and in the original functions those code segments were replaced with calls to the new functions. Code was therefore incrementally made more similar within the two subclasses. When the functions were completely identical, they were then moved to a common superclass.

These refactoring do however provide several near-term and mid-term benefits. Near-term benefits occurred during testing, errors found in the common code base needed to only be modified in one place. The overall code size was eventually smaller. Furthermore, the behavior specific to a particular file system format was cleanly separated from the code common to the two file system formats, making it easier to track down and fix behaviors specific to that file system format. Mid-term benefits occurred during; the abstractions that resulted from refactoring were often useful in defining subsequent file systems. Granted, the behavior common to the two existing file system formats might not be entirely common for a third format, however the existing base of common code was a valuable starting point, and subsequent refactoring could be applied to clarify what was common. The framework development team eventually found that over time, it took less effort to incrementally add support for a new file system format, even though the newer formats were more complex developments was done by less experienced staff.

With respect to physical health, in many ways, refactoring is like exercise and eating a proper diet. It is common knowledge to many of us that we ought to exercise more and eat a balanced diet. Such behaviour is highly encouraged. However, some of us get by, for a while, without doing this, perhaps even without visible effects. We can always make excuses for not performing this important routine. But the truth of the matter is, we will be only fooling ourselves if we continue to ignore it.

Some of us are purely motivated by near term benefits of exercising and eating a proper regular diet such as high energy levels, greater flexibility, higher self-esteem and other such benefits. Most of us are aware that these near term benefits are very real. Many of us make at least sporadic efforts in these areas. Others, however, are not sufficiently motivated to 'do something' until they reach a crisis point.

Yes, there are, of course, cautions that need to be applied – people should consult with an expert before embarking on a program. In the case of exercising and dieting, it is mandatory that they should consult with their physician before starting. In the case of refactoring, they should seek out resources such as this book and related papers elsewhere; staff experienced in refactoring can provide more focused assistance. Several people we have met are role models with respect to fitness and/or refactoring. We do admire their energy, commitment and productivity. Other, negative 'role models' do show visible signs of neglect. Their future – and the future of the software systems they will eventually produce – may not be good.

In a nutshell, refactoring can surely achieve near term benefits as well as making the software easier to modify and maintain down the road. Refactoring, therefore, becomes a means rather than an end. It is actually a part of a broader context of how programmers or programming teams develop and maintain their software over time.

13.9.6 Reducing Refactoring Overhead

Experiences reported by some object-oriented professionals and programmers suggest that the overhead of refactoring tends to be more than compensated for by reduced efforts and intervals in other phases of program development. While refactoring may appear a bit awkward and an overhead at first, as it becomes part of a software development regimen, it stops feeling like overhead and starts feeling like an essential. As refactoring becomes part of your constant routine, it seizes feeling like an overhead. Of course, it is easier said than done.

13.9.7 Refactoring Safely

Safety is a concern – especially for organizations developing and evolving large systems. In many applications, there are financial, legal and ethical considerations for providing continuous, reliable and error-free service. Many organizations do provide extensive training as well as attempt to apply disciplined development processes in order to help ensure the safety of their products. For many programmers, though, safety often seems to be of lesser concern. It is more than a little ironic that many of us preach 'safety first' to our children, nieces and nephews, while in our roles as programmers we scream for freedom – a hybrid of the wild west gunslinger and teenage driver. Grant us freedom, grant us the resources and then simply watch us fly. After all, is it our goal to let our organization miss out on the fruits of our creativity, merely for the sake of repeatability and conformity?

Here, we simply discuss approaches for refactoring safely. We will focus on an approach that is somewhat more structure/rigorous but which can eliminate many errors that might be introduced in refactoring. Safety is indeed a difficult concept to pin down easily. Intuitively, a safe refactoring is one that does not hamper a program at all. How can one refactor with the highest degree of safety? There are quite a number of options available:

1. Trust your coding abilities completely
2. Trust that your compiler will find errors that you miss
3. Trust that your test suite will catch errors that you and your compiler missed
4. Trust that code review(s) will find errors that you, your compiler and your test suite missed

Initially focus on the first three options in refactoring. Mid-to-large-size organizations tend to supplement these with code reviews. While compilers, test suites, code reviews and disciplined coding styles are all valuable, there are limits to all of these approaches:

1. All programmers are fallible – even you
2. There are subtle (and some not-so-subtle) errors that compilers cannot catch – especially scoping errors related to inheritance
3. While it is (or at least, use to be) common knowledge that the testing task is always made simpler when inheritance is used as an implementation technique. The truth of the matter is an extensive set of tests is often needed to adequately cover all the cases where operations that use to be requested on an instance of class are now requested on instances of its subclass(es). Unless your test designer is omniscient (or pays great attention to detail) there are likely to be cases your test suite will not cover. Testing all possible execution paths in a program is computationally not always possible. In simple terms, in general you cannot be guaranteed to have caught all of the cases with your test suite!
4. Code reviewers, like programmers, are generally fallible. Furthermore, reviewers may be too busy with their other work to thoroughly review someone else's code.

Another approach, is to define and prototype a refactoring tool to check if a refactoring can be safely applied to a program and, if it is, refactor the program. This minimizes bugs that may be introduced by 'human error'. Below, we provide a high-level description of the approach to refactoring safely.

The refactoring tool was a 'program analyzer' which is a program that analyzes the structure of another program (in this case, a C++ program to which a refactoring might be applied). That tool could 'answer' a series of questions regarding scoping, typing and program semantics (i.e., the 'meaning' as well as intended operations of a program). Scoping issues related to inheritance make this analysis more complex than with many non-object-oriented programs, but for C++, language features such as static typing makes the analysis easier than for, say, Smalltalk. Let us consider, as an example, the refactoring to delete a variable from a program. A tool can help determine what other parts of a program (if any) reference the same variable. If there happens to be any references, then removing the variable would leave dangling references – thus, this refactoring would not generally be safe at all. Apparently, when a user asks the tool to refactor their program, it would flag this as an error. The user might then decide that the refactoring was really a bad idea or the user may also be in a position to decide to change the parts of the program that refer to that particular variable and then proceed to apply refactoring to remove the variable altogether. There is quite a wide array of checks, most as simple as this, some even more complex.

Safety can be defined in terms of program properties (related to scoping, typing and so on) that need to continue to hold true after applying a refactoring. A lot of these program properties are quite similar to integrity constraints that must be maintained when database schemas change. Each and every refactoring has, with it, an associated set of necessary preconditions which, if true, would ensure that the program properties are preserved. Only if the tool is in a position to determine that everything is 'safe' then would the tool execute the refactoring.

Fortunately, determining whether a refactoring is safe is often trivial, especially for the low-level refactoring which comprise most refactoring. To be sure that all the higher-level, and more complicated refactoring are safe, we define them in terms of the low-level refactoring. For example, the refactoring carried out so as to create an abstract superclass is defined in terms of 'steps' which are simpler refactoring such as creating and moving variables and methods. By showing that each step of a more complicated refactoring is safe, we can know that by construction that refactoring is safe.

There are, however, some (relatively rare) cases where a refactoring that might actually be safe to apply to a program, but where a tool cannot be sure – in which case the tool takes the safe route and disallows the refactoring. For instance, consider again a case where you want to remove a variable from a program, but there apparently is a referencc to it from somewhere else in the program. However, it could be possible that, that reference is contained in a code segment that will never actually be executed. Consider the example; the reference may appear inside a conditional (e.g. if/then loop) which, of course, will never test true. If you could be sure that the condition would never test true, then you could remove the conditional test, including the code referring to the variable/function that you want to delete and then you could safely remove the variable/function. In general it is not possible to know for sure whether that condition will always be false. Suppose you inherited a project with code that was developed by someone else – how confident would you be in deleting this code?

In such a case, a refactoring tool could flag the reference and alert the user. It is possible for the user to decide to leave the code as it is, only if or when they are sure that the referencing code would never be executed, they could remove that code and then apply the refactoring. The tool makes the user aware of the implications of what and of the reference, rather than blindly applying the change.

In summary, quite a number of levels of safety are applicable to refactoring. Some are practically easy to apply but do not guarantee a high level of safety. Using a refactoring tool can avail many benefits – there are many simple but tedious checks that it can make, flagging in advance problems that if left unchecked would cause the program to malfunction as a result of refactoring. While the process of applying such a tool avoids introducing many of the errors that you otherwise hope will be flagged during compilation, testing and code review. These other corresponding techniques are still of much value, especially when developing or evolving real-time systems. Often, programs do not execute in isolation – they are often parts of a larger network of communicating systems. Some refactoring not only clean up the code but go further to make the program run more quickly. Speeding up a single part of the program might result in performance bottlenecks elsewhere. This can be compared with the effects of upgrading microprocessors that speed up parts of a system and require similar approaches to tune and test overall system performance. On the other hand, some refactoring may even slow down the overall performance a bit, but generally such performance impacts are minimal.

These approaches are mainly intended to guarantee that refactoring does not introduce new errors into a program. It should be understood that, these approaches do not detect and fix bugs that were in the program before the refactor. However, refactoring may make it easier to spot such bugs and subsequently correctly assist in correcting them.

13.10 Summary

Making refactoring real will mean addressing the 'real world' concerns of software professionals. Four commonly expressed concerns are:

1. They might not understand how to refactor
2. If the benefits are long-term, why exert all the effort now? In the long-term, you might not be with the project to reap the benefits!
3. Refactoring code is an overhead activity; they are paid to write new features
4. Refactoring might, unfortunately, may end up giving problems to the existing program

There are other issues that are of concern to some projects:

1. What if the code that is to be refactored is collectively 'owned' by several people? In some cases, many if not all of the traditional change management mechanisms are relevant. In some cases, if the software has been well designed and refactored, subsystems will be sufficiently de-coupled that many refactoring will only affect a small subset of the code base.

2. What if there exist multiple versions or code lines from a code base? In some cases, refactoring may be relevant for all of the existing versions, in which case all need to be checked for safety before applying the refactoring. In some cases, the refactoring may only be relevant for some versions, which simplifies the process of checking and refactoring the code. An effort to manage changes to multiple versions will often require applying many of the traditional version management techniques. Refactoring is useful in merging variants or versions into an updated code base, which may simplify version management downstream.

13.11 Implications Regarding Software Reuse and Technology Transfer

The 'real world' concerns addressed above do not only apply to refactoring – they apply more broadly to software evolution and reuse. For much of the past several years, focus has been on issues related to software reuse, platforms, frameworks, patterns and the evolution of legacy systems – often involving software that was not 'object-oriented'. The 'real world' concerns regarding a reuse program are very similar to those related to refactoring:

1. Technical staff may not understand what to reuse and how to reuse it.
2. Technical staff may not be motivated to apply a reuse approach unless short-term benefits can be achieved.
3. Overhead, learning curve and discovery cost issues must be addressed for a reuse approach to be successfully adopted.
4. Adopting a reuse approach should never be disruptive to a project; there may be strong pressures to leverage existing 'assets'/implementation albeit with legacy constraints. New implementations should interwork/be fully backward compatible with existing systems.

Geoffrey Moore described the technology adoption process in terms of a bell-shaped curve where the front tails includes 'innovators' and 'early adopters'. Apparently, the large middle hump includes 'early majority' and 'late majority', and the trailing tail including 'laggards'. In order for an idea and product to succeed, it must ultimately be adopted by early and late majorities. Put in another way, many of the ideas that appeal to the innovators as well as early adopters ultimately fail because they never make it across the chasm to the early and late majorities. The disconnection has its roots in the differing motivators of these customer groups. Innovators and early adopters are attracted by new technologies, visions of paradigm shifts and breakthroughs. Whereas, the early and late majorities are primarily concerned with the maturity, cost, support, and in seeing if the new idea or product has already been successfully applied by others with similar needs.

Software development professionals are impressed and or convinced in very different ways than software researchers. Software researchers are often referred to as innovators by Moore, while software developers and especially software managers are often part of the early and late majorities. Recognizing these differences is very important in reaching any of these groups. With software reuse, as is the case with refactoring, it is of prime importance that software development professionals are reached on their terms.

Keywords

source-to-source; refactoring; text editors; primitive tools; corrupted designs; extreme programming; Law of Demeter; class dictionary graph; subclassing; renaming; redefinition; surgery; versioning; reorganization; Self Language; Guru; namespaces; overriding; encapsulation; polymorphism; accessor functions; exclusive component; atomic refactoring; post-conditions; essential complexities; runtime; test suites; black-box; duplication; fixed-point; conservative approximation; static approximations; crude approximation; liberal approximation; method wrappers; method dictionary; bytecodes; delegation; aggregation; human error

Exercises

1. Define the term code refactoring.
2. Discuss in-depth why programs change.
3. Explain refactoring and its potential implications on a program.
4. What is the Law of the Demeter?
5. Elaborate on the impact of correctness.
6. Explain why developers are often reluctant to refactor their programs?
7. List and explain the principles guiding the use of test suites.
8. Compare and contrast dynamic and static analysis.
9. Discuss the feasibility of dynamic refactoring.
10. List and explain the characteristics of any refactoring tool you know.

Abbreviations

ANSI	American National Standards Institute
API	Application Programming Interface
ARDI	Access to Research for Development and Innovation
AST	Abstract Syntax Trees
BSD	Berkeley Software Distribution
CASE	Computer-aided Software Engineering
CFG	Control Flow Graphs
CM	Configuration Management
CMM	Capability Maturity Model
COBOL	COmmon Business-oriented Language
COTS	Commercial, Off-the-shelf
CRC	Class, Responsibilities, Collaboration
CSCW	Computer Supported Collaborative Work
CVS	Concurrent Versions System
DBMS	DataBase Management System
DD	Data Dictionary
DNA	DeoxyriboNucleic Acid
DOS	Disk Operating System
DSA	Dynamic Service Adaptation
EP	Extreme Programming
F/OSS	Free and Open-source Software,
FEAST	Feedback, Evolution And Software Technology
FLOSS	Free/Libre/Open Source Software
FORTRAN	FORmula TRANslation

GXL	Graph eXchange Language
HCI	Human Computer Interaction
HTML	Hyper Text Markup Language
IBM	International Business Machines
ICL	International Computers Ltd
IEEE	Institute of Electrical and Electronics Engineers
ISO	International Standards Organisation
IVV	Independent Verification and Validation
JCL	Job Control Language
LoC	Lines of Code
MAE	Mean Absolute Error
MIS	Management Information Systems
MS/DOS	Microsoft Disk Operating System
OCL	Object Constraint Language
ODC	Orthogonal Defect Classification
OO	Object Oriented
OOP	Object Oriented Programming
OOT	Object Oriented Technology
OS	Operating System
PDL	Public Documentation License
R & D	Research and Development
RSN	Release Sequence Number
SAAM	Scenario-based Architecture Analysis Method
SADES	Semi-autonomous Database Evolution System
SAP	System Application & Products
SATC	Software Assurance Technology Center
SCL	Standards Components Library
SCM	Software Configuration Management
SHRIMP	Scalable High-performance Really Inexpensive Multi-Processor
SIR	Synchronizing Interoperable Resources
SOM	System Object Model
SQL	Structured Query Language
TXL	Turing eXtender Language
UML	Unified Modeling Language
VDM	Vienna Development Method
Vim	Vi IMproved
VME	Virtual Machine Environment
XML	Extensible Markup Language

References

Abernathy, W.J., *The Productivity Dilemma: Roadblock to Innovation in the Automobile Industry*, John Hopkins University Press, 1978.

Adolph, W.S., Cash cow in the tar pit: Reengineering a legacy system. *IEEE Software* 13(3), 41–47, 1996.

Agrawal, H. and J. Horgan, Dynamic program slicing, *Technical Report SERC-TR-56-P*, Purdue University, 1989.

Aho, A.V., R. Sethi, and J.D. Ullman, *Compilers: Principles, Techniques, and Tools*, Addison-Wesley, 2000.

Ahrens, J.D., N. Prywes, and E. Lock, Software process reengineering—Towards a new generation of case technology, *Journal of System Software* 30(1–2), 71–84, 1995.

Albrecht, A., J. Gaffney, Software function, source lines of code, and development effort prediction: A software science validation, *IEEE Transactions on Software Engineering*, 11, 1983.

Alderson, A. and H. Shah, Viewpoints on legacy systems, *Communications of the Association for Computing Machinery* 42(3), 115–117, 1999.

Ball, T. and S.G. Eick, Software visualization in the large. *IEEE Computer* 29(4), 33–43, 1996.

Balzer, R. and Goldman, A fifteen year perspective on automatic programming, *Software Reusability—Volume II: Applications and Experience*, pp. 289–311, 1989.

Bates, S. and S. Horwitz, Incremental program testing using program dependence graphs, *Conference Record of the Twentieth ACM Symposium on Principles of Programming Languages, ACM*, 1993.

Basili, V.R. and H.D. Mills, Understanding and documenting programs, *IEEE Transactions on Software Engineering* 8(3), 270–283, 1982.

Beck, J. *et al.*, Program and interface slicing for reverse engineering, *Proceeding of the Fifteenth International Conference on Software Engineering,* 1993, also in *Proceedings of the Working Conference on Reverse Engineering.*

Beck, Kent *et al.*, Patterns postings related to aggregations.

Beecham, S., T. Hall and A. Rainer, Software process improvement problems in Twelve Software companies: An empirical analysis, *Empirical Software Engineering,* 8(1), 7–42, 2003.

Bellay, B. and H. Gall, An evaluation of reverse engineering tool capabilities. *Journal of Software Maintenance* 10(5), 305–331, 1998.

Bendifallah, S. and W. Scacchi, Understanding software maintenance work, *IEEE Transactions on Software Engineering* 13(3), 311–323, 1987, Reprinted in D. Longstreet (ed.), Tutorial on Software Maintenance and Computers, *IEEE Computer Society*, 1990.

Bennett, K.H., M. Ramage, and M. Munro, Decision model for legacy systems, *IEEE Proceedings Software* 146(3), 153–159, 1999.

Beyer, H. and K. Holtzblatt, *Contextual Design: A Customer-centered Approach to Systems Designs*, Morgan Kaufman Publishers, ISBN: 1558604111, 1997.

Bieman, J. and L. Ott, The relationship between slices and module cohesion, *International Conference on Software Engineering,* May 1989.

Biggerstaff, T.J., B.W. Mitbander and D. Webster, The concept assignment problem in program understanding, *Proceedings of the 15th International Conference on Software Engineering,* pp. 482–498, 1993.

Bisbal, J., D. Lawless, B. Wu, and J. Grimson, Legacy information systems: Issues and directions, *IEEE Software* 16(5), 103–111, 1999.

Blanchard, B. and W.J. Fabrycky, *Systems Engineering and Analysis*, Prentice-Hall, Upper Saddle River, NJ, pp. 557–602, 1981.

Boehm, B.W., *Software Engineering Economics*, Prentice-Hall, Englewood Cliffs, NJ, 1981.

Booch, Grady, *Object-Oriented Design.* Benjamin/Cummings, 1990.

Brant, John, and Don Roberts. Refactoring Browser Tool, Available at http://stwww. cs.uiuc. edu/~brant/RefactoringBrowser, The future of software development tools.

Brooke, C. and M. Ramage, Organizational scenarios and legacy systems, *International Journal of Information Management* 21, 365–384, 2001.

Brooks, R., Towards a theory of the cognitive processes in computer programming, *International Journal of Man–Machine Studies* 9(6), 737–742, 1977.

Brooks, R., Towards a theory of the comprehension of computer programs, *International Journal of Man–Machine Studies* 18(6), 543–554, 1983.

Bull, R.I. and M.-A. Storey, Towards visualization support for the eclipse modeling framework, A Research-Industry Technology Exchange at EclipseCon, California, 2005.

Burkhardt, J., F. Détienne, and S. Wiedenbeck. The effect of object-oriented programming expertise in several dimensions of comprehension strategies, *6th International Workshop on Program Comprehension*, pp. 24–26. Ischia, Italy, 1998.

Carl, Hewitt, Viewing control structures as patterns of passing messages, Artificial Intelligence Laboratory, Massachusetts Institute of Technology, Cambridge, MA, 1977.

Casais, Eduardo, Automatic reorganization of object-oriented hierarchies: A case study, *Object-oriented Systems* 1(2), 95–115, 1994.

Chalmers, M., K. Rodden, and D. Brodbeck, The order of things: Activity-centred information access, *Proceedings of 7th International Conference on the World Wide Web (WWW7)*, Brisbane, Australia, 1998.

Chikofsky, E.J. and J.H. Cross II, Reverse engineering and design recovery: A taxonomy, *IEEE Software* 7(1), 13–17, 1990.

Clayton, R., S. Rugaber, and L. Wills, On the knowledge required to understand a program. *The Fifth IEEE Working Conference on Reverse Engineering*, Honolulu, Hawaii, 1998.

Conradi, R. and A. Fuggetta, Improving software process improvement, *IEEE Software* 92–99, 2002.

Cordy, J.R., T.R. Dean, A.J. Malton, and K.A. Schneider, Source transformation in software engineering using the TXL transformation system, *Journal of Information and Software Technology* 44(13), 827–837, 2002.

Corritore, C.L. *et al.*, *A Comparison of the Comprehension of Object-oriented and Procedural Programs by Novice Programmers*, Elsevier, 1999.

Cubranic, D., G.C. Murphy, J. Singer, and K.S. Booth, Hipikat: A project memory for software development. *IEEE Transactions on Software Engineering*, to appear in the special issue on mining software repositories, 2006.

Curtis, B., By the way, did anyone study any real programmers? *Empirical Studies of Programmers* 256–262, 1986.

Curtis, B., Substantiating programmer variability, *Proceedings of the IEEE* 69(7), 846–846, 1981.

Cusumano, M.A. and D.B. Yoffie, Software development on Internet time, *Computer* 60–70, October 1999.

Davies, S.P., Externalising information during coding activities: Effects of expertise, environment and task, *Fifth Workshop*, 1993.

Dean, T.R., A.J. Malton, and R.C. Holt, Union schemas as a basis for a C++ extractor, *WCRE 2001—8th Working Conference on Reverse Engineering*, Stuttgart, Germany, pp. 59–67, 2001.

Debruler, Dennis, Review comments on this paper, PLOP '94.

DeLine, R., A. Khella, M. Czerwinski, and G. Robertson, Towards understanding programs through wear-based filtering, *Proceedings of Softvis*, Saint Louis, Missouri, pp. 183–192, 2005.

DeLucia, A. *et al.*, Program slicing: Methods and applications. *Invited Paper, IEEE Workshop on Source Code Analysis and Manipulation (SCAM 2001)*, Florence, Italy, 10th November 2001.

Détienne, F., *Software Design—Cognitive Aspects*, Springer Practitioner Series, 2001.

Deutch, P.L., Design reuse and frameworks in the Smalltalk-80, *Software Reusability—Volume II: Applications and Experience*, pp. 57–72, 1989.

Dilts, David, Personal communication, April 18, 2004.

Eisenbarth, T., R. Koschke, and D. Simon, Aiding program comprehension by static and dynamic feature analysis, *Proceedings of the IEEE International Conference on Software Maintenance*, Florence, Italy, pp. 602–611, 2001.

Eisenbarth, T., R. Koschke, and D. Simon, Locating features in source code, *IEEE Transactions on Software Engineering* 29(3), 195–209, 2003.

El-Ramly, Mohammad *et al.*, Recovering software requirements from system–user interaction traces, SEKE; *Proceedings of the 14th International Conference on Software Engineering and Knowledge Engineering*, vol. 27, ACM, 2002.

Erdös, K. and H.M. Sneed, Partial comprehension of complex programs (enough to perform maintenance), *Proceedings of the 6th International Workshop on Program Comprehension*, pp. 98–105, Ischia, Italy, 1998.

Exton, C., Constructivism and program comprehension strategies, *10th International Workshop on Program Comprehension*, Paris, France, pp. 281–284, 2002.

Ferenc, R., A. Beszédes, and T. Gyimóthy, Fact extraction and code auditing with Columbus and SourceAudit, *Proceedings of the 20th International Conference on Software Maintenance*, Chicago, IL, pp. 60–69, 2004.

Field, J., G. Ramalingham, and F. Tip, Parametric program slicing, *Conference Record of the Twenty-second ACM Symposium on Principles of Programming Languages*, pp. 379–392, 1995.

Fowler, M., K. Beck, J. Brant, W. Opdyke, and D. Roberts, Refactoring*: Improving the Design of Existing Code*, Addison-Wesley Professional, 1999.

Francel, M.A. and R. Rugaber, The relationship of slicing and debugging to program understanding, *Proceedings of the International Workshop on Program Comprehension*, pp. 106–113, Pittsburgh, PA, 1999.

Froehlich, J. and P. Dourish, Unifying artifacts and activities in a visual tool for distributed software development teams, *Proceedings of the 26th International Conference on Software Engineering*, Edinburgh, Scotland, pp. 387–396, 2004.

Gall, H., M. Jayazeri, R. Kloesch and G. Trausmuth, Software evolution observations based on product release history, *Proceedings of the 1997 International Conference Software Maintenance (ICSM'97)*, Bari, IT, October 1997.

German, D.M., Decentralized open source global software development, the GNOME experience, *Journal of Software Process: Improvement and Practice*, 8(4), 201–215, 2006.

Godfrey, M.W. and Q. Tu, Evolution in open source software: A case study, *Proceedings of the 2000 International Conference Software Maintenance (ICSM-00)*, San Jose, CA, October 2000.

Gonzalez-Barahona, J.M., M.A. Ortuno Perez, P. de lasHerasQuiros, J. Centeno Gonzalez, and V. Matellan Olivera, Counting Potatoes: The Size of Debian 2.2, *Upgrade Magazine*, II(6), 60–66, December 2001.

Gonzalez-Barahona, J.M., L. Lopez, and G. Robles, Community structure of modules in the Apache project, *Proc. 4th Workshop on Open Source Software Engineering*, Edinburgh, Scotland, May 2004.

Green, T.R.G. and M. Petre, Usability analysis of visual programming environments: A 'cognitive dimensions' framework. *Journal of Visual Languages and Computing* 7(2), 131–174, 1996.

Grudin, J., Partitioning digital worlds: Focal and peripheral awareness in multiple monitor use, *Proceedings of the SIGCHI Conference on Human Factors in Computing Systems*, Seattle, WA, CHI '01, ACM Press, NY, pp. 458–465, 2001.

Gupta, R. *et al.*, An approach to regression testing using slicing, *Proceedings of the IEEE Conference on Software Maintenance*, pp. 191–200, 1991.

Gutwin, C., R. Penner, and K. Schneider, Group awareness in distributed software development, *Proceedings of the ACM Conference on Computer Supported Cooperative Work*, Chicago, pp. 72–81, 2004.

Hammond, T., T. Hannay, B. Lund, and J. Scott. Social bookmarking tools (I): A general review, *D-Lib Magazine* 11(4), ISSN 1082–9873, 2005.

Hamou-Lhadj, A. and T. Lethbridge, A survey of trace exploration tools and techniques, *Proceedings of the 14th Annual IBM Centers for Advanced Studies Conferences (CASCON)*, IBM Press, Toronto, Canada, pp. 42–51, 2004.

Hannemann, J. and G. Kiczales, Overcoming the prevalent decomposition in legacy code, *ASOC Workshop at ICSE 2001*, Toronto, Canada, 2001.

Harman, M. and S. Danicic, A parallel algorithm for static program slicing, *Information Processing Letters*, 1996.

Holmes, R.T. and G.C. Murphy, Using structural context to recommend source code examples, *Proceedings of the International Conference on Software Engineering*, St. Louis, Missouri, pp. 117–125, 2005.

Hupfer, S., L.-T. Cheng, S. Ross, and J. Patterson, Introducing collaboration into an application development environment, *Proceedings of the ACM Conference on Computer Supported Cooperative Work*, Chicago, pp. 444–454, 2004.

Kersten, M. and G. Murphy, Mylar: A degree-of-interest model for IDEs, *Proceedings of the International Conference on Aspect Oriented Software Development*, Chicago, IL, pp 159–168, 2005.

King, J.L. and K.L. Kraemer, Evolution and organizational information systems: An assessment of Nolan's Stage Model, *Communications ACM*, 27(5), 466–475, 1984.

Koch, S. and G. Schneider, Results from Software Engineering Research into OpenSource Development Projects Using Public Data, Diskussionspapierezum Tätigkeitsfeld Informations verarbeitung und Informations wirtschaft, Hans R. Hansen und Wolfgang H. Janko (Hrsg.), Nr. 22, Wirtschafts universität Wien, 2000.

Koschke, R. and T. Eisenbarth, A framework for experimental evaluation of clustering techniques, *Proceedings of the 8th international Workshop on Program Comprehension*, Limerick, Ireland, pp. 201–210, 2000.

Laitenberger, O., Perspective-based reading: Technique, validation and research in future. *Technical Report*, University of Kaiserslautern, Germany, ISERN-95-01.

Lanza, M., The evolution matrix: Recovering software evolution using software visualization techniques, *Proceedings of the 4th International Workshop on Principles of Software Evolution*, ACM, 2001.

Laski, J. and B. Korel, Dynamic program slicing, *Information Processing Letters* 29(3), 155–163, 1988.

Lehman, M.M, D.E. Perry and J.F. Ramil, Implications for evolution metrics on software maintenance, *Proc. 1998 Intern. Conf. Software Maintenance (ICSM'98)*, Bethesda, MD, 1998.

Lehman, M.M. and J.F. Ramil, An approach to a theory of software evolution, *Proc. 2001 Intern. Workshop on Principles of Software Evolution*, 2001.

Lehman, M.M. and J.F. Ramil, *Software Evolution*, in this volume, 2004.

Lehman, M.M. and L.A. Belady, *Program Evolution—Processes of Software Change*, Academic Press, London, 1985.

Lehman, M.M., Programs, life cycles, and laws of software evolution, *Proc. IEEE* 68, 1060–1078, 1980.

Lehman, M.M., Rules and tools for software evolution planning and management, in J. Ramil (ed.), *Proc. FEAST 2000*, Imperial College of Science and Technology, London, 53–68, 2000. Also appears with J.F. Ramil in an expanded version as "Rules and Tools for Software Evolution Management," in *Annals of Software Engineering*, 11, 16–44, 2001.

Letovsky, S., *Cognitive Processes in Program Comprehension, Empirical Studies of Programmers*, Albex, Norwood, NJ, pp. 58–79, 1986a.

Letovsky, S. and E. Soloway, Delocalized plans and program comprehension, *IEEE Software*, 1986b.

Littman, D.C., J. Pinto, S. Letovsky, and E. Soloway, Mental models and software maintenance, in *Empirical Studies of Programmers*, Washington, DC, pp. 80–98, 1986.

Madisetti, V., Y.-K. Jung, M. Khan, J. Kim, T. Finnessy, On upgrading legacy electronics systems: Methodology, enabling technologies and tools, *IEEE Proceedings on VHDL International Users Forum Fall Workshop*, 7–14, 2000.

Mahaffey, W.R., J.S. Tomlinson, and M.D. Porter, Functional discovery to enable confident change, *15th International Conference on Systems Engineering*, 1–5, 2000.

Mandelin, D., L. Xu, R. Bodik, and D. Kimelman, Mining Jungloids: Helping to navigate the API jungle, *Proceedings of PLDI*, Chicago, IL, pp. 48–61, 2005.

Marcus, A., L. Feng, and J.I. Maletic, Comprehension of software analysis data using 3d visualization, *Proceedings of the IEEE International Workshop on Program Comprehension*, Portland, OR, pp. 105–114, 2003.

Mathias, K.S., J.H. Cross, T.D. Hendrix, and L.A. Barowski, The role of software measures and metrics in studies of program comprehension, *Proceedings of the 37th Annual Southeast Regional Conference, ACM-SE 37*, 1999.

Mayrhauser, A.V., Program understanding: Models and experiments. Colorado State University, CO, 1995.

Meyer, M.H. and J.M. Utterback, The product family and the dynamics of core capability, *Sloan Management Review* 34(3), 29–47, 1993.

Mockus, A., R. Fielding, and J.D. Herbsleb, Two case studies of open source software development: Apache and Mozilla, *ACM Transactions on Software Engineering and Methodology* 11(3), 309–346, 2002.

Moonen, L. Generating robust parsers using island grammars, *Proceedings of the Eighth Working Conference on Reverse Engineering*, Stuttgart, Germany, pp. 13–24, 2001.

Moore, Ivan R., Automatic restructuring of object-oriented programs, *Ph.D. Thesis*, University of Manchester, 1996.

Mueller, F. and A.L. Hosking, Penumbra: An eclipse plugin for introductory programming, *Proceedings of the 2003 OOPSLA Workshop on Eclipse Technology Exchange*, Anaheim, CA, pp. 65–68, 2003.

Muller, H.A. and K. Klashinsky, Rigi: A system for programming-in-the-large, *Proceedings of the 10th International Conference on Software Engineering*, Singapore, pp. 80–86, 1988.

Murphy, G.C., D. Notkin, and K. Sullivan, Software reflexion models: Bridging the gap between source and high-level models, *Proceedings of Foundations of Software Engineering*, Washington, DC, pp. 18–28, 1995.

Nelson, R.R. and S.G. Winter, *An Evolutionary Theory of Economic Change*, BelknapPress, Cambridge, MA, 1982.

O'Mahony, S., Developing community software in a commodity world, in M. Fisher and G. Downey (eds.), *Frontiers of Capital: Ethnographic Reflections on the New Economy*, Social Science Research Council, (to appear), 2003.

O'Reilly, C., D. Bustard, and P. Morrow, The war room command console—Shared visualizations for inclusive team coordination, *Proceedings of Softvis*, Saint Louis, Missouri, pp. 57–65, 2005.

Opdyke, William F., Refactoring object-oriented frameworks, *Ph.D. Thesis*, University of Illinois at Urbana-Champaign, 1992.

Pacione, M.J., M. Roper and M. Wood, A novel software visualisation model to support software comprehension, *Proceedings of the 11th Working Conference on Reverse Engineering*, Delft, pp. 70–79.

Parnas, D.L., Software aging, *Proceedings of the 16th International Conference on Software Engineering*, ACM, 1994.

Pennington, N., *Stimulus Structures and Mental Representations in Expert Comprehension of Computer Programs*, Elsevier, 1987.

Penny, D.A. The software landscape: A visual formalism for programming-in-the-large, *Ph.D. Thesis*, University of Toronto, 1992.

Perry, D.E., H.P. Siy, and L.G. Votta, Parallel changes in large-scale software development: An observational case study, *ACM Trans. Software Engineering and Methodology* 10(3), 308–337, 2001.

Petre, M., A.F. Blackwell and T.R.G. Green. Cognitive questions in software visualization, *Software Visualization: Programming as a Multi-Media Experience*, MIT Press, pp. 453–480, 1998.

Prechelt, L., B. Unger, W.F. Tichy, P. Brössler, and L.G. Votta, A controlled experiment in maintenance comparing design patterns to simpler solutions, *IEEE Transactions on Software Engineering* 27(12), 1134–1144, 2001.

Prechelt, L., B. Unger-Lamprecht, M. Philippsen, and W. Tichy, Two controlled experiments assessing the usefulness of design pattern documentation in program maintenance. *IEEE Trans. Software Enginering* 28(6): 595–606, 2002.

Pressman, R.S., *Software Engineering: A Practitioners' Approach*, 2005.

Reinertsen, R., Residual life of technical systems; diagnosis, prediction and life extension, *Reliability Engineering and System Safety* 54(1), 23–34, 1996.

Reiss, S.P., An overview of BLOOM, *Proceedings of the 2001 ACM SIGPLAN-SIGSOFT Workshop on Program Analysis for Software Tools and Engineering*, pp. 2–5, 2001.

Robbins, J.E. and D.F. Redmiles, Software architecture design from the perspective of human cognitive needs, *Proceedings of the California Software Symposium*, Los Angeles, CA, 1996.

Robillard, M.P. and G. Murphy, FEAT: A tool for locating, describing, and analyzing concerns in source code, *Proceedings of the 25th International Conference on Software Engineering*, pp. 822–823, 2003.

Robles-Martinez, G., J.M. Gonzalez-Barahona, J. Centeno Gonzalez, V. Matellan Olivera, and L. Rodero Merino, Studying the evolution of Libre software projects using publicly available data, *Proc. 3rd Workshop on Open Source Software Engineering*, Portland, OR, 2003.

Sage, A.P., *Handbook of Systems Engineering and Management*, A.P. Sage and W.B. Rouse (ed.), John Wiley and Sons, Inc., New York, 1999.

Scacchi, W., Understanding the requirements for developing open source software systems, *IEE Proceedings—Software* 149(1), 24–39, 2002.

Schach, S.R., B. Jin, D.R. Wright, G.Z. Heller, and A.J. Offutt, Maintainability of the Linux kernel, *IEE Proceedings—Software* 149(1), 18–23, February 2002.

Shneiderman, B., Human factors experiments in designing interactive systems, *ACM*, 1979.

Shneiderman, B., *Software psychology: Human factors in computer and information systems*, Winthrop Computer Systems Series, p. 320, 1980.

Sim, S.E., S. Easterbrook, and R.C. Holt, Using benchmarking to advance research: A challenge to software engineering, *Proceedings of the 25th International Conference on Software Engineering*, Portland, OR, pp. 74–83, 2003.

Singer, J., R. Elves, and M.-A. Storey, NavTracks: Supporting navigation in software maintenance, *Proceedings of International Conference on Software Maintenance*, Budapest, Hungary, pp. 325–334, 2005.

Singer, J., T. Lethbridge, N. Vinson and N. Anquetil, An examination of software engineering work practices, *Proceedings of CASCON'97*, Toronto, pp. 209–223, 1997.

Sneed, H.M., Economics of software re-engineering, *Journal of Software Maintenance, Research and Practice* 3(3), 1991.

Sneed, S., Planning the re-engineering of legacy systems, *IEEE Software*, vol. 1, 1995.

Solomon, R., P.A. Sandborn, and M.G. Pecht, Electronic part life cycle concepts and obsolescence forecasting, *IEEE Transactions on Components and Packaging Technologies* 23(4), 707–717, 2000.

Soloway, E. and K. Ehrlich. *An Empirical Investigation of the Tacit Plan Knowledge in Programming. Human Factors in Computer Systems.* Ablex Publishing Company, NJ, 1984.

Soloway, E. *et al.*, Knowledge and processes in the comprehension of computer programs, Available at www.psycnet.apa.org, 1988.

Storey, M.-A., *Designing a Software Exploration Tool Using a Cognitive Framework of Design Elements. Software Visualization*, Guest editor: Kang Zhang, Kluwer, 2003.

Storey, M.-A., F.D. Fracchia and H.A. Müller, Cognitive design elements to support the construction of a mental model during software exploration. *Journal of Software Systems*, special issue on Program Comprehension, 44, 171–185, 1999.

Storey, M.-A., K. Wong, and H.A. Müller, How do program understanding tools affect how programmers understand programs, *Science of Computer Programming* 36(2–3), 183–207, 2000.

Storey, M.-A., D. Cubranic, and D. German, On the use of visualization to support awareness of human activities in software development: A survey and a framework, *Proceedings of Softvis*, St. Louis, Missouri, pp. 193–202, 2005.

Systä, T., K. Koskimies, and H.A. Müller, Shimba—An environment for reverse engineering Java software systems. *Software Practice & Experience* 31(4), 371–394, 2001.

Tamai, T. and Y. Torimitsu, Software lifetime and its evolution process over generations, *Proc. Conf. Software Maintenance*, 63–69, November 1992.

Tilley, S.R. and D.B. Smith, Coming attractions in program understanding, *Technical Report CMU/SEI-96-TR-019*, 1996.

Tip, F., A survey of program slicing techniques, *Journal of Programming Languages* 3(3), 121–189, 1995.

Tonella, P. and M. Ceccato, Aspect mining through the formal concept analysis of execution traces, *Proceedings of the 11th Working Conference on Reverse Engineering*, Delft, the Netherlands, pp. 112–121, 2004.

Vessey, I., Expertise in debugging computer programs: A process analysis, *International Journal of Man–Machine Studies*, Elsevier, 1985.

von Mayrhauser, A. and A.M. Vans, From code understanding needs to reverse engineering tool capabilities. *Proceedings of CASE'93*, pp. 230–239, 1993.

Walenstein, A. Observing and measuring cognitive support. *11th IEEE International Workshop on Program Comprehension*, May 10–11, Portland, OR, 2003.

Weiser, M., Program slicing: Formal, Psychological and practical investigations of an automatic program abstraction method, *Ph.D. Thesis*, the University of Michigan, Ann Arbor, Michigan, 1979.

Weiser, M., Programmers use slices when debugging, *CACM*, 26, 446–452, 1982.

Wexelblat, A., Communities through time: Using history for social navigation, *Lecture Notes in Computer Science*, vol. 1519, T. Ishida (ed.), Spring Verlag, Berlin, pp. 281–298, 1998.

Wexelblat, A. and P. Maes, Footprints: History-rich tools for information foraging, *Proceedings of CHI*, Pittsburgh, PA, 1999.

Wiedenbeck, S. and C.L. Corritore, An exploratory study of program comprehension strategies of procedural and object-oriented programmers, *International Journal of Human–Computers Studies*, 2001.

Wong, K. The reverse engineering notebook, *Ph.D. Thesis*, University of Victoria, 2000.

Wong, K., S.R. Tilley, H.A. Muller, and M.-A. Storey, Structural redocumentation: A case study. *IEEE Software* 12(1), 46–54, 1995.

Zimmermann, T., P. Weißgerber, S. Diehl, and A. Zeller, Mining version histories to guide software changes, *Proceedings of International Conference in Software Engineering*, Glasgow, Scotland, 2004.

Index